SCATTERED
A PERSONAL STORY OF THE 1976 GENERATION

SCATTERED
A PERSONAL STORY OF THE 1976 GENERATION

KHULU MBATHA

Foreword by Sophia De Bruyn

All rights reserved

No part of this publication may be reproduced, stored in a retrieval system or transmitted in any form or by any means, electronic, mechanical, photocopying, recording or otherwise, without written permission from the publisher and the copyright holder.

© Khulu Mbatha
Published by KMM Review Publishing Company (Pty) Ltd
PO Box 782114
Sandton 2146

ISBN: 978-0-6399024-4-9

Published in 2022

Editors: Mokone Molete and Melody Emmett
Typesetting and layout: Quba Design and Motion
Printing and binding: Typo Colour Printing

CONTENTS

Acknowledgements iii
Foreword vi
Preface viii
Prologue xiii

Chapter One: My Roots *1*
    Western Native Township (1954 – 1962) 2
    Rockville, Soweto (1962 – 1976) 21

Chapter Two: A Frosty Beginning *73*
    Swaziland (1976) 74
    Tanzania (1976 – 1977) 83

Chapter Three: My Enlightenment *109*
    The GDR – my second home (1977 – 1987) 110

Chapter Four: Conquering the World *171*
    Zambia (1987 – 1988) 172
    Greece (1988 – 1990) 209

Chapter Five: My Return Home *231*
    Zimbabwe (1990 – 1991) 232
    My Repatriation and Homecoming (1991 – 1994) 235

Notes 281
About the Author 292

For
Dimitra Aretha & Nelson Stefanos

ACKNOWLEDGEMENTS

It has always been my dream to write about my life in exile – the countries I have been to and the people of the world I encountered and who became part of me. I would not have been able to make a start without the encouragement of my immediate and extended family, childhood friends – both girls and boys – I grew up with, those I went to primary, high school, and to university with. We spent the best of our times together, shaping each other's understanding of the social environment we were born into, and through all those years, our teachers shaped our ideas. I am deeply indebted to the friends and comrades I left the country with and lived with for many years in the wilderness, and on some occasions grieved with, not knowing if we would ever return home. At the same time, I and many others, benefitted from what exile offered and came home steeled by hope that our political struggle would not be in vain.

There are elder comrades I would like to recognise among the many who influenced me profoundly: Aunt Sophia Williams De Bruyn; Aunt Ruth Mompati; MaGertrude Shope; MaSeperepere; Kate Molale; Manto Tshabalala and Sis Jackie Modise. Others who influenced what I was to become include Alfred Nzo; Thomas Nkobi; Moses Mabhida; Timothy 'Tim' Maseko (ambassador); Lillian and Anthony Mongalo (ambassador); Bra Phiri; Reddy Mampane (ambassador); Ray and Jack Simons; Reg September; Professor Keorapetse William Kgositsile, and Max Sisulu (former speaker of parliament).

To those who inspired me to write this book, some of whom have since departed into the other world, I thank you sincerely for your untiring encouragement and support. I engaged many friends and comrades through research interviews and I have no words to thank you for your invaluable time and assistance in helping me recollect my memories and in recollecting yours. It would have been impossible to recap these experiences without your contributions. Any errors are, however, my sole responsibility as the author.

For many, remembering suffering, incarceration and torture at the hands of the enemy, and sometimes at the hands of those we regarded as comrades, was extremely psychologically and emotionally demanding. Names that come to mind are Miriam Duduzile 'Dudu' Zondo, Hilda Nompikiswano Mabuza (nee Matyobeni), Thabi Moloi, Welile Nhlapo (MK Andrew Mkhize), Zacharia Solomon 'Solly' Shoke (retired chief of the SANDF, and MK Jabu Lukhele), Derrick Sidney Sipho 'Siga' Pewa (MK Themba Mlotshwa), Omry Mathabatha Makgoale (MK Sidwell 'Mhlongo' Moroka), Suzman 'Kid' Nkopane Mokoena, Bransby 'Trizzer' Luke (MK David More), Lucky Lidlanga Moeketsi, Clement Fana Hlongwane, Richard Matwetwe Nyide. Others are Mandla 'Mbube' Mangethe (Ret. Gen. Mangethe), Joy Mojalefa Rathebe (MK Andrew Cindi), Justice 'Majase' Nkonyane (Ret Gen), Ernest Tshepiso Gumede (Ret. Col. Gumede), Dr Sphiwe Cele, Dr Teboho Josiash 'Tongogara' Lebakeng, Bada Maurice Olehile Pharasi, Meshack Ravuku, Jabu Mkhwanazi, Reuben Linda Zwane, Brian Luvuyo Hoga (Brian Hoga (MK Borifi 'Scratch' Ntathela), Abel Borole, David Mavuku, Richard Matwetwe Nyide, Juliana Makapan and Strongman Rampa.

I would like to make a particular mention of my cousin Happy Bhembe (Ret. Gen. Bhembe), who was supportive when I said writing this book is also good for our family. Happy was born on the same day, in the same year as my younger brother, Fana. He was a pillar of strength for me in exile. There was a bond between us because of our roots and we never forgot where we came from. My thanks go to my sister Maggie 'Nini', my son, daughters, nieces and nephews who also played a supportive role. When it came to family records, my cousins from my maternal family in Mamelodi were an invaluable resource and so was my sister-in-law Audrey Maki Mbatha.

A special honour goes to the martyrs of the 1976 uprising, in particular Kolisile 'Koli' Wycliffe Ngqase (MK Ephraim Gazelle), John 'Jannie' Magwegwe Vilakazi (MK Thabo Mkula), Selby Vuyani 'Svari' Chjivago Mavuso (MK Larry 'Bab' Makhaya) and Isaac 'Sakie' Motswasele (MK Oupa Moloi). Your sacrifices were a strong driving force for this book.

Among the people of Germany (both east and west) and Greece, I found new friends, mothers and fathers. The two 'Gs' of Europe – Germany and Greece, that's what I called them – became my home away from home.

My parents, like many other parents, inspired me to take education seriously and when I was forced into exile, they urged me never to give up no matter how tough things were. My family, friends and their families, will read about many incidents for the first time. I hope I have been able to close some of the gaps. It is possible that I have opened the door for more questions for friends and comrades to write their stories and fill in some of the missing pieces.

I am grateful to Mokone Molete and Melody Emmett for editing my manuscript and asking pertinent questions as we walked together through my past. I thank the publishers for their support.

FOREWORD

This is no ordinary record of life in exile. In this book, Khulu Mbatha, who I have known since our exile years, exploits his upbringing in Soweto, where the June 16, 1976 uprising started, to unveil a complex weave of socio-political and economic factors that were a constant feature in the lives of families and communities in black townships. He paints a holistic and well-researched context of the objective conditions that prevailed in the country which negatively affected black people and gave birth to a rebellion by students against the system of apartheid.

Khulu manages to weave his life story into the historic events of the time to create a distinctive account of his experiences. The multifaceted factors that contributed to the students' uprising make it evident that 'June 16' was a combustion waiting to ignite. There was a complex combination of political, social and economic factors that when fused together led to a social explosion. Extreme dysfunctional societal conditions in many black townships, devised by apartheid architects, became untenable.

Our oppressors needed an instrument that would over time control people both physically and mentally. Discriminatory apartheid and racist legislation served this purpose. Introducing Afrikaans as a medium of instruction under the Bantu Education Act, was a mechanism used to slowly erode the social fabric of black societies and impoverish education itself. Afrikaans, which was seen as the language of the oppressor, became a symbol of absolute conquest and evil, provoking immediate reaction and resistance. There is no doubt that the students felt this burden the most and it was evident that the students' revolts were not directed at the authorities in the education sector alone, but against the entire system of oppression.

Khulu Mbatha has managed to connect these events to the history of the struggle against white minority rule. 'June 16' in this sense was a social disruptor to the relative peace that the authorities wanted to portray to the white constituency and the outside world, especially after the banning of the African National Congress (ANC) and the Pan Africanist Congress (PAC). The book focusses on the aftermath of 'June 16' and takes us through Mbatha's journey into exile. He then reveals step by step, not only what happened there in general, but his own first-hand experiences and those of his many close friends, illuminating a life that was full of challenges. This book is worthwhile reading for both educational and historic purposes, and for posterity.

Sophia Williams De Bruyn
21 December 2021

PREFACE

> *There were other factors besides the rejection of Bantu Education and Afrikaans that were behind the uprising... They were the refusal to grant Africans permanent residential status; poor housing; restrictions on Africans trading rights in urban areas, and of course laws requiring all Africans to become citizens of one Bantustan or another. Each of these issues would have been enough to spark a riot; taken together they were the stuff of protracted civil wars...*
>
> *... the 1976 crisis drew in black parents and entire communities everywhere as few issues have ever done before. Organisations set up to deal with the crisis brought together adults from disparate political traditions, with different points of view and sometimes uneven understanding of the political situation, under the umbrella of Black Consciousness. Such was the case with Soweto's Committee of Ten, headed by Dr Nthato Motlana, and the Black Parents Association formed on 21 June, headed by Manas Buthelezi, to coordinate community responses to the crisis. Members of these bodies included Motlana and Winnie Mandela.[1]*

The June 16, 1976 uprising and its after-effects has troubled me for many years. At the 45th anniversary of this historical event in 2021, the familiar interpretation was that 'June 16' was an event involving students who resisted the introduction of Afrikaans in black schools. Unfortunately, this narrative, which is limited to immediate causes, such as grievances related to the Afrikaans language, Bantu education and the brutal reaction of the police, does not take into consideration the underlying factors. Some of the main proponents of this view are those that were directly in the forefront of organising the protests.

In this regard, the June 16 uprising, may perhaps be compared to the Sharpeville massacre of 1960, an event that is also widely understood as having been only against the carrying of passes (dom passes) by black people. One can also go back as far as the Bulhoek massacre of 1921:

> *The Bulhoek massacre remains a standard feature in accounts of South African history. Historians who wrote on the incident before the birth of the Popular or Peoples history movement and evidence submitted to Sir Thomas Graham, the presiding judge at the trial of the Israelites, made it clear beyond all doubt that the Israelites were religious fanatics who were driven by their fanaticism and blind faith in Enoch Mgijima's words to attack the Police. In the 1980s, with the birth of the Popular history movement, the massacre was reinterpreted by social historians, especially those associated with the University of Witwatersrand (Wits) History Workshop to fit into the perspective of the Popular history approach. The Israelites were seen as political heroes who stood against an oppressive system. The two different approaches to the massacre leads to the historical distortions of the event.*[2]

It is not my intention to undermine recognition of the youth and organisations that were in the forefront of the uprising primarily sparked by the language question, or the role of those who led and participated in the mobilisation and execution of marches and demonstrations. Without such leaders, these actions would not have happened. However, to see these events from this perspective only is short-sighted, since there were other structures opposed to the government's policy regarding Afrikaans in black schools including parents, teachers and community leaders.

The struggle against colonialism, oppression and the denial of human rights was only separated by epochs, the changing face of politics and the terrain of struggle. It is important to see the events of 1976 as a culmination of previous actions and setbacks that black people experienced in the fight against white minority rule, from the wars of resistance to the struggle led by the ANC for many years and later by the PAC, which was formed in 1959. Understandably, ANC and PAC members were arrested and tried after June 1976.

I am often asked by my children, nieces and nephews, and the youth in general, what made us, the youth of 1976, leave the country, and whether we informed our parents, and what we expected to find in the countries we fled to. I explore these questions in this book.

My book is also about the conditions surrounding my birth, the social milieu I grew up in, the culture that formed me. The implementation of forced removals, which was intrinsic to the implementation of apartheid rule, was part of this. To appropriately contextualise the 'June 16' uprising in its multifaceted form, it felt important to tell my life story. Skipping the country, jumping fences or crossing rivers and borders and going into exile would not have been the first choice for my peers and myself. The truth is that while marches and demonstrations were planned, the outcome and the direction that the uprising took, to a great extent, was spontaneous.

As the impact of the 1976 uprising reverberated throughout Africa and the world, the revolutionary atmosphere that energised the youth rebellion, was changing the course of history for South Africa.

For most black families life was never going to be the same again. Friends were separated from friends and families were torn apart. Girls and boys transitioned into adulthood, in detention and prisons, and the world of exile.

The journey started for some and ended for others, some were strong and some were not; some survived and others did not. Many families, buried their children.

Going into exile or staying in the country were both precarious. For future generations to appreciate the myriad of obstacles we faced and the tough decisions that had to be taken, the events of 1976 must be deconstructed. This is what I have attempted to do in this book.

I believe that this detailed account of my experience of going into exile in 1976, and how my life played itself out as a result, also offers insight into the experiences of others of my generation who followed in the footsteps of the then banned ANC and PAC. Scattered across the continent and the world, our survival to a large extent hinged on where we ended up. Many suffered irreparable physical, emotional and psychological damage. I am reminded of Tsietsi Mashinini, Tebello Motapanyane, George Wauchope (Reverend) and many others – may their souls rest in peace!

How prepared were the ANC and the PAC to welcome the youth of 1976 into their fold? How much influence did the Black Consciousness Movement (BCM) have in exile? These critical questions, which shaped the thinking of the 1976 youth, are explored as my narrative unfolds.

The liberation movements were not immune from the divisions that our people experienced under apartheid, both racial and tribal, as these organisations were a microcosm of South African society. How were these divisions dealt with in exile? Some of the political differences in both the ANC and PAC came to the fore in the tenuous conditions of life in exile. To maintain unity within these organisations for their survival proved to be one of the biggest tests and undertakings the leaders of the ANC and PAC faced.

My experience as a student in a then divided Germany was decisive. Germany was the quintessence of the Cold War and the division of the world into East and West. Like some of my compatriots, I spent many years of my life in this environment, studying and at the same time being active in politics and world affairs. This is the background that shaped my understanding of the world. Moreover, I dealt with living without parents, siblings and friends, sometimes facing the very harsh winters of Europe as a stateless refugee wishing I had never left my own country, and often dreaming about the unknown. Normally dreams reflect what you have seen before and have experienced. In exile, you dreamt about what you imagined.

Even before I left the country, my ideals and those of my close friends had been strongly influenced by the vision of the ANC. Yet this book is neither a history of the ANC, PAC or any other organisation, nor an assessment of their principles, what they stood for, what they accomplished or not. Rather, it is a personal story about my generation – the youth of 1976. Some of the stories woven into my narrative are horrific and painful and told for the first time in this book. Even today, they arouse anger and outrage, but they need to be told.

The circumstances I found myself in, dictated that I never lost sight of the fact that the struggle was about liberating South Africa. The ANC, PAC or the BCM were political and organisational vehicles through which South Africans hoped to free themselves from social oppression. The friends and comrades who influenced me as a young man and in my adulthood are found in all these organisations. However, the ANC is the political organisation in which I was able to develop and become the person I am today. Besides the bonds I had with comrades I worked and lived with, I also found new friends, uncles, mother and father-figures who became part of my life and shaped the values that became my own.

Dr Khulu Mbatha
January 2022

PROLOGUE

In Book I of *Politics*, the Greek philosopher, Aristotle, writes:

> *Nature, as we say, does nothing without some purpose; and she has endowed man alone among the animals with the power of speech. Speech is something different from voice, which is possessed by other animals also and used by them to express pain or pleasure; for their nature does indeed enable them not only to feel pleasure and pain but to communicate these feelings to each other. Speech, on the other hand, serves to indicate what is useful and what is harmful, and so also what is just and what is unjust. For the real difference between man and other animals is that humans alone have perception of good and evil, the just and the unjust, etc. It is the sharing of common view on this matters that makes a household and a state.*

In *Anti-Dühring, a critique of Professor Dühring's absurd theories* Friedrich Engels wrote:

> *When we consider and reflect upon nature at large or the history of mankind or our own intellectual activity, at first we see the picture of an endless entanglement of relations and reactions in which nothing remains what, where and as it was, but everything moves, changes, comes into being and passes away. This primitive, naive but intrinsically correct conception of the world is that of ancient Greek philosophy, and was first clearly formulated by Heraclitus: everything is and is not, for everything is fluid, is constantly changing, constantly coming into being and passing away.*

> *But this conception, correctly as it expresses the general character of the picture of appearances as a whole, does not suffice to explain the details of which this picture is made up, and so long as we do not understand these, we have not a clear idea of the whole picture. In order to understand these details we must detach them from their natural or historical connection and examine each one separately, its nature, special causes, effects,*

etc. I am a product of the things I learned in life through my own experiences and the influences of my studies on me.

At the time of writing this book the country where I lived most of my years in exile no longer exists. I went to the GDR (German Democratic Republic) or East Germany and studied philosophy as my major subject. My studies were a big contributor to my perspectives and how I see the world today. The country I lived in was a direct outcome of World War Two, a divided Germany, occupied by the four victors of that war. East Germany, the part occupied by the Soviets, became the GDR and formed part of socialist bloc countries.

No struggle has been victorious and successful without some form of solidarity. The people of the GDR stood side by side with the oppressed people of South Africa in their struggle against the evil system of apartheid that killed black children like flies. They contributed to the liberation of South Africa by making sacrifices. Our freedom was theirs too, as it was for all those in the international community that gave their support.

It was also the understanding within the ANC that we as an organisation and as individual members would not interfere in the internal affairs of the countries that supported us: Swaziland, Lesotho, Botswana, Mozambique, Zambia, Tanzania, Algeria, Ethiopia, Egypt, GDR, Hungary, and the Soviet Union among many others. Doing so jeopardised our presence in some of these countries as was the case in some of the southern African countries.

The ANC's struggle was waged under the banner of the Freedom Charter with a preamble that states: 'We, the People of South Africa, declare for all our country and the world to know: that South Africa belongs to all who live in it, black and white, and that no government can justly claim authority unless it is based on the will of all the people...' This was our lodestar and it was my belief that the preamble of the Freedom Charter was universal.

As a result of the divisions between East and West, the people of the GDR and other socialist states had many of their freedoms curtailed. I do not intend to deal with the causes of the collapse of the socialist system here as they were many and complex. With this book I pay tribute to the sacrifices made by the international community in supporting the struggle to bring about freedom and democracy in South Africa, not least the people of East Germany and the Anti-Apartheid Movement in West Germany.

Chapter One
MY ROOTS

WESTERN NATIVE TOWNSHIP (1954 – 1962)

I was born in Johannesburg, in what was formerly the Transvaal, and in those days my father worked as what was called 'a delivery boy' and his tool at work was the famous Italian Lambretta scooter. There was one for his workplace and he owned one too.

My mother did domestic work in the northern suburbs of Johannesburg – around Dunkeld and Rosebank. Despite their meagre salaries my parents sent all of their seven children to school.

Not all managed to finish school. I was the only one out of the seven to obtain a matric certificate and to attend a tertiary institution, the University of Zululand.

Parents, My Birth and Relocation

I was named Mkhulu Zephania and my mother always reminded me that I was born on a very cold Sunday, 20 June, 1954, in the Western Native Township, popularly known as 'Western' (now called Westbury). In those days births happened at home or at hospitals nearest to the neighbourhood – in this instance Coronation Hospital (now Rahima Moosa Mother and Child Hospital) and Bridgeman Memorial Hospital (now Netcare Garden City Hospital). The Bridgeman Memorial Hospital was the largest hospital intended explicitly for African women in the southern hemisphere before the 1960s. Because of apartheid it was forcibly closed in 1965. Later, on the same plot the Netcare Garden City hospital was built. Reverend TP Mokoena conducted my baptism on 19 September at the Apostolic Faith Mission Church in Western.

All my siblings were born in Western, and I was the fifth of seven children – five boys and two girls. The eldest was Joseph Ngomela (18

April 1942 – 6 December 1994), followed by Jotham Mhlophekazi (19 November 1944 – 21 June 1980) and Jeremiah 'Jerry Cooper' Limaphi (5 March 1948 – 14 April 2009). They were known as the '3Js' among their peers and in the soccer fraternity. At one time they all played soccer for leisure or for an amateur club in the township. After my brothers came Florah Sizakele, shortened as 'Siza' or 'Sizi', (1 April 1951 – 7 January 2020) as the fourth child. Then it was me (1954) followed by Moses Bafana 'Fana' Madoda 'Slow' (1 January 1957 – 26 September 1995) and Magdeline 'Maggie' Nomthandazo 'Nini' (30 January 1959), the last born.

My father, Ephraim Zamcolo Mbata[1] (6 January 1907 – 8 February 1981) was born at a place called eNhlazatshe, near Ulundi, the capital of Zululand. Ulundi, the heart of the Zulu nation, witnessed one of the greatest battles against the British Empire during the Anglo-Zulu War. In the Zulu language 'Zamcolo' means heavy rains that can uproot trees and move houses. We were told that heavy rains accompanied my father's birth. He was the eldest of nine children born to Jessie Bholi and Zephania Mbata. I was named after my grandfather Mbata, who was always referred to as 'Mkhulu', which means 'grandfather', whenever he was spoken about.

Hence my original name is Mkhulu and not Khulu. But the mocking that came from my peers while growing up in the township was unbearable. I always rushed to my mother crying, 'they say I am an old man'. One day she calmed me down and said to me, 'don't worry my son, Mkhulu means 'big', so you are a 'big man', that's 'Khulu'. From that day on, I was happy as ever! But there was a problem with my second name too. As a child I could not pronounce it properly. When asked what my English name was, instead of saying 'Zephania' my tongue got twisted and in the end I said my name was 'Vaseline' to the amusement of people around me.

I never knew Mkhulu Mbata, as he died before I could understand what was happening around me. All the stories I heard about him as I was growing up made me realise that these Mbatha people were prominent among the Zulu people. The name of Manyosi kaDlekezela waseMambatheni (Manyosi, the son to Dlekezela from the Mbatha clan) is exceedingly popular among the Zulu people. Manyosi was the most celebrated, incredibly talented, skilled, and greatest warrior of all times in the history of the Zulus. He brought this renowned reputation to the Mbathas. He was also lucky to have lived through Shaka's, Dingane's and Mpande's reigns. When Manyosi led his warriors to war, victory was certain and so he became known as Ndabezitha. 'Ndabezitha', translates into 'the one the enemies talk about all the time' or 'the undisputed one, even among enemies'. It is this celebrated name that the Zulu kings, after Shaka, later adopted, and which today is used when addressing the King of the Zulus and the Mbatha people.

Mkhulu Mbata married Jessie Bholi, fondly called 'Gogo MaMbata' as she was married emaMbatheni (into the Mbatas). She was born Jessie Bholi Zulu in 1885. Her birth was a year after the death of King Cetshwayo kaMpande (Cetshwayo the son of King Mpande) in 1884. King Cetshwayo is widely known as the man who made history by defeating and humiliating the British army on African soil at Isandlwana in 1879. Therefore, Jessie's birth coincided with the beginning of the reign of King Dinuzulu ka Cetshwayo (Dinuzulu the son of Cetshwayo). She was born close to Ulundi, the then capital of Zululand that was established by King Cetshwayo and where the last battle (Battle of Ulundi) of the Anglo-Zulu War occurred.

Jessie was the fifth child of seven children; she had four older sisters and two younger brothers, named Daniel and Petros. I came to know Gogo MaMbata well as I lived with her for nearly a decade before she died in October 1963, at the age of 87. Jessie Bholi and Mkhulu Mbata had nine children, my father being the eldest followed by Meshack (son), Enny (daughter), Jessie (daughter), three more siblings (whose names I do not know), then Petros (son) and Daniel (son) the last born. The last two were named after Jessie Bholi's two younger brothers, Daniel and Petros. With my father's assistance, all his siblings followed him and settled in Johannesburg. Gogo MaMbata used to take me with her when visiting her children, my father's siblings, as I was her devoted bag-carrier. Her remains are buried at the Nancefield Cemetery in Soweto.

My grandfather owned a lot of cattle, He became, a pastoral farmer, and in later years, he became a nomad, moving great distances and selling livestock for a living. His remains are buried near a town called eNhlangano, in Swaziland (now Eswatini), which lies right on the border with South Africa. Swaziland remained a British protectorate after the Union of South Africa was formed in 1910.

Following the creation of legislative structures and the holding of the 1967 elections, Swaziland became a protected state preparing for independence. On September 6, 1968, the Kingdom of Swaziland became independent and joined the Commonwealth, a body that South Africa had left in 1960. As a result, border gates and fences between the two countries were erected, which left my grandfather's grave on the Swaziland side of the border. From this point onwards, citizens of both countries entering and leaving each country were to do so through the newly established border posts. For the first time they had to carry passports.

I was a child and never understood what was happening, but I remember very well how my father moaned and grumbled that he had to carry this 'special book' when visiting his own family in Swaziland. He would on certain occasions report that he was forced to go over a fence into Swaziland. I was left wondering how possible this was, my father jumping a fence? I could not conceptualise the idea of two countries then. Now and then he would visit his uncle, Petros Zulu – the youngest and last-born brother to his mother, Jessie Bholi – in

Swaziland. Petros Zulu, like Mkhulu, had also settled at Nhlangano with his family and children before the two countries were separated. My family still has blood relatives in Swaziland stemming from my father's generation and lineage.

My mother, born Elizabeth Siphelile Nhlapo[2] (6 March 1925 – 21 July 2008) was the third out of nine children born to Lena Mbono 'Mbom' (1 March 1906 – 3 September 1984) and Jacob Makhubalo Nhlapo who was born in the 1890s and died in November 1969, and was buried on November 16, 1969. Her mother, Lena Nhlapo, was born Mabuza in Ermelo, Eastern Transvaal. I have no recollection of her siblings. Her father, Jacob Nhlapo, was the younger of two children; his elder sister married Israel Nkosi.

Nhlapo also came from the Eastern Transvaal apparently around Ermelo too. It is recorded that the Nhlapo (Nhlapho) clan originally came from near the Thukela River (also known as Tugela) in Mgungundlovu, Natal. Apparently, during the 18th century they moved to a place that was known as Sheepmore in the Ermelo neighbourhood (Eastern Transvaal). There were skirmishes over grazing land and at the end the Nhlaphos won, and the place was renamed Mpisikazi.

As the third born out of nine, my mother's other name Siphelile means 'we are finished', in the Zulu language. It so happened that the first two children before her, didn't live long after birth. As a result, when she was born, they named her Siphelile, signalling that 'we are finished', but also expressing a wish that my mother can live longer. For this reason, my mother was treated like the first born, as her other siblings after her, also lived longer. She was followed by Emma (daughter), Job (son), John (son), Jumaimah (daughter) Hezekiel (son) and Hazel (daughter).

In the 19th century, African families being robbed of land by the colonisers, had to seek work around cities like Johannesburg. As a result, my maternal grandparents slowly migrated from place to place, to somewhere near the eastern part of Johannesburg known as East Rand and settled there. When Jan Smuts International Airport (now OR Tambo International Airport) was built in 1952 near the town of Kempton Park, named so in honour of Smuts who had died two years earlier, the communities in the area were relocated. Jan Smuts International Airport replaced Palmietfontein International Airport, which had been there since the end of the Second World War in 1945. After this, Palmietfontein first became a motor racing circuit where the Rand Grand Prix was held. Eventually the apartheid authorities decided to build a black township on the same spot and named it Katlehong.

That is how my maternal grandparents were affected and were among the first to be settled on a farm known as Vlakfontein near Pretoria that people called 'eFlaga'. In the 1950s the name was changed to Mamelodi Township.[3] They lived in Section Q.

I came to know both my maternal grandparents. I remember very well that my maternal grandfather had for many years worked for the South African Railways (SAR) and wore those distinct reddish-brown overall uniforms with a sizeable SAR embroidered at the back. The old man never spoke much and in summer, he always relaxed with his sorghum beer under the peach trees in the yard. When the peaches were ripe, he didn't eat the peaches from the tree but always picked the over ripe ones that had fallen on the ground and were gathering insects. I learned later in life that those peaches were richer in proteins than the ones still hanging on the trees. It was fun listening to him telling stories about life in general.

My maternal grandmother was a disciplinarian and a workaholic. When she came for a visit, she woke us up incredibly early in the mornings to help with whatever chores she had started. Both my maternal grandparents, Lena and Jacob Nhlapo, who were real pillars of strength to my parents are buried at the old Mamelodi Cemetery in Pretoria.

Chapter One

I have no idea how my mother and father met, but it was in the City of Gold, Johannesburg. The city came into being after gold was discovered on farmlands in 1886. It was not until the Anglo-Boer War (South African War) of 1899–1902 that calm came back to Johannesburg, which colloquially came to be known as Joburg.

In 1897 a speculator named Tobiansky, whose wife was Sophia (after whom Sophiatown is named), had bought the land on which Sophiatown, Newclare, Martindale and Western lie. In 1905 the government of the day, under the British who had won the Anglo-Boer War, wanted this area to build a township for whites, but they discovered there was a municipal sewage plant nearby which devalued the properties in the area. In 1918, towards the end of the First World War, there was an outbreak of influenza, the Spanish flu, and the authorities used this opportunity to remove Africans, who had been attracted to the booming city because of work opportunities, from the inner city. Following the influenza outbreak, the Johannesburg Town Council made a small concession and bought Western to accommodate Africans specifically. Between 1919 and 1922, they carried out a municipal housing scheme that provided homes for 5 000 people.

Up to this time, Johannesburg did not offer Africans any form of housing. The Gold Laws[4] inherited from the South African Republic province, which became the Transvaal after the Union of South Africa was formed in 1910, prohibited 'persons of colour' from owning land anywhere in the city. The large, unskilled and predominantly male Africans who laboured in the mines around the city were accommodated in a 'compound system' of housing. These were single sex hostels with rooms accommodating in some instances up to 18 people. They barely had any facilities other than sleeping quarters and a large hall for selling sorghum beer.

Along with the Native Land Act (1913), this system was inhuman in many ways. Men from the rural countryside were uprooted and accommodated in these single-sex hostels – between eight and 16 men per room. This is how the African rural economy was destabilised, which led to the destruction of rural life and culture, and the eventual impoverishment of Africans. With no leisure time, alcohol abuse, prostitution and venereal diseases became common among mine workers.

At this stage there were very few African women in Johannesburg. In 1902 out of a population of 64,664 African men there were only 7 615 women on the Rand (the collective name for the mining areas in and around Johannesburg). By 1918 the population of Africans had risen to 116,120.[5] Still there was a disproportionately high ratio of men to women. A few African women found jobs as domestic workers in the new suburbs around the city, and it was up to their employers to provide them with sleep-in quarters. The rest had to squat in and around the city.

Besides the mine workers and these domestic workers, as the city developed, or more appropriately the economy, skilled and semi-skilled workers were in demand. These people were going to be of service to the City of Johannesburg and all businesses in the surrounding areas. These ranged from office cleaners, bus-drivers, teachers, lawyers and policemen to those who worked for the municipality, including the agricultural, manufacturing, construction, mining and maintenance sectors.

Western was the first place in Johannesburg where African people could legally reside. It accommodated Africans of all origins: Xhosa, Zulu, Pedi, and Sotho and became a mixed ethnic and cultural setup. Its history gives insight into the experiences of the early African working class in Joburg. It was first called 'Newlands Location'. Nearby white residents of the real Newlands objected to the name and in 1919 it was changed to Western Native Township.

Western was state-owned. There was no apartheid. The segregation legislation which discriminated against Africans in this period recognised class differences among the African population. It accorded different urban rights to middle class and working-class Africans. For example, middle class Africans had access to elite educational institutions; they could avoid movement restrictions in the cities; get better jobs, and own property.

After 1948, under apartheid, class divisions within urban African communities were done away with by a range of discriminatory policies. No level of education, occupation or wealth counted anymore, instead a mere piece of paper called a 'passbook' dictated where you belonged. This piece of paper was a permit that identified whether you were born in the city or; whether you had a work permit or not. You either had it or you didn't, and there were no in-betweens.[6]

I guess after falling in love and getting to know each other, my father paid lobolo (dowry) and my parents' marriage took place. When I look at their wedding pictures, I always wish I were there, because I realise they had a 'white wedding' – that is, a formal wedding where the bride wore white. Although the pictures are in black and white, it is obvious my mother was wearing a white tulle lace wedding gown and a lace head covering with a young boy carrying the train of her dress. My father is immaculately garbed, looking his best in a well-fitting suit.

My mother would have been in her late teens or early 20s and my father in his mid-30s. They were both blue collar workers, married and qualified to legally occupy house number 849 Malotane Street in Western Native Township. Both had gone to school and could read and write in both English and Zulu. They had probably gone up to standard six (Grade 8 today), for those days a great achievement.

As blue-collar workers, my parents were dedicated to their jobs. For as long as I can remember, my father had been employed as a scooter delivery driver with a printing company. It was a stationery company that produced and supplied office material in the Johannesburg area. In those days this was a safe, secure and to a certain extent well-respected job.

The company had a production factory in Boksburg and some of the material was imported from the UK. Ownership of the company had changed hands while my father remained in the company's employ. The last owner was someone who had found my father in the company. His name was David Shimmin (Mr Shimmin – as my father always referred to him) and he came from Britain as an immigrant with his wife. He had divorced and married a South African Afrikaner woman, named Valerie 'Val'. As a result of my father's loyalty to the company, my family developed a close relationship with Shimmin's family.

My mother used to do domestic work on specific days of the week, mainly around Dunkeld, Rosebank and Parktown. For African women, this was the norm in those days. Others, if they were not nurses, teachers or social workers, worked in factories around Johannesburg. On Thursdays, most women doing domestic work were off duty to attend church services. This day became popularly known as 'Sheila's Day'. The women in their splendid black and white (Anglican) or red and white (Methodist) uniforms looked elegant and dignified in the streets of the townships.

My mother was a staunch member of the Apostolic Faith Mission Church. She could speak almost all African languages, as well as English and Afrikaans, and was an interpreter at our church. Both my parents were Christians, but I do not remember my father ever going to church or praying.

My father was an ardent reader of newspapers, even those older than a month. He would then seek an audience to tell anyone visiting or just passing, about what was happening in the world. He was strongly conservative and hated to see half-naked pictures of women in bikinis in newspapers or magazines. While reading, he would carefully cut these pictures out and continue to read, thus rendering the paper useless for anyone who wanted to read it afterwards.

For cutting, he used big 'multi-purpose' scissors that you put into a cowhide or goatskin leather case that old people used to carry with them like a pet, cutting anything from nails and papers to cloths.

When my father came across a piece of news he disagreed with, he would shout out very loud, 'This is first class rubbish!' You would think he is talking to someone, but he was all alone and talking to himself. My friends always teased me by asking me to explain to them what 'first class rubbish' meant?

What I treasure most are the love letters between my parents, mainly from my father to my mother. He had such a wonderful handwriting and could express himself so pleasantly, his heart was always for my mother. Those days writing was a golden treasure.

During my mother's pregnancies she would leave home just after giving birth so she could be with our maternal grandmother in Mamelodi. In this way she had the necessary support she needed to look after the baby. Some weekends she paid us visits and cooked a delicious meal for the family. On Sunday afternoons she left the family in the care of my father. This was the general practice after the birth of almost all the children.

A few days after my mother left, my father wrote six-page letters by hand as if my mother had been away for years. These are such amazing letters to read today. They give me a sense of belonging. My elder sister Sizakele was born on 1 April 1951 and in one such letter my father penned in 1952 after my mother had visited, he wrote:

Original in Zulu:

849 Malotane St
W. Native Township
Johannesburg
6th – 8 – 52
Dear Heart
Isikati engikulobela ngaso ngu 10 o'clock evening. Ngiyabingelela ku Sizi ingane yami esengiyikumbule kabi ngithi nipila njani? Tina sisapila sonke ekaya. Kakuka biko luto olubi. Kakulu into nje yinye engi ngaku tyela tshela yona. Ikaya malingena mninilo kakubi kaya laluto. Into sibulawa sizungu senu nje…

Translation:

849 Malotane St
W. Native Township
Johannesburg
6th – 8 – 52
Dear Heart
As I am writing to you, the time is 10 o'clock in the evening.
I pass my greetings to Sizi my daughter that I miss so much, how is life on that side? We are all okay here at home and there is nothing bad to report about. One important thing that I can disclose to you, is that a home without its owner can never be a home. One thing, your absence is killing us…

My parents and all the grandparents on both sides were particularly strict. They tolerated no misbehaviour. There was always a sjambok (whip) ready to deal with any mischievous or negative behaviour. I became a victim of that sjambok because of whistling, which was a way of connecting with my friends. If my friends were looking for me and wanted to find out if I was home, they didn't come in, they whistled a certain tune. If I was home, I had to leave whatever I was doing, go outside and whistle back the same tune. They waited for me outside and if I didn't respond, they knew I wasn't at home and that was it.

When there was a death in the neighbourhood, I first got to know of it from my father because my whistling had to stop immediately. Whistling when there was a death was taken as a bad omen. They first warned me, but as a teenager I always forgot. The minute I opened the door and entered my home, the sjambok was on me. I screamed and apologised, but my friends never knew what I was experiencing at home. Because of this experience, with time whistling became part of my life and whenever it was quiet around me, automatically the whistling started without me being conscious of it. It's been like this till today.

Western, like many state-owned and built houses in big cities, was surrounded by a steel fence and there was only one entrance controlled by blackjacks (suburban police) for those coming in or out. The 'blackjack' name for black urban policemen derived from the truncheon or baton they carried which in other countries is known as a blackjack. These policemen were notorious and you never messed around with them. When they called, you responded immediately, otherwise a baton knocked on your head like thunder.

Those driving cars who were not residents, had to park at the entrance, get out, and report at the offices of the blackjacks. They registered how many were in the car and which house they were visiting. On weekends you were allowed to have sleepover visitors. If they overstayed, it created a big problem. The blackjacks raided houses with sleepover visitors in the early hours of the morning and either arrested the culprits or chased them away.

The design of the houses in Western was the same design for houses later built in Orlando East and Orlando West. They were built of red bricks with corrugated iron roofs and were either one- or two-bedroom houses with a small kitchen and a veranda. It is in this milieu that Elizabeth and Ephraim raised and gave us the best we could get from their meagre salaries. Both came from relatively large families with sizeable extended families, but they spent the best times with us, the children.

There was never a dull moment over the weekends. One or other relative or group of relatives would come and visit. We had many feasts and some of them slept over as they wished. I was born here and so my life is rooted here. As children we were encouraged to pay attention to our education and schoolwork. My siblings and I were all born in Western and started school there, except for those coming after me, Fana and Maggie, as they were still too small for school when the apartheid forced removals started. At the time, all schools were still under the missionaries.

'Freehold' status caused many Africans to rush here. Part of the rush though, was driven by the fact that the Native Urban Areas Act' of 1923 proclaimed most of the inner city as a place for 'whites only'. In Sophiatown there was no race that was not represented. Human beings are social animals, they move into each other's lives of necessity.

The mingling and association were fuelled by life in the big city and of course the politics of the day. Young men who grew up here spoke the original 'tsotsi taal' – the Sophiatown or Kofifi (the colloquial name for the township) style of speaking that was common through the 1940s, 1950s and 1960s. It is a pidgin-type language made up strongly of elements of Afrikaans and mixed with local African languages. This language matched with a clothing style associated with gangs, in fact, typical of an Americanised lifestyle.[7]

When the Second World War broke out, all white males, unless handicapped, had to leave for the war front. Although Africans were not conscripted, they could enrol to be carriers of essential goods but not guns. At the beginning the ANC and the then Communist Party of South African (CPSA), now the South African Communist Party, did not support enrolment. With the positive signals coming from the government of the day that they would address the basic concerns of

Africans in the country, the ANC decided to support the war effort on the side of the Allied forces.

The war made it possible for more Africans to come to Johannesburg to occupy what were deemed to be white men's jobs. South Africa experienced rapid industrialisation in many sectors, especially in the steel industry. After the Second World War, because of industrialisation and more Africans coming to Johannesburg, the city's population ballooned. Before the full establishment of Soweto, many people in the Western Areas were now Africans. The politics in the country were changing too.

Partly because of these developments and other factors, places like Sophiatown soon became overcrowded and this led to sanitation problems, rent racketeering and the formation of gangs, which in turn gave rise to political discontent among the rulers of the land. The apartheid regime ascended to power in 1948. They wasted no time in coming up with forced removal plans.

The Western Areas were the most popular in Johannesburg and were experiencing vibrant political activities related to the ANC and the Natives Representative Council, following the Representation of Natives Act No. 12 of 1936. Leaders like PQ Vundla, JB Marks, Gaur Radebe, Robert Resha and Agnes and Meinrad 'Mendi' Themba Msimang (ambassador), some of whom were members of the executive of the ANC and the CPSA in the Transvaal, were Western residents

Ida Mntwana, the first official president of the Women's League, and a prominent teacher during those days, also popularly known as 'Mistress June', whose real name was Motlalepula Chabaku, came from Western too. (Chabaku later became a church minister.) At some stage in the 1950s the strongest branch of the ANC was also from Western.

Across the Main Road in Sophiatown there was Dr AB Xuma, the ANC president from 1940 to 1949 and the man who introduced a new constitution to the ANC and planted the idea of Africans' Claims in 1943, a document drawn up by a committee of 28 members and sympathisers of the ANC who on 16 December 1943 unanimously accepted the document at the ANC's Annual Conference.

There was also Kate Molale, an activist against the Bantu Education Act and forced removals, who became a secretary of the Sophiatown ANC branch and the ANC Youth League, in the Transvaal.

Suddenly, in terms of the Group Areas Act of 1950, the state had the absolute right to expropriate, demolish and forcibly remove non-whites from the Western Areas. From around 1955 to the early 1960s Sophiatown was gradually demolished and was named Triomf – an Afrikaans word that means 'victory'. Africans, rich and poor alike, were moved first to Meadowlands in 1955, and in the following years, some were allocated 'matchbox' houses in various parts of Soweto: Chiawelo, Diepkloof, Meadowlands and Moroka (Rockville). This was orchestrated according to which ethnic groups people belonged to. For example, Venda and Tsonga speaking Africans were taken to Chiawelo, Meadowlands or Diepkloof, Sotho speakers to Moroka Sotho-section, and Zulu speakers to Moroka Zulu-section.

As Africans were being relocated to the various areas, other nationalities – Chinese, Asians and coloured people – were also separated into groups and moved accordingly around Johannesburg. By the 1960s the Western Areas had been cleared for 'sanitary and safety reasons', and space was created for whites and coloureds to move in, while Indians were forcibly removed from Pageview and part of Vrededorp (together known as Fietas) and Fordsburg – areas that are close to the Johannesburg city centre, to Lenasia (also called Lenz), the largest area where people of Indian origin could legally live in the Transvaal Province. Lenasia was built from 1958 to 1963 and is close to the Lenz Military Base, south of Johannesburg. The place is named after a Captain Lenz who owned the plot on which the township was established. The name 'Lenasia' is a combination of the words 'Lenz' and 'Asia'.[8]

For employment and business, new laws were introduced which aimed to exclude Africans from middle class occupations, and new restrictions on African businessmen were imposed. Job reservation regulations came in to prevent Africans from being employed in so-called 'white collar' jobs and skilled trades.

My family was among the last to be moved, in early 1962, before I was eight-years old. I remember the ride so well in that big open overloaded truck provided by the city council. I sat on top of the family load as if I was on top of the world. The big truck gently meandered out of Western with my family's worldly possessions. Days after that ride, with the naivety of a child, I kept asking my mother: 'When are we moving again?' I longed for another ride but it never came.

Following the forced removals of Africans to accommodate coloureds from Doornfontein and Pageview, Western Native Township, my birthplace, was proclaimed the Western Coloured Township in 1963. It was renamed Westbury in 1967.

Associated with these forced removals, two incidents remain embedded in my memory and psyche. The first is the aftermath of the Sharpeville massacre of Monday 21st March 1960. I was five years old and had no clue what had happened. Days after these killings, I accompanied my eldest brother, Joseph, to the shops. Our usual crossing place to reach the Chinese shops on the Newclare side, was blocked by policemen – black and white – clad in the old khaki uniform with matching helmets, carrying all sorts of weapons.

Our usual crossing place was an opening on the damaged steel fence that surrounded Western – two steel lines had been removed, allowing a person to go through. This made it easier for people to reach the shops across the road quickly. The police instructed us to turn back. I heard nothing and understood nothing, and I went straight up to them signalling that I want to cross over.

They laughed, noting that this little boy was not taking instructions from any stranger. The police waved to Joseph, who had already stopped and was preparing to turn back, to follow me. He obliged and followed me to the shops.

Joseph bought his cigarette, and I got my stock sweet. On our way back I waved my stock sweet at the police to show them that they had no authority to stop me from getting what I wanted. I even dared to play a little on an electricity pylon next to where some policemen were standing. The only time I felt there was something abnormal, was when my mother gave my brother a stern warning never to take me to the streets when there was danger looming.

The first state of emergency under apartheid was imposed on 30 March. The ANC and the PAC were banned on 7 April, and by May 1960 almost 18,000 people had been arrested and detained

A few months before my family's relocation to Rockville, Soweto, my father was involved in an accident that nearly took his life. Again, I was too young to understand what had happened. As I grew up and saw the injuries that my father sustained, I became more inquisitive about what had really taken place.

My father had stopped at a traffic light somewhere in the CBD. A white male driver who didn't pay attention to the traffic lights, hit his scooter from behind and caused my father to be flung metres high in the air. He landed head first on the road. He sustained a gaping hole on his head and both his legs were broken. He only regained his consciousness after a few days at Baragwanath Hospital (now Chris Hani Baragwanath Hospital). This was the most devastating moment for my family. The incident occurred on the eve of our departure for Soweto.

Days after the accident we were told our father was injured and was in hospital. As children, in the first few months we could not visit him. This was an extremely frustrating time. It would take long before my mother took us to visit my father at hospital. It was difficult to see him motionless with both legs hanging in the air and wrapped with gypsum plaster (plaster of Paris).

From this time on, our fortunes as a family changed forever. Every weekend we spent at Baragwanath Hospital visiting my father. We even relocated to Soweto without him. He was in hospital for six to nine months. The doctors suggested that he should consider amputating both legs. My father refused this ludicrous proposal and was obviously angry.

We started school in Soweto without him and without his support. With only my mother working and seven children to be looked after, this situation took a heavy toll on my mother. Up to this point my younger siblings and I didn't understand what had really happened or who had caused this almost fatal accident. It was almost three to four years after the accident that the truth started filtering through. Our parents never involved us in serious conversations. As children we would sense that there was something wrong or difficult to handle when our parents stopped talking as we approached them. We sensed that they were talking about the accident and my father's injuries. They spoke about papers that were not forthcoming and someone who was not prepared to do this or that.

Slowly the truth was coming out. Investigations by the traffic cops indicated that the white man driving the car that hit my father was at fault and he was doing everything he could to make sure the accident didn't go to court.

The details of the driver's discussions with my father's employer never came to light, but tricks and bribery were alluded to. I was too young to be involved or even grasp what was happening. All I know is that by the time I reached high school, and I was debating the politics of the day, I was an angry man regarding this accident. Every time my father had to go to hospital for this or that check-up, it was a painful moment, and someone had to accompany him.

ROCKVILLE, SOWETO (1962 – 1976)

Settling in Moroka/Rockville

My father's injury affected the family negatively. When the head of the family is not there, things go wrong. My elder brothers who were still at school when my father got injured started playing truant. My younger siblings and I were not aware of this as my mother tried to keep everything to herself. By the time my father came back from hospital my eldest brother, Joseph, was in jail for robbing an ice-cream vendor of his stock. When paying visits to him, my mother just said she was visiting Pretoria, because the Baviaanspoort Prison was not far away from Mamelodi. We thought she was visiting our relatives and wondered why she left us behind.

Jotham had also stopped going to school. When my mother tried to exert pressure on him, he tried to commit suicide by drinking caustic soda and his throat was partly damaged. Some years later he threw himself out of a moving train and was left crippled for life. Jerry started his classes at Sekano-Ntoane High School in Senaoane. I am not sure if he finished a year or two, before he was out of school. With a father who was no longer able to direct his children on what to do, things just went in their own direction with my elder siblings. My sister Sizakele started school at Ndondo Higher Primary and my mother found me a school at the edge of Rockville and White City, named Jabavu East Community School. Fana would later start school at Sipho Lower Primary in Dlamini Number Two. Some years later, Maggie followed him at the same school.

Extended family members who were living with us were also affected. During the relocation to Rockville, my grandmother, Gogo Jessie, went to stay with my father's other siblings moving between

Ennie, Petros and Daniel. Sydney Mafutha Zulu, our cousin and son of Petros Zulu in Swaziland (my father's uncle) had been with us for a long time in Western and attended the same schools as my brothers. My younger siblings and I grew up thinking we were eight children in the family and never knew that he was not one of our siblings.

We learnt later that he had been taken away from Swaziland because there was a belief that Petros Zulu's boy-children were dying at an early age because someone was poisoning them with 'muti' (African traditional medicine, sometimes associated with witchcraft). To save his life, he was brought to Johannesburg to stay with us. During my father's absence Mafutha started playing truant too. After the relocation to Rockville, he was sent packing back to Swaziland. He was already a big boy by this time. Overall, a new chapter in the family's life started.

Schooling and Student's Politics

Just as Johannesburg grew out of farms, so did Soweto. When Johannesburg was booming, the squatting around it became a problem. That is how Western, Sophiatown, Newlands, Newclare, and Martindale were created. With time the population increased and with segregation the criteria for spatial planning and occupation (the Natives Urban Areas Act 21 of 1923) changed and more farms were bought by the Johannesburg City Council (JCC) to relocate more people.

The mining sector through the Chamber of Mines (COM), which was mainly British, built Johannesburg. The JCC together with financial support from the COM, built Soweto. They went out to buy farms and created 'settlements' for Africans – that's what Soweto was called at the time. The Klipspruit Settlement was the first to be built on the Klipspruit farm in 1904. Kliptown, the oldest residential area with squatter camps had already been established in 1891.

Following an outbreak of the bubonic plague in the city (in 1904), the authorities burned down the compounds – where Africans lived – for health reasons and executed the 'first forceful removal' action. A large part of this settlement became known as Pimville in 1937.

The Department of Non-European Affairs (NEAD) was established in 1926 by the JCC to manage all these native settlements. In 1932 planned settlements 'to improve accommodation' started with Orlando East, followed by Orlando West, Mofolo, Jabavu (White City), Moroka North. Poor surroundings and squatting conditions started developing in Shanty Town near Orlando and Moroka near Nancefield. As time went on, formal settlements kept on increasing. These developments were taking place under the 'segregation laws' and under the United Party rule in the country.

Then in 1946 the JCC had a dream to create a middle-class African village on the Klipspruit farm next to the other settlements already built. It happened that in the same year the first popular president of the ANC, John Langalibalele Dube, died. In his honour this 'dream land' was named after him. However, the dream had many nightmares before Dube became a township in 1954.

Firstly, the National Party came into power in 1948 and halted all these developments. The hope remained that at least this first and only project would be implemented but in 1952 Dr Hendrik Verwoerd became the Minister for Native Affairs. The message was clear: Africans cannot have permanent settlements in the cities.

NEAD built a new head office in 1954 at 80a Albert Street, in the centre of town. This was the hub and nerve centre for controlling African people's lives in and around Johannesburg. Controlling the movement of Africans stretched throughout South Africa.

From 1954 onwards, no one coming to or born in Johannesburg, could avoid passing through Albert Street to get an official permit to work or reside in the area. Permit stamps in your 'dom pass' (the name given to the official document that African people had to carry with them to prove their identity and where they could live or work) were non-negotiable. Housing issues, marriages among black people, births and death certificates, everything was controlled and registered here. This place was officially called the Natives Affairs Department – 'Kwa-Ndabazabantu'.

After a stalemate, a 30-year-leasehold scheme was consented to for the middle class. They could do improvements on structures, but the property was still owned by the government. The concession of a 30-year leasehold was also extended to other townships, for example Orlando West and later Moroka – Rockville. Not everyone took up the scheme and in 1968 the apartheid regime stopped it.

Initially the plan envisaged bigger stands for Dube, but Verwoerd directed that the sizes of the stands be decreased. It is claimed that some people privately negotiated with the JCC for double stands.

The dream of Dube being a residential area with recreation, sport, education, and trade facilities, and with roads, water reticulation, sewerage services, was already proceeding in 1951. This was stopped and adjusted. Dube could not be exclusive. Nonetheless, residents who moved in 1954 gave Dube its own identity. It had a mixture of match box houses, 30-year-lease homes, a little bit bigger in size, and others with running water and installed sewerage-piping, especially in Dube Village.

The apartheid authorities never failed to show who was in charge. A year after residents moved into their homes, they erected the first single sex hostel for migrant labourers next to the houses in Dube, just to prove that Dube was not special. The township had been reserved for Nguni speaking Africans, but this was not enforced, and the residents were a good mixture of black South Africans. Noteworthy people from diverse backgrounds and cultures came to live here, like Andrew

Mlangeni (Rivonia Trialist), Dr Richard Gugushe (educator), Richard Maponya (entrepreneur) and Gibson Mthuthuzeli Kente (dramatist/playwright). Others were M Tebatso Moerane (World newspaper editor 1962/68) and Leslie Sehume (journalist/boxing coach).

After the forced removals in Western, Sophiatown and surroundings, Dr Nthato Motlana (doctor, business leader and political activist) and Sally Motlana (leader and businesswoman), Dr Benedict Wallet Vilakazi (academic/poet), Dr Alfred Bathini Xuma (former ANC President) and Ben Mabuza (businessman) resettled here.[9] Philip Qipa 'PQ' Vundla, who had become a nonconforming ANC leader, educationist, trade unionist and journalist, was a member of the Western Native Township advisory board and a principal organiser of resistance to the removal scheme, came to live here.

The number of townships kept increasing as more settlements were added. The 'Soweto' name for the area was only officially adopted in 1963 following a tense competition by the JCC. SOWETO is an acronym for South Western Townships. More than 10 years later this name made headlines after the June 16 shootings and killings of school children.

Officially the name for Rockville is Moroka, named after the former ANC President, Dr James Moroka. The origins of the name Rockville had to do with the rocks and stones found in most parts of the township when we first arrived there. The municipality used dynamite-blasting machines to remove some of the rocks and flatten the ground. In some places the rocks were inside the houses. We were fortunate at my home as the rocks were only outside in the yard. The noise of the blasting machines was unbearable. In the early days, the blasting was a daily occurrence and caused the walls of some houses to crack. People started saying this place is 'Rockville', we were fooled by the authorities to come here and live among rocks. The name stuck.

There were temporary fences dividing houses, and no gates. There were no trees, no streetlights, and no electricity in the houses. These were only fitted and built when we were already living in the houses. The roads, like almost all streets in Soweto at the time, were not tarred except for the main roads. Zulu-section lies on the northeast and Sotho-section on the northwest of the famous Moroka Dam, also called Rockville Dam. Some people here used to say that apartheid authorities were bad, but for the first time they thought that black people deserved to have a dam of their own. Others would counter this by saying it was a trap because they wanted us to all drown in it as most people did not know how to swim. The area around the dam is now popularly known as 'Thokoza Park'.

We were lucky that my father's accident happened after he opted for the 99-year-leasehold. These houses are situated south of the dam, and they are called 'eziTandini' (stands). They were much bigger than ordinary houses in Soweto, especially those in Dube. At this time all houses had water and sewerage inside. The plots were relatively large too. After the expiry of the 99-year-lease period, the owners were promised ownership. Although this applied to those people 'eziTandini' only, it made all residents of Rockville think that they were better than others in Soweto.

Once the streetlights were erected, these houses were amongst the first to be provided with electricity. I remember very well that in my neighbourhood, families who could afford to have electricity installed, were the envy of the day. Electricity meant buying a fridge. Having a fridge meant having ice cubes, and ice cubes meant having 'ice-squinches' – the compacted ice made from a cool drink using 'Kool-Aid' powder, the most popular brand in those days. Right from the beginning the area was earmarked for anyone who could afford to sign for the leasehold. This became a mixed ethnic and cultural environment, just like in Western, and most families knew each other from there. We occupied stand number 2018 Budaza Street.

Everything looked and sounded new. South Africa had just pulled out of the Commonwealth of States. The regime got rid of pounds and pennies and introduced rands and cents in early 1961, before 31 of May. This was the day the new constitution declaring South Africa a republic came into force. 'Umsakazo', the old radio system with wires connecting through houses was being discarded and radios with batteries were coming into fashion. The gramophone with needles was being replaced by a compact hi-fi system. The music of Mahlathini and the Mahotella Queens was bellowing from the new houses. The name change from the Union to the Republic of South Africa was printed everywhere.

Rockville is surrounded by Moroka North and White City (Jabavu) in the north, Mofolo South in the east, Dlamini and Senaoane in the south and Molapo on the north-west side. Just past Dlamini is Kliptown, which is also a walking distance away. On Saturdays, as kids, we used to go to the old and famous Sans Souci cinema (built in 1948) in Kliptown. This cinema used to host many prominent artists like Miriam Makeba, Kippie Moeketsi and Dollar Brand (Abdullah Ibrahim) in the 1950s.

I was exactly one year old when the Freedom Charter was adopted on the sports grounds of Kliptown, where later during my childhood days we used to watch football matches between various Soweto soccer teams.

On weekends, especially after rainy days, as young boys, and girls, we went swimming at the Moroka Dam, which is part of the Klip River wetlands that run through Soweto. This was a risky affair as we relied on those who could swim for our safety. Many a times, life threatening scenes occurred. If it happened to you, you prayed that your family never came to know of it. You would receive harsh punishment for this escapade. We went to catch river crabs in the tributaries to these wetlands, and had fun opening the carapace, the shield-like dorsal part of the exoskeleton. There was a legend that we would find coins inside. That never happened.

On freezing days in winter the boys would play truant and go hunting for a special rat called 'imbiba', or the 'reed rat', which was brownish in colour and had two or three strongly distinct stripes at the back. After removing the head, we carefully skinned it with our hands, then removed the insides and put it on a fire made from pieces of wood. This was a delicacy if you added salt.

I completed my Standard II at Jabavu East lower primary school in 1964 and went to Ndondo Higher Primary School, a mere three minutes' walk from my home. Starting with Standard III in 1965 I finished standard VI in 1968. In these formative years, it was clear that progress was measured by learning and mastering three languages – your mother tongue, English, and Afrikaans. English and Afrikaans were obligatory, but funnily enough, you could change your mother tongue language to whatever you wanted. It all depended on the school you chose or where you succeeded in finding placement.

At Ndondo there was a teacher, Frederick Mbatha, who had come from Newcastle, Natal and immediately connected with my family. In those days it was easy for teachers from outside Johannesburg to find temporary accommodation and later permanent places to stay in Soweto. The regime was slowly turning education into an instrument to control our minds. With 'Teacher Mbatha', one of the strictest teachers I ever met, I had the toughest time of my life at school. I had to get everything right or face the worst punishment. In any test he gave, my marks had to be ninety percent or higher. Suddenly I was treated differently from other kids.

'Teacher Mbatha' had reconnected with Jabulani Mazibuko, the principal and famous choirmaster, as both had qualified from the Marianhill Teachers Training Institution in Natal. As a teacher and choral music conductor, Mazibuko conducted the Jabavu Choristers.

He founded the Johannesburg Teachers Choir in 1969 and later formed the Soweto Teachers Choir and the Baragwanath Choir, thus becoming a force in choral music. The combination of the two and another dreaded teacher called Sydney Motingoe, who taught the Sotho language class and was responsible for handwork for all Standard Five and Six scholars, symbolised discipline of the highest order. Those who schooled at Ndondo during those years, know that the school became a testing ground for resilience. When you were given physical punishment from any of these three individuals, you dared not repeat the same mistake again. This experience was not unique. All teachers had to produce students who mastered the teachings of Bantu education heart and soul. We were the pawns they tested with.

My schoolmates and friends here were: Dennis Mxolisi 'Bucs' Ngqase, Selby Vuyani 'Svari' 'Chivago' Mavuso (MK nom de guerre; Larry 'Bab' Makhaya), Derrick Sydney Sipho 'Siga' Pewa (MK nom de guerre Themba Mlotshwa) and Oupa Nyathi (Reverend Cecil Mangedwa Nyathi), Edward Panka Malvern and George Nkosinathi 'Sonke' Twala, all from Rockville. There were also girls from Rockville: Faith Nomaqule Titi Malinga (nee Ndzekeli), Florence and Nomvula Ndaba, Lawukazi Budaza, Miami Welile Twala, Cordelia Dlodlo, Kuki Sibiya, Vera 'Fufu' Ngwenya, Cynthia Thabile Sithole, Queen Maguba, Miriam Duduzile 'Dudu' Zondo[10] and Patricia Moipone Mokoena. From Dlamini and Senaoane there was Elias Mandla Hlophe (Mandla 'Dlamini'), Dr Theophilus Mandla Nyembe (Mandla 'Senaoane'), David Mavuku, Abednego Tito Zwane, Lauretta Zethu Sibisi, Ephraim Gama, Sdakwa Majola, Clement Hlongwane, Stephen Mngomezulu, Steven Njoko, Sydney Bongani Ngwenya, Archibald Duma Ngcayi, among others.

Ndondo was a preparation ground for high school. I mastered schoolwork and assignments given to us by all the teachers. What I appreciated most, even today, were the handiwork classes. Although it was time-consuming, producing trays out of wood and décor figures out of a cow's horn, these achievements contributed to my versatility, later in life, and equipped me to do many things for myself.

It was also during this time that I, together with a few friends, developed an interest in gardening. At home I took over from my father who was interested too, but he mainly cared for the trees – peaches and plums – and the grapevines. I established a rockery in the front yard which proved to be time-consuming so I flattened it so that I could concentrate on keeping the lawn in good shape. In the summer the garden became a haven of relaxation that not only provided shade but also bore fruit.

My first year – Form I – at Sekano-Ntoane High School in 1969 was laissez-faire. I mingled with my new peers from all around Soweto. There were only four high schools – Madibane High, Musi High, Orlando High and Sekano High – in the whole of Soweto for over three-million or more people. There were a few secondary schools – Orlando West, Morris-Isaacson, Naledi, and later Molapo and Senoane.

Many parents who could afford to send their children to boarding schools so that they could escape the volatile political environment and many other challenges and tribulations of township life. Some of the popular destinations were high schools with boarding quarters like KwaDlangezwa, Ohlange, Amanzimtoti and Inanda in Natal, and some were in the Cape Province. Among my peers from Rockville the brothers, Bangile and Sabelo Neku (the sons to Eunice Ntsiki Kabane, popularly known as Sis' Ntsiki, a socialite in those days), went to KwaDlangezwa and Mandla Nyembe left Sekano after passing JC with many distinctions, for Amanzimtoti.

My peers and I came from strict and very conservative families. We never looked our parents in the face, and most of the time we never questioned them, even in instances where we felt they were wrong.

Bangile and Sabelo had a different relationship with their mom and spoke with her as if they were talking to their sister. It was unusual and as kids we were envious of this relationship. Sis' Ntsiki, being liberal, allowed all types of freedom in her house, the boys drove her work-car for errands around Rockville. We hung around her place as we got free rides and learned how to drive when the occasion presented itself. Her attitude was rewarding when it came to general knowledge as her children were always ahead when it came to world affairs and collected banned literature which was revolutionary. Sis Ntsiki was the elder sister to Patricia Kabane, who was the mother to Wandile Thamsanqa Kabane and a cousin to Bangile and Sabelo.

Other parents sent their children to high schools in the Northern Transvaal, for example, Cyril Matamela Ramaphosa (current President of South Africa) started his high school at Sekano-Ntoane and went to complete his matric at Mphaphuli High School in a village of Sibasa in Venda. Naturally, it was every child's dream to go to a boarding school, but for many families, like mine, financial circumstances did not allow for it.

I had chosen mathematics and physics as my subjects, because my mother's dream was that I would become a medical doctor. As I progressed at school, from Sub-A, Sub-B, Standard One and so on, this dream was being fulfilled. Every time there was a visitor of some reputation at home, I was directly asked, 'what do you want to be?' And I had memorised the answer, 'I want to be a doctor'. This response made my mother feel proud that her investment in me was bearing fruit. I could see her smile and the twinkle in her eyes.

Form II and III (1970 and 1971) were known as the Junior Certificate (JC) level and I was with: Abednego 'Tata' Ngwenya, Juliana Makapan, Thelma Mapule Mbhalati (nee Mkhabela), Elizabeth Mkhaliphi, Angee Netshiheni (nee Mkhwanazi), Queen Maguba, Beverley Madiale Mashile, Patricia Moipone Mokoena,

Abednego Tito Zwane, Papi Kubu, Duma Ndlovu (playwright, producer and director), Mandla Nyembe, among others.

These were my eye-opening years. I was getting into my mid-teens now and started to look at life quite differently. The Native Education Act of 1953 (later known as the Bantu Education Act or Black Education Act) which became operational in 1954 was now encroaching on the lower levels of schooling from higher primary levels. To start with, from the late 1950s, many qualified teachers left the profession and went to start business enterprises, while others left for neighbouring countries like Bechuanaland, Basutoland, Swaziland, North and Southern Rhodesia, up to Kenya and Tanganyika. Moving to these places was easier then as these colonies were all under Britain and had a similar educational system to South Africa.

Through the Extension of University Education Act of 1959, the regime managed to take control of and tribalise universities. The law directed that 'white' universities be inaccessible for black students and those designated for black people were divided into different ethnic groups. New universities were established for 'non-white' groups. In the Cape, the University of the Western Cape was created in Bellville for Coloureds, the University of Zululand for Zulus, the University of Durban-Westville for Indians, Turfloop for Sotho and Tswana speaking Africans, and Fort Hare, after all the years of enrolling blacks from all over the continent, was turned into a place for Xhosa speakers. The 1960s were the amalgamation of the old and new, which would give birth to new paradoxes and conflicts. Therefore, it was not a mistake that the turn into the 1970s gave rise to resistance by students at universities.

The Bantu Homelands Citizen Act of 1970, which robbed Africans of their South African citizenship and the brutal enforcement of Section 10 [10] of the Urban Areas Act worked against the requirement for better skills that the economy needed.

Having taken a decision not to build schools in places like Soweto, the Bantu Education Department was forced to reverse these choices and build more schools, which in any event were insufficient. To save money, the department even reduced the number of years from 13 to 12 years for Africans at school. Enforcing the Bantu Education Act and having succeeded in introducing Afrikaans as a subject at higher primary levels, for the JC years 1970 to 1971, the department commenced with at least one subject in Afrikaans that we, as students, had to master.

As the apartheid state was now in charge of education, it allowed no political activity at schools and universities. The teachers that had remained in the profession had to do what the state wanted. With a pupil-to-teacher ratio that was remarkably high and increasing every year, sometimes there was one teacher for 50 to 60 pupils. This was a demanding task for teachers in places like Soweto. The only way that principals and teachers could maintain discipline and control among students was through excessive corporal punishment. Many a principal or teacher became notorious as executors of the worst punishment.

Students without the prescribed books, stationery or uniform and those who could not learn by memorisation and regurgitating everything taught by the teachers, were brutally punished. The same applied to those who were late or had not paid their school fees. If you were chosen as a prefect at school, you had to help teachers with the maintenance of this type of discipline.

In this context, the authorities allowed the teaching of religious classes to continue as part of education. At both Ndondo primary and Sekano-Ntoane, morning gatherings of students opened with prayers said by our teachers. At Ndondo, there were special scripture lessons on Wednesday afternoons that were always led by white women, who came to school only for this purpose. Attendance was compulsory.

At Sekano, on Tuesday or Wednesday mornings, the prayers at the morning gatherings were led by mainly male white scripture teachers. Some of these teachers would come back on specific days and meet with students organised under the banner of the Students Christian Movement (SCM). At least it was not compulsory to attend these meetings. The SCMs had been in existence in South Africa for many years before apartheid came into existence. Since this was one of the only few organised structures allowed by the authorities to freely mobilise, organise and hold functions in schools, it became the basis upon which future student' organisations were established.

This applied to universities too and can be traced back to the existence of the University Christian Movement (UCM), the National Union of South African Students (NUSAS) and the South African Student Organisation (SASO).[11] At high schools in Soweto, it was the existence of these SCMs, the influence of certain teachers who resisted the changes that apartheid was imposing on our education, and other factors that made it possible to establish student' organisations that were politically inclined. I know many of my peers who used these SCM gatherings to discuss political matters.

This is where another teacher, Thomas 'Tom' Madikwe Manthata, who won my attention as well as that of other students, comes in. He was a no-nonsense teacher who earned the name 'Killer' from students. Tom Manthata taught English and wanted us to come to class in the morning having read the *Rand Daily Mail* (RDM). For most students, the paper was expensive and the English in it was of a higher level. He wanted us to improve our English language knowledge. Later, we found out that there was another reason, which was that of the contents of this newspaper. Unlike popular township papers like *The World*, originally named *The Bantu World*, a black daily of Johannesburg, the RDM carried a variety of themes in politics, economics and world affairs.

Teacher Manthata commenced his class by asking about any issue or event from the RDM. If you could not answer correctly, all hell broke out. He would admonish the class and challenge them, saying, 'Some of you were loud during the prayer meeting in the morning and yet you can't tell me what's in the paper today'. He then wanted to know what was on this page or that page of the prescribed English literature book under discussion for that month, usually from one of Shakespeare's writings. If you did not know, the punishment was severe.

Radio in South Africa at the time was a non-starter, including SAFM (called English Service then), Radio Bantu, etc. It was all about local insignificant matters, no political discussions or reports, and no perspective. Unless of course you listened to BBC or VOA.

The early 1970s were characterised by the intensification of political conscientisation in the country and the RDM carried reports of what was happening in every corner of South Africa. For example, the students' strikes at universities organised by the South African Students' Organisation (SASO), the emergence of the Black Consciousness Movement (BCM), the launch of the Black People's Convention (BPC) at Edendale – all in 1972; the death of Ahmed Timol in 1971; the Durban strikes and the release of Jacob Zuma in 1973 and that of Joe Gqabi in 1975; the banning orders imposed on PAC leaders like Robert Sobukwe after his release from Robben Island and on Zephania 'Zeph' Lekoane Mothopeng; and the Pro-Frelimo rallies. The harassment of Winnie Mandela by the state and numerous trials during this time, such as the trial of Harry Gwala, were also covered by the paper

> *The state's trial of Gwala became a site of a countervailing discourse, a site of establishing historical narratives that simultaneously questioned the authority of the apartheid state and legitimised the liberation struggle. The trials present the*

> *paradox of the oppressive South African state using the law in politically biased courts to deny justice to the majority. These trials were characterised by state censure intended to disconnect and vilify Gwala, but which instead aided the liberation movement's efforts through providing publicity, thus gaining much-needed public sympathy, international expressions of solidarity, and widespread exposure of the brutality of apartheid.*[12]

Later when I was politically ripe, I reflected on the role that Manthata played. He was encouraging us to engage with the daily political and concrete happenings in the country. He opened my eyes to many things about my country.

Ernest Hlabane was another teacher who left me with remarkable impressions as a physics and mathematics teacher. He stayed in or hired a room at a house in Rockville, Sotho-Section. One afternoon in his physics class, while explaining how matter can change from one state to another, he he told us a story related to the Second World War in Germany. He described the crematoria built in the concentration camps and how the Nazis incinerated corpses of prisoners. Before the incineration process started, the hair of the victims would be removed and burned separately to make soap. And, from the dead, they removed teeth with gold fillings. This was probably the scariest part of the narrative and it remained with me for many years after I left school.

I had been given a solid base for my political awareness by the time I began my matric.

After JC I abandoned physics and mathematics because I was now more attracted to history and geography. I did not tell my mother that the road to becoming a doctor had been abandoned. If I worked hard and passed my classes this would be good for my parents and my family, I convinced myself. Maths and physics did not help me understand the world so I dropped these key science subjects at the beginning of 1972. I now wanted to know more about the Germans and the Napoleonic wars and so on.

There was another reason for this switch. It was from observing senior students in matric carrying big volumes under their arms after school. This fascinated me as these books were bigger than the bible. What was written inside there? This provoked interest in me. I imagined they might be carrying some serious stuff. One of these voluminous books was by Boyce (Professor Arnold Napier Boyce).[13] He specialised in European and South African history.

The events that were about to unfold before me were a catalyst for my political growth. As the school year started, new teachers arrived. Their approach to teaching was more engaging with students than anything we had experienced before. I call these teachers the 'BCM' graduate teachers as they were mainly influenced by the philosophy of the Black Consciousness Movement (BCM), and they were rebellious against the system of Bantu education. These teachers were questioning the edifice of education for African children, and they made it their mission to influence students differently.

As the debates in class became more interesting, I was forging new friendships with other students. This was happening to some of my peers from Rockville too. Our circle of friends soon multiplied. Suddenly we were able to gain access to banned literature, books about the Black Panther movement of the late 1960s in the United States of America. There was also literature on the inspiring struggle of black Americans (we called them Afro-Americans then) led by Martin Luther King Jr. These books were harder to get, and some were banned. You got a book and over two nights you needed to have finished reading it and passed it 'under the desk' to the next in line.

I remember very well how my classmates from Rockville, Dede Mokgemi and Thabo Nkhumise, Michael Mike Mashinini from Diepkloof and I used to swap some of these books. Nkhumise was also a good storyteller, especially movie-stories like that of actor Sydney Poitier in *To Sir, With Love* or *Guess Who's Coming to Dinner*. If one were caught reading a book, there were serious repercussions, especially with teachers who were pushing the 'old line' of teaching. To finish on time, one had to carefully choose which periods gave you space to read while the lesson was going on.

A flood of African literature arrived in our township libraries, books like, *Things Fall Apart* and *Arrow of God* by Chinua Achebe. At higher primary, during my years at Ndondo, all literature – from grammar to novels and poetry – was written by black authors, in African languages: Sotho, Xhosa, or Zulu. Suddenly literature from the continent was in English and depicting real life stories. We rushed to libraries to get hold of the books and we stopped concentrating on literature such as that of author James Hadley Chase, which was very popular then.

Sharpeville

One day our history teacher Pat Chabane (Professor Patrick Chabane)[14] came to class and straight away started talking about the shootings of Sharpeville in 1960. He spoke about the burning of passes and the police opening fire on demonstrators. Destroying a passbook! Wow! Many of us had never imagined such a thing. A passbook in those days was the almost sanctified, and a must-carry document if you wanted to avoid police harassment. Without a passbook, you faced jail.

During school holidays as boys, we carried special school permits that proved to the police when stopping you in the streets, that you were not a 'wanderer', but a good citizen and had permission to be where you were. Girls had no such harassment in Johannesburg unless they were arrested for a concrete illegal act.

The day was the 21st of March in 1972. The class was so silent, you could hear a pin drop. Teacher Chabane remained calm and composed, he never flinched. Listening to him aroused a lot of anger among us students, which, I think, was his intention. The message was clear. The way he described Sharpeville and what had followed days after the shootings, reminded me of the incident with the police in Western when my brother and I wanted to cross over to the shops. My mind just stopped there. Yes, that was it, Sharpeville!

1972 and the University of Turfloop

Nelson Mandela, in the first powerful and revolutionary self-defence address in court in 1962, which was later termed the 'Black man in a white court' speech, among other things, said:

> *The white man makes all the laws, he drags us before his courts and accuses us, and he sits in judgement over us ... Why is it that in this courtroom I face a white magistrate, am confronted by a white prosecutor, and escorted into the dock by a white orderly? Can anyone honestly and seriously suggest that in this type of atmosphere the scales of justice are evenly balanced?*[15]

In the 1964 Rivonia trial he said:

> *During my lifetime I have dedicated myself to this struggle of the African people. I have fought against white domination, and I have fought against black domination. I have cherished the ideal of a democratic and free society in which all persons live together in harmony and with equal opportunities. It is an ideal which I hope to live for and to achieve. But if needs be, it is an ideal for which I am prepared to die.*[16]

In 1962 and 1964 I was eight and 10 years old respectively, too young to have comprehended the above scenarios. As we were growing up there was a political vacuum caused by the banning of the black political parties and many leaders had fled the country. Others were incarcerated on Robben Island. There was no literature about these events. What was worse, there was no word of mouth sharing of information as that was too dangerous. The media was totally gagged and those leaders that were among the people were muzzled. Everything was said in whispers. Apart from those coming from involved and affected families, many of us had not heard our own leaders speak or address an audience, a rally in the streets or in a hall.

Year after year those in attendance during the graduation ceremonies at the University of Turfloop were always white administrators, their wives and children in the front rows while black parents of those graduating were seated at the back or left outside as it was claimed that the hall was full. For this reason, these graduation ceremonies were considered non-events, except for the families of those graduating and receiving their certificates of achievement.

Then on one Saturday, 29 April 1972, the son of an unknown domestic worker took to the podium to deliver the valedictory speech. Traditionally the purpose of this speech was to thank the authorities and the university, which was almost endorsing their policies. What makes events historical is never predictable. No one anticipated that things were about to be turned upside down. The graduate, Onkgopotse Abram Tiro, spoke:

> *How do Black lecturers contribute to the administration of this University? For if you look at all the committees, they are predominantly White if not completely White. Here and there one finds two or three Africans who, in the opinion of students are White Black men...*
>
> *Right now, our parents have come all the way from their homes only to be locked outside. We are told that the hall is full... My father is seated there at the back. My dear people, shall we ever get a fair deal in this land? The land of our fathers. The system is failing...*
>
> *In the light of what has been said above, the challenge to every Black graduate in this country lies in the fact that the guilt of all wrongful actions in South Africa, restriction without*

> *trial, repugnant legislation, expulsions from schools, rests on all those who do not actively dissociate themselves from and work for the eradication of the system breeding such evils. ...*
>
> *We Black graduates, by virtue of our age and academic standing are being called upon to bear greater responsibilities in the liberation of our people.*

That was it, the end of the ceremony. The red faces, the rant and rave in the front rows were a spectacle to behold. At the back and outside there was jubilation. For such a stand there were grave consequences. On Monday morning Tiro was summoned to a mock disciplinary hearing and expelled on the same day.

One could not tell of the effects this would have on the turn of political events in the country. Slowly the news filtered through, and we got to know what had taken place at 'Turf' as the university was known. The progressive teachers started whispering, the core coming from the Northern Transvaal and they galvanised us towards action.

Tiro's expulsion sparked nationwide protests and had far-reaching consequences that almost crippled the entire tertiary education sector. From May to June there were solidarity actions at institutions of higher learning across South Africa. One afternoon at school we were told that Tiro was going to address us at Phiri Hall. On the day there was euphoria everywhere as we marched to this place which was a kilometre away from Sekano.

The progressive teachers were still a minority, so not all teachers were enthusiastic about this. We already knew which teachers were tolerant and which were very conservative. The Phiri Hall event left a lasting impression on me. After being introduced by Tom Manthata, Tiro took to the floor amid thunderous applause and started addressing us. Every sentence that he uttered struck a sympathetic chord among the students. It was a single conscientising moment that would last forever. After this, at our morning gatherings before school started, during break intervals and after school, we spent time discussing our education and the circumstances we black people lived in.

The most outspoken student among us and my classmate was Amos 'Ambi' Masondo from Senaoane (a former prisoner of Robben Island and a former mayor of Johannesburg, and current Chair of the National Council of Provinces – NCOP). Ambi never lost an opportunity to urge us to act or do something. Already in 1974, he wanted us to destroy bottle stores and other apartheid infrastructure in the township that held our people in perpetual disillusionment.

My other class- and schoolmates besides those from Rockville, like Lordwish 'Otis' Letsoalo, were: Mirriam Nuska Thobeka Zwane (nee Fumile), Moses 'Steyn' Hadebe (Senoane), Andrew Ndzonga, Abednego Nkula, David Mavuku, Amos Ramaphakela, Steve Pelle, Moses Tholoane, (Dr) Richard Lekhotla Monare, Brutus Molefe, Abednego 'Tito' Zwane, Joseph 'Hu' Xaba, Joel Mpshe and Abel Thabo Borole.

In later years of exile, it became clear to me that Masondo was already linked to underground operations of the ANC. Very slowly the seeds of revolt were planted. The process of conscientising led to a broader awareness of our social and political conditions in society.

To expose and interpret this reality that surrounded black people's lives was one of the most important influences BCM philosophy had on Africans' political thinking. It happened under very repressive conditions. I should also indicate that this BCM philosophy at this point in time in our history had nothing to do with the political organisations that were later founded in the name of black consciousness. This awareness alone (or the philosophy), did not always lead one to challenge the inequalities that surrounded black people's lives, but surely it laid the basis. It was not long that this foundation became the platform from which a political voice emerged to express the sentiments of the disenfranchised.

In my family, the injury my father suffered negatively impacted on us all. My father never returned to work. There was no court case, and no one was arrested. There was no compensation of any sort for his injuries. Now and then he experienced this or that problem with his legs. At one stage we thought the wounds on both his legs had healed, and the next thing the wounds were emitting maggots. Whenever he took off the bandages and exposed his wounds, the scene in the kitchen was a distressing spectacle. He and all of us, the children, did not understand what was happening to him.

Some years later, when I was based in East Germany (the German Democratic Republic – GDR), there were comrades who had been injured in the military camps in Angola and were brought to Germany for treatment. Some had leg injuries as a result of grenade explosions and their wounds emitted maggots, just like my father's wounds had. I had a personal interest in finding more about the cause of this.

One day I sat down with Aubrey 'Bushy' (retired Lt. Gen. Aubrey Sedibe) who was a student and had a wound like my father had, and I asked him to explain what was happening. He told me that the broken pieces of bone made the wound septic and this resulted in maggots growing inside the wound. That is why the wound needed to be opened every five to six weeks or so, to remove the pieces of bone until the wound is fully healed. As there were no means of communicating with my family back at home, I always hoped that they had also found the cause of my father's problem.

Because of his injuries, my father limped and used a walking stick for the rest of his life. Jobless as he was, he did not want to stay at home and do nothing. He joined the fah-fee (Chinese numbers game) – a form of gambling in the townships which was illegal and was from time to time disrupted by the police – and became a 'runner'. In the mornings and afternoons, every day during the week, he was up and about around the township, collecting players' bets and distributing the winnings afterwards.

My mother had continued doing 'piece jobs' (casual or ad hoc employment) for my family to survive. My elder brothers were now out of school. At times they would have jobs and the next day they would be unemployed. This put a lot of strain on my mother. I kept telling myself that one day I would address my family's needs.

My elder sister, Siza, had left school too in 1969. School ended for her when she got pregnant. In those days pregnancy was seen as an evil and an unacceptable thing for a schoolgirl. One day I came back from school, and she was screaming from the punishment she was getting in my parent's bedroom. I did not understand then what wrong she had done. From that day on, I noticed that she no longer attended school. When the time arrived, she gave birth to a baby girl, and she was named Jessie Lindiwe. Jessie was my paternal grandmother's name.

As things stood, Siza had to look for a job. Her first and only workplace for many years was the popular five-star Carlton Hotel at the Carlton Centre complex that was built by Anglo American and started operations in 1972. The 50-storey skyscraper and shopping centre in downtown Johannesburg was the tallest building in Africa until the Leonardo was built in Sandton, Johannesburg in 2018. Siza was a self-taught cook having learned all the skills from my mother. In those times girls had to master cooking skills at home. As her older siblings were boys, the task of cooking and baking fell on her. Over the years, it is this skill that made her one of the best sous-chefs at the Carlton and always in demand for special occasions when rich and famous South African and international guests were in town. Fana and Maggie were also doing well with their education.

I had to ponder over many things now. I resolved to finish my studies and to repay my parents' investments in me. Although there were many challenges in the family that year, I never thought this would affect my performance at school, as I was convinced that I had given my best attention to my books but at the end of the year when I received my results, I had failed.

I was very angry about this, and I remember well that I walked to my class teacher's house (Teacher Segoni) in Dube during the holidays in early December and asked for an explanation regarding my results. He was calm with me and told me simply that there was a quota system that was applied by the authorities which allowed for a certain number of students to proceed to the next class. It was not his fault. I was shocked by this revelation. I learned later that the quota system applied in other areas of black people's lives too. For example, in the legal practice, the system didn't allow for an influx of blacks into the profession and encouraged them to go to the homelands.

I repeated Form IV the following year (1973) and made sure I received more than average results. In the intervening time, African parents, teachers, school principals, and even some of the homeland leaders, were raising their voices on this issue of imposing Afrikaans in African schools.

> *In 1973 the Department of Bantu education issued a policy document, Circular no. 2 of 1973, entitled 'Medium of Instruction in Secondary Schools (and Std 5 classes) in White Areas'. Section A of the circular, referring to 'Policy to be applied and arrangements to be made in the white areas', accorded both English and Afrikaans 50:50 status as official languages of instruction from the year of primary school until completion of high school.*[17]

I only completed my matric, Form V, in 1974.

Gangsterism

To talk about growing up in Soweto is not complete without pointing out at another reality that was part of our lives – the prevalence of gangsterism. As a young boy one was not spared. If you were sent to buy bread, you were warned, 'make sure you hide the money from the 'tsotsis' (thugs)'. As you started school and become independent, your parents would caution you, 'Hide your pocket money from the tsotsis'. When you were old enough to be sent to town, using buses and trains, you were cautioned, 'Don't speak to strangers, hide your money and make sure you are safe from the tsotsis'.

With time you become experienced and streetwise. Your circumstances such as your family, your location in the township, where you attended school, who you befriended and of course where your girlfriend or boyfriend resided influenced how you adapted. At some stage during my childhood and growing up, it seemed impossible to survive without belonging to a gang, especially as a boy. I first associated this with being black but gradually realised that it was an urban phenomenon, although the intensity differed from one township to another or from city to city. I began to see that it was directly connected to the social milieu we lived in; to poverty, inequality, and unemployment, especially in densely populated areas.

From the early years of the development of the City of Gold, this phenomenon was there. For example, legislation of the time indicates that:

> *Anyone caught in possession of unrefined gold after 1895 without 'proof that he obtained the possession' lawfully was presumed guilty of the crime of Illicit Gold Buying and subject to harsh penalties.*[18]

It is not surprising that with the rise of Western, Sophiatown and the surroundings, gangs started swelling too. There were groups like the Americans, the Gestapo, the Berliners, and the Vultures.

As a school student in Soweto, crime and violence became my reality of urban life and culture. The poverty, misery, violence, and lawlessness in the city was reflected and captured in musical theatre pieces like *Sikalo (The Cry,* 1965*)* and *How Long* (1973), authored by the prominent playwright, composer, director, producer and father of township theatre, Gibson Kente. He was one of the first writers to confront the oppressive system by dealing with real life issues using township popular culture, dialects, fashion, song, dance and topical issues.

How Long, the theme and song of the musical bravely asked, *'how long, must we suffer?'*

> *How long must we suffer this way, Oh Lord?*
> *How long all this misery, each day, Oh Lord?*
> *How long, the tears?*
> *Tell me Lord, how long, Oh Glory, how long?*
> *Tell me Lord, why pick on me, Lord?*
> *Tell me Lord, why pick on me,*
> *When I am hopeless and down and down ...*

Themba Limbi, a song in the same musical succinctly captured the state of the African family in the township during this period:

THEMBA LIMBI (Zulu/Xhosa)

>*Themba limbi, asinalo,*
>*ngexesha le' nhlupheko*
>*Nguwe, nguwe wedwa somandla,*
>*Ithemba lezintandane!*
>*Thuthuzela abafelweyo,*
>*Pholisa abagulayo*
>*Sula, suli' nyembezi zabo*
>*Themba lezinkedama!*

Translation:

NO HOPE

>*We have no hope,*
>*during this time of tribulation.*
>*You, and you alone, the Almighty,*
>*are the Hope for all the orphans!*
>*Comfort the bereaved,*
>*Heal the sick,*
>*Wipe away their tears,*
>*Hope for all the orphans!*

Kente followed with *I Believe* (1974) and *Too Late* (1975) and while he was filming *How Long* in early 1976, just before the outbreak of the uprisings, he was arrested.

In most families both parents had to work long hours in town and far away from Soweto. The instability of the urban African family, which had no right to be in the city except for selling its labour, was reflected in the minimal parental control and guidance exercised, especially with regard to schoolwork. Juvenile delinquency rates were particularly high.

There were numerous youth gangs or tsotsis, mostly territorial in character. Some of the tsotsis or gang members attended school with us. I remember very well that during my years at Sekano-Ntoane High

School there were two murders involving students, one from Rockville and another from Mapetla. Some of these gangsters were small-time criminals, having 'respectable' jobs during the day, but at night and on weekends they were criminals.

One of the popular music groups of our time, the Temptations, from the United States, released a song that instantly became trendy in places like Soweto, as it describes life in the township so well. The song, *Masterpiece* was written and produced by Norman Jesse Whitfield, one of the creators of the Motown Sound and the psychedelic soul, and it was released in early 1972.

> *MASTERPIECE*
>
> *… Thousands of lives wasting away*
> *People living from day to day*
> *It's a challenge just staying alive*
>
> *'Cause in the ghetto only the strong survive*
> *Broken down homes, kids strung out*
> *They don't even know what life's all about*
> *Stealin' cars, robbin' bars*
> *Mugging drugs, rat infested*
> *And no one's interested*
>
> *Kids dodging cars for recreation*
> *Only adds to a mother's frustration*
> *Breakings, folks comin' home*
> *And finding all their possessions gone*
> *Oh it's an ev'ry day thing – well well – in the ghetto*
> *Oh it's an ev'ry day thing in the ghetto*

It was common to wake up on a weekend morning and hear about someone you knew very well, running away from the police because he raped a girl in the neighbourhood. Although gangs were everywhere, the townships were not the same. Densely populated areas like White

City, Zola, Meadowlands Mzimhlophe, Orlando East and Pimville, were notorious. If you had a girlfriend in some of these areas, it was always risky and dangerous to go there unless you were accompanied by friends, and this made the visit awkward.

There were disputes about the football sports grounds in Rockville that had been used by clubs from Senaoane and Dlamini – locations that were there before Rockville. The people from Rockville presumed the football grounds belonged to them and they had the right to determine who played there and who should ask for permission to play.

Because there were no co-ordinated plans, this caused bitter rivalry between football teams like Hungry Lions and Rangers that were from Western and Sophiatown, and Dlamini All Blacks and Senaoane Gunners.

One day these clashes led to the stabbing and killing of a youth named Clot Moloi from Rockville, who was also an amateur golf-player. Moloi was a close friend of Strongman Rampa, whose mother was an ANC activist in Western before the banning of the ANC.

At some stage township gangs went on the rampage, terrorising communities and youths from Rockville who were being prevented from hawking their goods on certain trains between Soweto and the city. Tensions were aggravated because, students from Rockville attended school at Sekano-Ntoane and the route to school was through Dlamini and Senaoane.

Territorial gangs started harassing students that were either going to or coming back from school. This led to the formation of the 'Japanese', comprising mainly boys from Sotho section in Rockville, who were students at Sekano-Ntoane (Senaoane) and Morris Isaacson (White City).

As the situation worsened, my peers in eziTandini decided enough was enough; we had to do something to protect our territory too. We established the 'Ocean's 11', named after the 1960 American film starring actors like Frank Sinatra, Dean Martin and Sammy Davis Jr, among others. There were other gangs like the Bazins, Kwaitos, Hazels (MaHazels) and others. I belonged to the Ocean's 11. The group was made up of all my school friends, and a few of our peers who were already working, like Molefe 'Scruntsh' Motsei (MK Ezra Makhosini), Samuel Mango Nyathi, Welcome 'Dover' Oliphant, Sydney 'Zola' Mxakatho and Joseph 'Fajie' Sefefe. One or two friends who came from outside Rockville, like Mandla Hlophe also joined us.

One day, the Ocean's 11 decided to attack the other gangs inside the train. Some of us boarded the train from Park Station; others boarded at New Canada station. When the train was between New Canada and the first station in Soweto, we attacked. This forced some of the other gang members to jump out of the moving train, thus forcing the train driver to stop the train from continuing its journey. We clashed with many gangs and with the police. Some of the Ocean's 11 members escaped while some got arrested.

It was the nature of gangs that they did not last for long. A year was too long for a gang to exist. It would then disappear or mutate into another gang focusing on other issues of the day. My gang collapsed too, but we remained close friends forever.

Arts, Sports and Culture

Notwithstanding all these happenings, for me, Soweto was the best place to have grown up as it was alive with everything associated with development and modernity. Time moved faster here, buses and trains moved on time here, if you overslept you missed your transport. You learned how to outwit police surveillances and controls. At least apartheid did not have enough tools to control our cultural expression through music, dance, sports, arts, performances, and narratives – provided these were promoted among us as blacks and did not encourage interracial activity.

The number of modern churches in the townships grew and many families converted to Christianity. After our arrival in Rockville new churches were built, including – the famous St Francis of Assisi, Anglican Church and the Wesleyan Methodist Church next to my home. My siblings and I and most of our peers grew up in Christian families, attending church, especially Sunday school, and some were devoted servants of their churches.

There were vibrant sports and music competitions at schools. Soccer, tennis, dancing, softball and basketball were the main activities. One could travel from one end of the country to the other when participating in music and sporting activities.

In the late 1960s we listened to radio LM from Mozambique, with its beautiful sound of pop music. We played the latest 45s and LPs of the Mahotella Queens, Letta Mbuli, Miriam Makeba, Percy Sledge, Aretha Franklin, Brook Benton and many others. We danced to the music of The Temptations, Rare Earth, Hugh Masekela, Caiphus Semenya, Jonas Gwangwa (members of the Union of South Africa music ensemble) and Booker T and the MG's. The music of the Staple Singers, Marvin Gaye and Roberta Flack became legendary. But then again, we also loved gospel, blues and jazz from the likes of Louis 'Satchmo' Armstrong, 'Champion' Jack Dupree, and Winston 'Mankunku' Ngozi to Houston Person, Jimmy Smith, Stanley Turrentine and Shirley Scott.

There were local jazz groups spread throughout the country but Soweto was better positioned to host live competitions, especially at Orlando Stadium, which hosted many 'battle of the giants' jazz festivals. The 1964 Castle Lager Jazz Festival, which was organised by the Union Artists and attracted 40,000 jazz lovers on September 26th, 1964, stands out. Coming from Rockville, the township of jazz lovers and 'die ouens' (the guys) who tightened their trouser belts just above the waist so that they could dance in style, this festival remained on everyone's lips, whenever there was a discussion on jazz.

Some of our peers like Sipho 'Hotstix' Mabuse, Khaya Mahlangu, and the late Selby Ntuli started their careers in music while still at school, playing for Boys Scouts or cadet bands. With time some, like Mabuse, left school to pursue music full time, and founded the first of its kind pop-group with township soul, the Beaters in 1968. There were numerous groups before this, playing jazz, marabi, mbaqanga and so on. The Beaters emerged with original Afro soul being heavily influenced by the Manhattan Brothers, Miriam Makeba, The Ink Spots and other foreign artists such as Jimi Hendrix, Nat King Cole, Elvis Presley, Wilson Pickett and Otis Redding.

Besides the various genres of international music, the music of that time – called 'Soweto Soul' – greatly inspired township youth who were slowly being influenced politically by the BCM. Other soul icons of the time were Babsy Mlangeni and Steve Kekana. Groups also came from Alexandra Township: the Flaming Souls and The Movers. In those days, they all performed at Mofolo Hall and later at the nearby Eyethu Cinema in Soweto, owned by Ephraim Batana Tshabalala, a self-made millionaire who died in 1994 at the age of 84. Eyethu also hosted impressive concerts of international artists like Brook Benton, the Staple Singers and the Commodores; and our South African Sophiatown-born Stella Starr performed with Percy Sledge at the same venue.

At high school level, soccer was strongly supported and a source of pride as some players competed in the professional soccer league. At Sekano-Ntoane there were players like George 'Best' More, George Makapan and Baldwin 'Groovin' Molope, who first played for Rockville Hungry Lions, one of the oldest teams in the country. It was formed in Western in 1924 and is older than Orlando Pirates, which was founded in 1937 and is my favourite team. The two Georges went on to play for Kaizer Chiefs, Pimville United Brothers (Pubs) and

Orlando Pirates, with Makapan later becoming the first black player to play for Wits University.

James 'Akulalwa Egigini' Mabena and Molope, who were both my classmates, became seasoned players of Moroka Swallows, joining Irvin 'Pepe' Dire, whose family had been moved from 'Western' to Meadowlands. Then there was Ephraim Matsilele Jomo 'The Black Prince' Sono, the son of Eric Bhamuza "Scara" Sono – a soccer legend of Orlando Pirates. With the death of his father, and as a student at Musi High, he went on to fill his father's shoes at Pirates.

Now and then at Sekano-Ntoane we had to put out fires relating to the school soccer teams, as boys from Rockville liked to bully their way into all the squads, A, B and C. Then others from Dlamini, Senaoane and Phiri would complain. Mxolisi 'Bucs', Mandla 'Mendoza' Mtselu, Selby 'Vuyani', Sipho 'Siga' and I, my peers from 'eziTandini', always stood together when there were disagreements at school. In these soccer disputes we would, most of the time, take sides with the guys from Senaoane and Dlamini. We would then be accused of 'selling out' to 'turkeys' or 'kalkoens' (in Afrikaans). One of the people who liked to accuse me of this was Peter Mashego, an intimate friend whose family was very close to mine as we were opposite neighbours in Malotane Street when we lived in Western. This culminated in real squabbles between us boys from Rockville. Boys from 'eZitandini' would end up losing positions at Hungry Lions. As was always the case, there was reconciliation because of the Western connection, which was stronger than anything else, among people from Rockville.

In the early 1960s, there was a modern cycling racecourse called Elkah Stadium next to the sports grounds.[19] The cycling entrepreneur John Hurwitz, owner of the cycling business LK Hurwitz & Sons, defied apartheid South Africa and paid for its construction under exceptionally difficult conditions. It is not clear where the name Elkah came from, but it looks like 'LK Hurwitz' was shortened and pronounced 'eL-Ka-H'. Today the whole sports complex in Rockville is called Elkah Stadium. Whites like John Hurwitz and South Africa's 'Mr Cycling' Basil Gordon Cohen, wanted to promote cycling and involve black cyclists in the sport at a time when South African laws were being tightened to enforce racial classification and separation. They succeeded in promoting and expanding cycling activities among black miners around the mining areas in Johannesburg. Black cyclists did not mix with their white counterparts.

My friends and I liked ballroom dancing and table-tennis the most. We even established a professional table tennis squad in Rockville called the Rockgrip Table-Tennis Club, which was led by Bra Thami Mda who resided in my street. Our clubhouse was situated at the Elkah Stadium and we participated in regional competitions. These activities contributed immensely to boys from Rockville forming strong bonds with youth from around Mapetla, Moletsane, Tladi, Senaoane, Chiawelo, Dlamini, Phiri, and Mofolo.

We had sports clubhouses in Dlamini, Rockville – Chiawelo Centre and Elkah Club – and Dube. On Tuesdays and Thursdays after class, we spent most of the time at the Dlamini clubhouse. Members of this club like Ingram Gcobani Mazibuko (Lt. Col. Mazibuko), Willie Ndlovu (Mazibuko), Samuel Shaluza Sikhakhane, Zacharia 'Zakes' Nkosi, Mahlasela Majola and David Mavuku, were at Sekano, Morris Isaacson or Musi high schools. That is how, besides our peers, we established close relationships with many families, like the Wauchope family in Dlamini Number One. George and Windy were our seniors at Sekano. I got close to Maki and Kuku Wauchope, Jenny Kaloate (now Jenny Ngwenya), Natalia 'Nat' Kaloate (now Natalia Sifuba), and Sindiswa Dlamini (now Sindiswa Mbatha), who were like my younger sisters.

During my last years at school, I became the main organiser of all outings and picnics during Easter and 'December 16' holidays.

That is when I developed a love of photography and collecting music. I had won the trust of my peers as I was responsible for collecting money, two months before the event, and prepared every detail of the outing, from the hiring of a bus or kombis to organising food and any other necessities. Sometimes we took livestock with us, like a sheep, and slaughtered it at the destination. We usually spent three days on these outings, and included our peers who had already left school and were working. Our favourite places were in Munsieville, outside Krugersdorp and Wilgespruit in Roodeport.

Working Years

For most black students, passing or failing matric was the end of formal education. I found myself facing the same predicament. I tried my best to apply for a bursary but I was unsuccessful. I had to kiss university a goodbye and look for a job. Until then, it had always been a sad moment to see a friend dropping out of school because of financial deprivation. Although I had completed my matric, it felt the same as dropping out.

In the three years before completing my matric, Selby and I had joined Mandla Nyembe doing piece jobs on Saturday evenings in town. We worked for the Sunday Times, the sister publication of the Rand Daily Mail at 174 Main Street, binding bundles of newspapers for delivery throughout Johannesburg and the townships, and also Jan Smuts Airport for distribution in major cities in the country. This meant we had cash during the week at school and could save money for whatever we needed – shoes, trousers, or shirts. I became totally independent from my family financially. When I got back from school, I washed the shirt I had on that day and the next morning I pressed it myself before leaving for school. In those days we used the coal stove to heat the iron. The handiwork skills I learnt in Standard V and VI were useful.

My elder brothers had become a burden and were unreliable in assisting my mother and the family. My sister Siza's earnings were not enough to keep the home fires burning and savings could not get me to university. I had to go find a job too. Armed with a matric certificate, I soon found a job with a bank, the Allied Building Society,[20] shortened to 'Allied'.

First, I had to visit 'kwaNdabazabantu', the Labour Bureau, Efflux and Influx Control and Registration section, to change the status on my passbook. Since I first carried a pass, the stamp I got from my local municipal offices stated: 'Permitted to be in the prescribed area of Johannesburg for the purpose of Scholar'. Before starting with any job in Johannesburg you had to come here. Whether you were born here or not, it was compulsory to have a stamp, and mine now stated: 'Permitted to be in the prescribed area of Johannesburg while employed by Allied Building Society as a Filer', stamped on 24th April 1975.

Before acquiring this stamp you had to go through the notorious section known as 'Vula, Vala' (open and close). Here, men of all ages, young and old, entered in groups of 10 to 12, naked as the day they were born, clothes and belongings in one hand and in the other papers to be stamped by the doctor. You put your belongings on the floor, stepped forward in a row, raised your hands straight up, and the white doctor came with a stethoscope and quickly, almost touching each one's chest with it, moved on. The doctor signed some papers and rushing back to the beginning of the row shouted loudly, 'Vula, Vala'. At this stage you held your penis up with your right hand and allowed the doctor to check if you had any diseases by opening the foreskin. He never touched anyone and quickly beckoned everyone to dress up while he put his stamp on your papers as proof that he had examined you. Out you went to the next queue to collect your passbook with a stamp that confirmed that you were in decent shape and could start work in Johannesburg.

From that day on, somewhere in your passbook, your employer signs every month-end as proof that you are alive and working. Without this signature, if stopped by police, you could end up with a fine, in a police station or imprisoned until your employer sent proof that you were still employed.

The bank's headquarters were in Commissioner Street, and I was employed at a branch at the corner of Fox and Rissik Streets where I started work in April 1975. A new world opened for me. At Allied, Frank Hetem was the manager responsible for putting the golden' signature on our pass books on behalf of the company.

In 1975 there was not a single black teller in any bank in the country. The highest and most advanced job for a black person in the employ of a bank or building society, was to do filing set apart and hidden behind the offices. I was a filing clerk. All the transactions of the day, people depositing and withdrawing money, were filed by black people. Those days there were no computers to do this, so filing was essential and so was a clerk's job. Although all banks and saving institutions belonged to and were run by whites, many blacks put their money into savings accounts with little interest, but they had easy access to their deposits.

The computerised machine that had been introduced by IBM a few years earlier in South Africa, was as big as a two-ton truck occupying a room. I joined a team of about five other blacks out of a staff component of thirty whites and we did filing work crammed in the basement of the building, as no black person could be accommodated with whites on the ground-floor or upper floors. We sported dark blue suits with matching ties on sky-blue shirts, courtesy of the company. We looked very smart and dignified in those uniforms and drew attention wherever we went. Since we collected files from other branches close to us, we had cute two-piece plastic rain-suits to protect our smart garb on rainy days. That was the face of the company for its black employees who were all male as black women were only employed as 'tea girls' (irrespective of age) and cleaners.

When we entered the building on the side of Rissik Street, which had a beautiful glass-front, transparent from the outside all the way around to Fox Street, we used the stairs to go down to the basement. All 'Non-White' people entering the building and going to upper floors, were strictly only allowed to use the goods-lift. In those days, this was the convention in all buildings in Johannesburg. The 'Non-White' people who used the lift were those doing deliveries, cleaning, or like us, the company staff taking files for further processing upstairs. Only when coming down from the upper floors were black people allowed to use any lift.

To make sure these rules were adhered to, there was always a guard, 'uMatshingelani' at the entrance of every building in Johannesburg. A literal translation of 'uMatshingelani' is 'marching-in line', which means that the guard was there to make sure there was order. In those days most of the guards were Zulu-speaking and were regarded as more dependable because they listened to no excuses when they found someone breaking the rules. These guards carried knobkerries – a short stick with a knob at the top. If you dared take a lift for 'Whites-Only' going up you landed in serious trouble, with a possibility of injury, arrest or being banned from a place.

Meshack Ravuku was one of the five colleagues I found at Allied. We had known each other from early childhood through our parents, who attended the same church. The others were Jackson Khumalo, William Zikalala, Solly Tshabalala, Leslie Ngubane and Joseph Mboweni. It was pleasing to meet at least someone I knew in this place. It made it easier for me to learn the job. When I first came, Hetem introduced me to my new colleagues and they showed me the table we shared for filing and that was it. Within a week I had grasped the filing system. We never mixed with the white colleagues.

Chapter One

Whites didn't wear uniforms. The only whites we interacted with were those we collected files from on the ground-floor and those that processed them further after we had finished with them.

The head-office of Allied on Commissioner Street had a restaurant for white staff members only and on Thursdays it sold fried fish. It was located on the third floor. Since we were not allowed to eat there, one of us would go and buy fish for the others. For black people, the only way to reach the company's restaurant was through the main ground-floor entrance, going past the lifts on both your left and right sides, and getting to the back of the building. Once there, we used the outside fire escape stairs to go up. On reaching the third floor, we stood metres away from the restaurant's entrance so as not to disturb the whites that came out of the lifts. A black person came out to collect orders from us and we paid and waited for the food. When the food was delivered to us, we went back the same way we came in. It was the most demeaning practice to feed ourselves.

On the same floor as the restaurant, there was a table-tennis room. After eating, some white girls would go there and play a game. As I was a table-tennis player myself, it was funny that I could join them and play while waiting for my food. This was the only time I interacted with white staff members as an equal, in this secluded space far away from the public eye. We touched the same balls and used the same bats, but never interacted beyond this. I did develop a friendship with one or two white girls, but it all started here and ended here in this isolated space.

I was earning almost R100.00 a month. That was good money, but not good enough for me to have savings that would send me to university any time soon. At least I could give something to my mother and look after myself. The price of Star Press trousers was R7, good shoes, like a pair of Saxone, R31, and Crocket & Jones were R25. An Arrow shirt was R6, and a Pringle T-shirt was R13. A weekly train ticket was about R12 and a monthly about R38.

My mother was by now fully employed by the Shimmins. She had replaced my father as the main breadwinner, but of course she was not doing any deliveries on a scooter. Shimmin kept enquiring about me, and my mother told him that I was interested in furthering my studies at university. A discussion ensued between the two, and later I got involved. Shimmin volunteered to finance my studies on the understanding that I would pay back the money when I finished. In those days, employment after studies was guaranteed and the only professions to pursue after university were teaching, becoming a lawyer, a medical doctor, or a health inspector. Changes were taking place in the corporate sector as South African and international businesses were beginning to take in educated blacks in their junior management positions. I accepted the offer from Shimmin and after 10 months at Allied I resigned in mid-February 1976, to take up studies at the University of Zululand in Natal.

University of Zululand

In 1976 I undertook what was the first and longest journey in my life. I was all by myself, without my parents or siblings. Going to university for the first time with me were two homeboys, Stanley 'Stan' Mngadi from Rockville and Abednego Themba 'Thiza' Ntsibande (Ret. Gen. Ntsibande) from Dlamini Number Two. Before this I was much closer to Thiza's older brother, Norman 'Nox' Ntsibande, who was my peer at school. Stan and Thiza were my juniors at Sekano-Ntoane High and both had completed their matric after me in December 1975 and were accepted for studies in 1976 like me.

Embarking on this most captivating adventure, the train left Johannesburg Park Station late in the evening and arrived in Durban the following morning. We ventured into town, reached Victoria

Street market and unexpectedly from a distance, the ocean came into view for the first time, live and awesome. In the evening we boarded another train bound for Richards Bay, known as eMpangeni. I was a Sowetan and had never been outside the Transvaal. Along the coast of Natal, the train made stops at some weird stations with no real platforms like in Johannesburg. We reached our destination on the morning of the third day. Transport had been organised to drop us at the university.

After collecting our belongings – big new trunks with our clothing, some tinned food and so on, off we went to campus. The registration process went smoothly and was followed by the allocation of accommodation and other formalities. A new life began for the three of us. We settled in quickly and met other 'Joburgers' or 'Skomfanas' (ons skom van – Afrikaans), as students mainly from the Transvaal were labelled by their counterparts from Natal, who were considered 'amaMoegoe' (backward people) by the Skomfanas.

The people I knew were Cynthia Thabile Sithole and Thami Mnguni from Rockville, Ephraim 'Skojo' Zulu and his sister Grieselda Thandile 'Thandi' Mateya (née Zulu), were my cousins, and I got introduced to Thandi's friend Thuthukile Ntombana Skweyiya (née Mazibuko). Others were Favourite Nonhlanhla Morekure (nee Mabaso) from Senaoane, who was a classmate with Stan and Thiza, Mafika Mkwanazi – a friend to Skojo and Penuell Mpapa Maduna (former minister) from Rockville. Years later I got to know that Tseko Nell (MK nom de guerre Steve Rantso), the late Manzini Manala, Masiphula Mbongwa and the late Jabulani Nobleman Nxumalo (MK Mzala) were also here at the same university.

Right from the beginning it was evident that there were also territorial gangs here. Coming from Soweto with all that I had gone through, I made up my mind that I was not going to tolerate any form of harassment. I had had enough of gangs in Johannesburg. The same attitude was adopted by my two homeboys. We downplayed any temptation to get involved in petty squabbles. Every morning when we lined up for food at the dining hall, there were small skirmishes about who came first and who came last. The amaMoegoe would forcefully put themselves in front of the queue whenever one of them was ahead of the Skomfanas. Naturally, this led to some scuffles, as the Skomfanas retaliated by doing the same.

We understood that these acts were an adaption of what was inherited from boarding schools in Natal, like KwaDlangezwa which was in the neighbourhood of our university. It was not a bullying behaviour per se but an irritation of some sort. After a few weeks at the university we woke up one morning to the sad news that a student from Johannesburg had been seriously stabbed and had suffered injuries that required him to be sent back home. The victim was Mondli Kubheka from Pimville. This incident alone raised tensions on the campus and from that day, we made it clear that this type of behaviour would no longer be accepted by us.

Thiza found accommodation in prefabricated dormitories on the campus that were close to stagnant waters. We dubbed the place '*eMatilosini* (a place for sailors). The noise from the bullfrogs was intolerable. He shared a room with three other colleagues. One of them was Derrick Sipho Ciko Mbatha (MK nom de guerre Simpi 'Gatsha' Mthobi) from KwaMashu, Durban. I immediately connected with Ciko because of the common surname. One day, while visiting Thiza, Ciko said to me, '*Hey Shandu, isiZulu sakho esikathayela*', meaning that my Zulu sounded weird. 'Shandu' is my clan's name and 'esikathayela' refers to a tyre. This means my Zulu was from the streets. I understood him, and I confessed to him that I have never heard the type of Zulu that was being spoken in Natal. We laughed at each other and Thiza also joined in the laughter.

Since we were at school, under apartheid laws, we had to know which ethnic groups we belonged to. Because of my parents and mainly my surname, I had always regarded myself as a Zulu. I had never questioned this but from that day onwards I knew that I was not a 'full Zulu'. This encounter stayed with me forever and I took it with me into foreign lands.

I had randomly chosen philosophy as one of the subjects to complement those that were obligatory in my first year of a BA degree. The course was taught by a white lecturer, Professor Van der Merwe, and in one of his first lectures he introduced us to the philosophy of German thinkers like Immanuel Kant. In the brief time I spent at univesity – from February to June – what I learned had such immense influence on me that I was eager to read more about the German philosophers. In my mind I was trying to reconcile this philosophy with what I learned at high school and what I knew about the Germans up to then, especially the events of the Second World War.

The waves of the uprising that started on June 16 in Soweto found fertile ground at the university. I had been involved in two student boycott actions. The first action took place during the Easter holidays in April and was over the quality of food we were being fed. After some days of disruptions and not eating properly, the matter was resolved. The following month there was protest action against the chancellor of the university, Prince Mangosuthu 'Gatsha' Buthelezi.[21] Since the 1972 expulsion of Tiro and especially after the Frelimo Rallies of 1974, black universities had become key sites where student protests were rife.

One of the targets against which protest action was directed, was the Bantustan system of government. Therefore, Buthelezi's presence during the graduation ceremony on campus, triggered fierce clashes between the students and his bodyguards and the police.

After this incident, serious discussions took place amongst us students. We questioned South Africa's future and our role in it as black people. Hence, when news of the June 16 killings reached the university through radio broadcasts on the morning of Thursday, June 17, it found fertile ground among the students. We gathered in the main hall that evening and tried to assess what had happened in Soweto and what our response was going to be. In those days, there was no TV news and we did not have access to newspapers. The meeting lasted until the early hours of Friday, June 18 with no clear direction or resolution. Some wanted boycott action immediately and for us to join with the students of Soweto, while others called for radical steps like the closure of the institution. All indecision was put aside with the arrival of a respected and very charismatic SRC (Students' Representative Council) leader on campus that night. His name was Mental 'Panel Beater' Mkhonza.

By chance Stan and I had been allocated a room at Block M, Blue Waters, at the same residence hostel as Mkhonza. Before his arrival we had befriended Bra Mandla, who was from Diepkloof in Soweto. Bra Mandla, had told us some stories about the vibrant Mkhonza. Mkhonza did not disappoint. He electrified the meeting that had been dilly-dallying on action to be taken. The meeting had, amongst many proposals, concluded that the administration would be confronted straight on. With the arrival of newspapers that Friday morning carrying the first pictures of the students who had been mowed down in Soweto, havoc followed. Hector Pieterson's body was the most heart-breaking image to see. Within minutes, buildings at the university were burning. The flames could be seen a distance away. Police helicopters started hovering above the university campus.

Thiza, Stan, Gilbert Mazibuko[22] from Phiri had joined us after our arrival and I decided it was time to go and pack our suitcases and leave. As we approached the main entrance police were arresting students. From amongst us, they picked on Gilbert and arrested him. We never saw him again, and when we went into exile later that year, he was still in detention. We left Empangeni by train in the evening and arrived in Durban on the morning of June 19. We departed the same evening for Johannesburg.

Back in Soweto

On the morning of a very cold Sunday, 20th June, the train zigzagged into the surroundings of Johannesburg until it reached Park Station. On this day, exactly twenty-two years ago under similar settings – a cold Sunday morning – I was born. Since my family was relatively large we didn't celebrate birthdays with a special cake. When we knew that one of us was going to have a birthday or once my mother reminded us of this, we looked forward to dinner time because on everyone's birthday, my mother would wait for dinner time and tell a relevant story of what happened the day that specific individual was born. This was a most educative moment in the family.

As children this is how we got to know the family and its origins. My mother was exceptionally good at relating these family stories. It kept the family bonded together. After describing how they guessed whether it was going to be a boy or girl, who was there and who was visiting from where, there would be a delicious meal. In my case my mother never forgot to say that I was born on a very cold Sunday morning. This might be the reason why later in life I fell in love with winter and snow. This day too was very cold.

At Park Station we took the train to Soweto and when it reached Mlamlankunzi, Orlando and then Nancefield stations, there was a stench that came through the doors of the train as they opened and closed at each station. The smell was from burnt, damaged, and smouldering beer halls, administration buildings, buses, trucks and cars. Because of winter and the cold, the stench hung in the air, a reminder of what had taken place here since that past bloody Wednesday.

I reached Rockville and in the yard of Moroka police station, not far away from my home, I saw corpses laid on the ground waiting to be taken to the funeral parlours. I arrived home unannounced and the sigh of relief as I came in was written on everyone's face in the kitchen. Everyone was sitting around the coal stove because of the cold. There were no cell phones in those days for me to warn them about my return. Everything had happened so fast and there was no time for any forewarnings. I had been away from home for almost five months, but it felt like years – it was the longest period in my life I had been away from home.

While the police had killed black people in the past, as with the 1960 Sharpeville massacre, for the first time the bullets were aimed at school children. This was to be the trend after June 16. From this day life changed for the worse in Soweto. Demonstrations became routine occurrences and school children were losing their lives. The demonstrations soon spread throughout the country. The shooting of school children and their ensuing mass exodus into exile were the two phenomena that made the events of June 16, 1976 different from all previous clashes with the apartheid system.

The song, *Senzeni na? Isono sethu, ubumnyama?* (What have we done? Is it our sin to be black?), encapsulates both the emotional side and the predominant political consciousness of many of the students. Without the heavy influence of the BCM philosophy, there would have been no June 16 uprising. Given the history of Soweto and the politics in the country, the place was a bomb ready to explode any time. The Afrikaans language issue gave a spark to the fire.

After I came back home from university, every day was eventful. Having connected with all my friends and former schoolmates, everyone was speaking the same language. There were demonstrations, marches, and meetings and at home, I could sense that my parents were worried about what the end of all this would be. I got into arguments with my father about what the government could do next. Like many parents at the time, he was of the view that the demonstrations were leading to more deaths and that we should consider bringing them to an end. For the first time in my life, I had a political exchange with my father. It followed with my mother too. When I went to my friends' homes I found the same discussions, were happening with their parents. Many parents were indeed worried. At home my brother, Fana, had already started with matric at Orlando High School and my younger sister, Maggie was now in JC. They were both deeply involved in the marches and demonstrations. I could understand the concerns from my parents.

One day Koli (Kolisile Koli Ngqase, MK nom de guerre Ephraim Gazelle) and John[23] (John Magwegwe Vilakazi, MK Thabo Mkula) sat me down for a talk that changed my life forever. Both were peers of my brother Jerry, and Koli was the elder brother to Mxolisi, who was my peer and one of my bosom friends. The meeting took place under the tree in the back yard of the Ngqase family home. The talk with Koli and John focused on the outcomes of what was taking place in the streets of Soweto. They explained that what was happening in the country had no end and we had to deal with the cause of the problem.

Since I was the only one among my peers who was already at university, they said I had to play a constructive role and understand that the system was not going to change unless we brought matters under our control. They too had fears about the future, but unlike our parents they believed there was a way out. From that day on, at specific times and on certain days, we listened to Radio Freedom, the underground broadcast of the ANC. The message was clear: we must fight back by all means possible because everything was in our hands.

More meetings followed with more clarity about what the next move should be. I brought two more friends at different intervals to engage with Koli and John. The first was Isaac Sakie Motswasele

(MK Oupa Moloi), who quickly understood the gist of the meeting. If there were better opportunities to deal with our situation let it be, he would say to me. The next person I came with was Stan as he was with me at university. Koli and John had prepared themselves very well and handled all the questions we had for them and what needed to be done, very well. The emphasis was of course on education, but, if necessary, those who want to join MK must understand that the country will need educated soldiers too. In, years that followed when I was alone in Germany, I used to reflect on these discussions and it became clear to me that Koli and John were involved with the underground structures of the ANC long before the uprisings.

After some weeks of political work among close friends and others from the neighbourhood, Koli and John indicated that it was time to 'skip'. Again, we had to handle the sensitive matter of leaving the country carefully. As a result of many youths wanting to leave country, on the day of our departure there was a mix-up with transport arrangements. The kombi that arrived to fetch us was already full and only Koli, John and Stan were able to squeeze themselves into the vehicle. I was left behind.

After two days, their disappearance started raising questions and Koli's sister, Rose – also known as Lolo – stopped me in the street and said to me, 'Khulu, where is Koli?' 'You were the last person with Koli.' She was correct and it meant that she had taken note of our meetings. Koli wanted these meetings to be as casual as possible so as not to arouse suspicion but his sister, Lolo had been watching us. I mumbled something to Lolo telling her I had also not seen Koli. I knew then that I had overstayed.

Left with Thiza and Sakie, we immediately went out searching for transport and landed in Dube at the house of Khosi and Alexander Mbatha. After quick introductions and meeting the family, we got down to the business of the moment. Unfortunately, the structures under their control had also run out of transport. We moved on and got transport somewhere in Zondi or eMndeni. We arranged for the time of departure and came back to Thiza's place in Dlamini Two. We had left about six people at Thiza's place and when we arrived there were about fifteen people. I got cold feet because of the previous experience with transport but there was nothing I could do.

One of the most difficult things that I had to do, was to say goodbye to my girlfriend, Chriselda Refilwe Tshabalala. She stayed a mere 600 metres away from Thiza's place and was a next-door neighbour to Mandla Dlamini. Since our schooldays at Ndondo Primary, Mandla Dlamini spent most of his time with us in Rockville. He never smoked and was a teetotaller whose view carried more weight than anyone else's in our group He was one of the eldest among us and was also among the first to leave school to start working. He had gone to Musi High in Pimville and one day he confided to a few of us that the financial situation in his family demanded that he leaves school. His closeness to the Tshabalala family who were his neighbours, was the reason I ended up in a relationship with Refilwe, whose father once came to my family to warn them that I should keep away from his young girl. My family was left traumatised because of the threats he made to them if they didn't stop me. I discontinued going to Mandla's place for a few months after this. It was Refilwe who came to visit me in Rockville.

I gathered my strength and rushed to her place to give her a last kiss. At that moment I felt life was being turned upside down. I could not tell her I was seeing her for the last time. On these issues, as Koli and John had warned me, one had to be sure there was no mistake as this could spell danger for everyone, including my family and hers.

I quickly rushed home for the last time to make sure all my essential belongings, photo albums, records (LPs), books and whatever else was tucked away and locked in the trunk I had bought when I left for the university. I had already done this on the day I was supposed to have left with Koli and the others but because of what had happened, I had to open it again to change clothes. Now it was another goodbye. I went to fetch Mandla 'Mendoza' first, and as we were crossing the road in the direction towards Dlamini, my mother got out of a PUTCO bus. She was returning from work and normally on such occasions I would rush to her and assist with her bag and walk her home. On that day, I watched from afar knowing it was probably the last time I would see her. That picture too, of her walking home alone, remained with me for many years in exile.

Evening came and we were waiting at Thiza's place, and I was praying that this time there would be no disappointment. Just as I was beginning to lose hope, a truck, big enough to carry all of us, arrived. On this journey, no one brought extra things to carry; you only took what you had on you. The trek to an uncertain destination had begun. There was one determination only, that we would come back and free South Africa. Koli and John had emphasised that schooling was to be priority number one for whoever was with me.

The truck made a few stops collecting more students along the way out of Soweto. It travelled the whole night and none of us had a clue where we were going. This was the night of 12 October 1976. As daylight broke, the truck stopped close to a hill. The old man driving the truck instructed us to get off and follow the route that he showed us. 'Jump the fence!' he instructed.

Chapter Two
A FROSTY BEGINNING

SWAZILAND (1976)

Manzini and Mdutshane Prison

What the youth and students found happening in Swaziland was preparation for things to come on their journey to liberate our people.

When we reached the bottom of the hill on the other side, the same truck was waiting for us. We jumped back onto it and departed. As the truck was moving, we realised that this place and its surroundings looked totally different. The cars on the road had registration numbers starting with SD and immediately we knew we were in Swaziland. At that moment, my memory started working backwards and so fast that the stories of my father jumping a fence in Swaziland came back.

The truck delivered us to a house in Manzini. When we arrived, a big man in his late forties – wearing black trousers, a white shirt and a red tie – was there to welcome us. He was preparing to leave and quickly showed us where to make tea and the location of the shops where we could buy bread. We were about twenty or so. He invited us to settle in and as he left, we started familiarising ourselves with the new situation. Within an hour, the truck that brought us here also disappeared forever. Later, a Coca-Cola truck came to deliver drinks.

The house belonged to the chief representative of Coke in Swaziland, Joseph 'Joe' Mkhwanazi, the man we found when we arrived. Not long after settling in, a few of us took a walk to the shops. We had not gone far when we came across a group of boys of our age. We didn't need to ask where they came from; everything about them indicated that they were from Soweto. In a quick exchange with them about why we were there they told us they were with 'Uncle'. What about us? At that time we didn't know much about Joe Mkhwanazi, and we didn't say who were staying with. Sakie looked at me and quietly whispered that Koli had told us, we would meet 'Uncle' on the other side. He was the only person in this group who was part of the discussions with Koli and John. I pulled him aside and indicated that we must wait. We left the group in the park and moved on while I pondered if we had been dropped at the right place.

We made our way back to the house. We found Themba Nkenene and Benjamin Thomas Setshedi Zobane (Col. Zobane) there. They were also new arrivals in Swaziland like us. In the following days more students arrived. One group came with Richard Matwete Nyide, Fannie Mazibuko, Justice Ntshuntsha, Gerald 'Gerry' Malinga (Ret. Gen. Malinga) and Ernest Tshepiso Gumede (Ret. Col. Gumede). Another group included my cousin, Happy Bhembe (Ret. Gen. Bhembe), and Phillip Norman Phiri (Lt. Col. Phiri, MK nom de guerre Bongane Matwa). More familiar homeboys landed, among them Ephraim Mbulelo 'Ali' Phako (Ret. Gen. Phako and MK nom de guerre Makabokwana Makhosini) and Brian Luvuyo Hoga (Brian Hoga and MK nom de guerre Borifi 'Scratch' Ntathela).

An elderly man arrived to fetch Thiza, Mandla 'Mendoza' and myself. We went to a house a few kilometres away from Mkhwanazi's house. At this house, the man told us about the next mission we would be undertaking: military training in China. According to him, the ANC was being influenced by white communists and Russians not to fight whites in South Africa. He narrated to us that the PAC was the only genuine liberation movement fighting the racist regime. This short encounter greatly influenced Thiza and Mandla 'Mendoza'. I could tell by their enthusiasm that they were captivated by what this man had told us and their resolve to do military training was hardened. At the right moment I shared with Sakie what had happened and that we were housed in a PAC house. I made him aware that Thiza and Mandla 'Mendoza' were enthralled.

The following day, Sakie and I went back to the park and as luck would have it, we found the same group at the same place. We quickly asked them to see 'Uncle'. 'Uncle' was the name used to disguise the 'ANC', pronounced as 'ENK'. They took us to a house where we found two gentlemen, one of them I later came to know as Bab' Maseko (Ambassador Timothy 'Tim' Karikari Maseko). We quickly explained that we had been delivered to a PAC house. I was adamant I could not leave the other young boys who came with us. They were too young to be taken for military training, I argued. Some of them were 12 or 13 years old. Bab' Maseko concurred. We agreed to take them in small groups to another house where Bab'Maseko assured us they would be safe. We went back to Mkhwanazi's house.

Bab' Mkhwanazi was very smart and full of life, but he didn't say much about us leaving Swaziland. He organised more PAC members to come and interact with us. These were people like Pitika Ntuli (Professor), Daniel Makhiyana, Zwelonke Mdluli and Joe Moabi, who were based in Swaziland. We should have been talking about how and when we would be leaving Swaziland to be trained to come back and face the Boers. This worried Sakie and me; it was the opposite of what the other man had told us.

Either Thiza or Mandla 'Mendoza' had informed some in the group that we were going for military training in China, and that this was imminent. This alone captivated the spirits of many while a few got cold feet and started enquiring about going back to South Africa. It made me feel uneasy to think of what the system (the Boers) would do to you if you were to jump the fence and return home.

One day we woke up short of one person. When we did not see him, we knew that he had gone back home. That was the late Pat Seboko from Rockville. He had been extremely uncomfortable since hearing about the military training in faraway China. When the others were singing songs that depicted us coming back with our own guns to avenge the killing of students, Pat couldn't take it. I realised that he was not alone, but the others were afraid to speak out. The consequences of skipping – jumping the fence – and leaving South Africa, were now beginning to sink in for some of the youth. It was too late.

The reality of the situation was that Bab' Mkhwanazi never expected such large numbers of young recruits to arrive at his house or at PAC houses. In fact, we were the first of many youth to arrive from South Africa and a few days later, the numbers had doubled.

Students had been leaving the country, especially after the 'Frelimo Rallies' of 1974, seeking ways to fight against the white regime. Others were studying in Botswana, Lesotho and Swaziland (BLS states), where they attained passes in O and A levels under the British education system taught in those countries. They came back to South Africa during their holidays. The 1976 exodus was different. As the fires continued to burn inside South Africa, thousands of students skipped the country, crossing the borders into Botswana, Lesotho and Swaziland, not knowing who or what they would find.

Out of the blue the neighbouring states found themselves hosting thousands of young refugees. The immediate consequence of this was tension between the apartheid regime and these states. Prime Minister John Vorster asked parents to fetch their children from these countries. Jimmy Kruger, the notorious Minister of Police, even offered to help parents wishing to bring their children back home. A few parents took up this offer. At the same time, the South African regime threatened neighbouring states with reprisals if they failed to return the students.

We heard later from new arrivals that Pat Seboko visited one or more families in Dlamini and told them that their children were in Swaziland. The threats from the regime were enough to cause panic in many black households and Pat's appearance added more distress, which led to some parents taking risks and arranging to fetch their loved ones from these neighbouring countries. Hilda Nompikiswano Mabuza (nee Matyobeni) was among many young girls, most of them from around Dlamini and Senaoane, students at either Junior Secondary or Sekano-Ntoane High, whose parents brought them back from Swaziland.

Some parents succeeded in convincing their children to return to South Africa. Others, whose children had no intention of returning, had to accept this reality. The police hunted for those helping with the organisation and provision of transport that took the youth across the borders. Jabulani Mkhwanazi, from Soweto, nephew of Joe Mkhwanazi, was a dedicated cadre who out of sheer commitment to the struggle transported the youth. Even after his arrest and imprisonment, he continued with underground work. Some of his daring acts included single-handedly transporting ammunition for the Azanian People's Liberation Army (APLA), the PAC's armed wing and cadres from Botswana into the country, as well as taking ammunition to Swaziland, to arm those that were operating from there.

On another front, there was an undeclared battle between, the ANC and PAC. It was not only ideological, but also involved resources, funding and support. The ANC was better resourced and had greater recognition throughout the world. Little was known about the BCM grouping during our time in Swaziland, or the frontline states of southern Africa. It didn't feature on the agenda of the Organisation of African Unity (the OAU, now the African Unity, AU) or even on that of the Frontline States, later the Southern African Development Coordination Conference (SADDC from 1980 to 1992, and since then SADC).

Botswana was a safer route to the rest of Africa; compared to the partially surrounded Swaziland and landlocked Lesotho. This was why most students fled to Botswana's capital of Gaborone, and were taken up by the ANC and the PAC. The overwhelming majority went to the ANC. Before 1976, Gaborone had been invaded by former university students that left South Africa after the expulsion of Abram Tiro in 1972 (killed by a bomb in Gaborone 1974) and the Pro-Frelimo Rallies of 1974. In addition to the ANC and PAC, there were various groupings, like the Unity Movement (Non-European Unity Movement which was dominant in the Cape province) and an Africanist group known as the Gang of Eight, which was led by Tennyson Makiwane who was expelled from the ANC in 1975.[1]

Most of the BCM groups and their members were reluctant to join either the ANC or the PAC, mainly because they did not understand why these two organisations had spent so many years outside South Africa without waging a visible armed struggle. So, they decided to be neutral. Some of them wanted to undergo military training so that they could come back and fight, and this could only be provided by either the PAC or the ANC. Some joined the PAC as full members; while others were convinced by the PAC that they could go for training without necessarily becoming members. Welile Nhlapo (MK nom de guerre Andrew Mkhize), Papi Otukile Moloto, Tebogo Mafole (MK nom de guerre Dan Cindi) and Tim Williams, were among those who accepted this training. The training was done in Libya and some even went as far as Syria.

On their way to Libya, flying via Lusaka and Dar es Salaam (Dar), they met people they knew, like Joseph Snuki Zikalala of the ANC who left after the 1969 failed 'trial of 22', which included among others, Winnie Mandela, Rita and Lawrence Ndzanga.[2] They also met Keith Mokoape (Ret. Gen. Mokoape) also in the ANC, who had been with some of them at university.

They did their training under extremely difficult conditions in Libya, with the Libyans and other fighters not understanding how this group came with the PAC but considered itself independent.

When they were given the Green Book to study, they demanded all available literature, including Soviet literature, which they could only get from the Soviet embassy. They were given what they asked for. They also demanded a radio with international stations so they could follow what was happening in the world. After they volunteered to do further training in Syria and still wanted to retain their independence, relations with the host soured and they were kicked out of Libya and left for Botswana, where they had come from.

Flying back via Dar and Lusaka, it gave them enough time to interact with PAC and ANC leaders, and again with Zikalala and Mokoape, and this time also with Thabo Mbeki, until they reached Gaborone. They had enough time to make their own assessment of the situation in southern Africa, Africa and in the world. By the time they arrived in Botswana, some of them were convinced that the ANC provided a better solution to the questions they had about the liberation of South Africa.

The group I came with in 1976 was caught up in this confusion in Swaziland. The number of youth coming from South Africa kept increasing and the Swazi government ran into trouble because there were no resources to cater for these unannounced arrivals. With the intervention of the United Nations, the Swazi government took a decision to move all the male youth to Mdutshane Prison, now called the Juvenile Prison and Correctional Institution, in Luyengo. The girls were taken to the Matsapha Correctional Centre.

This did not affect those under the care of the ANC, as they continued to be taken to Mozambique. There is no doubt that the ANC machinery was better organised. The Mozambique Liberation Front (FRELIMO) was at this stage in alliance with the ANC, and this explained the efficiency of moving people relatively quicker from Swaziland through Mozambique to Tanzania. The PAC had no such ability to take people out of Swaziland. I only became aware of this when we arrived in Tanzania and was exposed to the alliances among liberation movements in Southern Africa.

Before the move to Mdutshane Prison, we had managed to move some students from Mkhwanazi's house over to the ANC house with the assistance of Nzima Aaron Nobanda (Ret. Gen. and MK nom de guerre Tom Mazibuko). Among those who left in this way was Joseph Mlungisi 'Lungi' Daweti from Rockville. He left behind his intimate childhood friend, Bongani Makoa, who cried for days. I tried to quieten Bongani and make him understand that Lungi was gone and that he should have left with him. I felt sorry for him as he was one of those young boys, who at that stage of our journey into the unknown, needed psychological counselling.

The Mdutshane Prison was emptied of its inmates to accommodate us. Bab' Maseko was close to the Commissioner of Prisons and was a frequent visitor to the prison. This made it possible for us to coordinate the removal of youth to ANC houses. At the Mdutshane Prison I continued to be in charge of the youth and was the liaison officer working with the Swazi authorities, the Commissioner of Prisons and the United Nations High Commission for Refugees (UNHCR), which was now in charge of us. That is when I earned my other nickname 'Boss'.

The immediate priority was to deal with food and blankets. They had removed the inmates but continued serving food. It was terrible food and the Sowetans were up in arms. After a few days the matter was resolved. We had to learn to cook for ourselves using huge pots that I had never seen before in my life.

As Bab' Maseko frequented the prison he introduced me to Joshua Nxumalo, known as 'General Zhukov'. With Nxumalo's assistance, more students were able to move from the prison to ANC houses and taken out of Swaziland. Among these were my homeboys Mbulelo Phako and Brian Hoga. They were neighbours to my relatives, the Nhlapo family, in Dlamini One.

In early December 1976, the UNHCR came up with a plan to fly all the refugees out of Swaziland to Tanzania. We had to get everyone a UNHCR passport. For Sakie, who besides myself and Bab' Maseko knew what we were doing, this created a serious problem. Do we fly with the group or was it time for us to leave this place for the ANC? When Bab' Mkhwanazi came to enquire about the departure plans, I told him I was not leaving with the group. He tried to find out what the problem was, as this whole process was in my hands. I could not tell him the truth. Bab' Maseko came in and advised that considering that we had coordinated the affairs at Mdutshane Prison, Sakie and I should consider flying with the group – more than a hundred people. The idea was, when we got to Tanzania, we would get in touch with the ANC offices. This proposal made sense and, Sakie and I, settled for it.

The process took off and on Friday, 3 December half of the youths were flown by UN-flagged helicopters to Maputo, Mozambique. The rest were flown to Maputo the following day. I was in this last group. On the afternoon of the same day a big jet – a Zambian Airways plane – took off with all of us, first time flyers – to Dar, Tanzania. When the plane stabilised mid-air, there was a very loud clapping of hands as many shouted, 'Thanks to John Vorster for making it possible for us to fly for the first time!'

TANZANIA (1976 – 1977)

Travelling on an aircraft for the first time in our lives was both exciting and scary. Landing in Dar in the early evening was even more extraordinary. When the plane's doors opened, the heat that came through was overwhelming. Dar is the largest city in Tanzania and is located on the eastern coast of Africa along the Indian Ocean. It has a natural harbour with white sandy beaches. It lies next to the equator and has a tropical climate – hot and humid throughout the year. About 45% of Tanzanians are Christians. Islam is the religion of about one-third of the people on the mainland and is dominant in Zanzibar. Swahili and English are the official languages of Tanzania.

From the airport and along the way, traveling at the back of military trucks organised by the UNHCR, seeing so many women covered in black from head to toe presented a shocking sight from where I was seated. Some of us even thought there was a worse 'June 16' here than in South Africa where we came from, because all the women dressed in black seemed to be in mourning. Only later did we understand the truth about the dress code for Islamic women.

We arrived in town in Dar when it was already dark. We saw people under the street lights and others relaxing on the pavements as if it was a holiday. We did not understand anything about night life outside South Africa. A debate ensued among us, about whether this was in fact Dar. Some suggested that we were just sleeping over here and we would continue with our journey to Dar the following day. We were accommodated in about three or four hotels, the largest being the group at Zanzibar Hotel. I was at the Holiday Inn where I shared a three bed suite with Sakie and Norman.

The following day we had our breakfast and were told to relax, officials were seeing us later in the afternoon. They came and we were assembled at one of the hotels, most probably at the Zanzibar, where Potlako Leballo accompanied by other PAC leaders addressed us. He did not hesitate to inform us that the PAC was the only authentic liberation organisation of Azania and that his organisation refused to take instructions from Moscow. The leaders were joined by the Commanders of the Zimbabwe African National Liberation Army (ZANLA), which was the military wing of the Zimbabwe African National Union – (ZANU) and other organisations of Southern Africa that were aligned to China. After they had addressed us, we returned to our hotels.

I then discussed with Sakie – with Norman present – that we really were in trouble. We had now heard it from the horse's mouth that everyone would be going for military training. I made it clear that my understanding was that all those who came with us were under the auspices of the UN and should first be asked which organisation we wanted to join. Sakie advised that we should not waste time on this matter because many among us were already in favour of going for military training. This was not a problem for me, but I was concerned about the many young boys in the group, especially those I knew from Rockville, Dlamini and Senaoane, whose lives could be ruined if they were forced into military training at such a tender age.

The following day, together with Norman, we went looking for the ANC offices. It was not long before we located them. We were ushered into a building, and we asked to see the chief representative. We were told to wait, and we sat on a bench next to the entrance. While seated, suddenly, some young men of our age came in followed by a man in a checked safari suit, with long trousers, walking upright and fast. He stopped beside us and remarked, 'Is there a protest today?' We looked at each other puzzled, but he moved on without waiting for our response.

After some time, we met the Chief Representative, Mabuse

Mampane (MK nom de guerre Reddy Mazimba). With the formal introductions done and after listening to our story he asked where the others were. They were at the hotels, we said. We agreed on when Mampane was going to fetch us, and that we were going to do our best to convince the others. As we were walking out, Mampane informed us that the man we saw coming in was President Oliver Reginald Tambo (then Acting President-General of the ANC, also known as OR). He was surprised that when he entered, we did not stand up and that is why he asked, 'Is there a protest today?' We did not recognise him, and it was too early to have understood the protocols then. Deep inside me, I was happy to have seen the man.

We went back to the hotel and that afternoon I called a meeting with those that were close to me. I had hoped to persuade them that the ANC was the best choice to address our needs. I was still convinced that I could influence some of my friends and I started by explaining that the initial understanding was that the UNHCR was going to be responsible for us here in Tanzania, and individuals would decide which organisation to join. I said, it was obvious that the whole group of more than a hundred people were handed over to the PAC.

The immediate reaction shocked me. Most had already made up their minds and they wanted to do military training with the PAC and nothing else. I lost the game when those closest to me like, Mandla 'Mendoza', Mandla 'Mbube' Mangethe (Ret. Gen. Mangethe), Thiza and others sided with the rest. Even when I tried to convince them that there was also training in the ANC, they were unbending. Sakie, Norman and I, decided that was it, we had done our best. I must confess, this was my most heart-breaking moment since leaving South Africa. Separation was not easy among friends and especially from my relatives Happy Bhembe and Joe Bhembe.

On the agreed day and time, Mampane took us directly to a house in Temeke, one of the suburbs in Dar, where we joined other youth who were being prepared for travel to Angola. The man in charge here was Graham Gadimphelele Morodi (MK nom de guerre Ntate Mashigo). He was from Rockville, and I knew one of his two sons, Ronnie, and where they stayed. I never raised this with him as there were strict rules that you did not identify yourself or your friends, or discuss such matters. On arrival wewere given paper and pen and told to write our biography and sign it with a nom de guerre.

I knew someone who was close to Ntate Mashigo and was cared for by him. He was epileptic and had terrible seizures. He was also from Rockville. The first time our eyes met it was as though we had seen each other yesterday. This person was Emmanuel Phetho Moloi (MK nom de guerre Edmund Khoza). Ntate Mashigo became more interested in me. After exercise, we got talking. He was happy that there was someone Phetho could connect with emotionally. We discussed Phetho's situation and the issue of education. It became clear that the ANC found it difficult to convince young people to go to school because of peer pressure.

After engaging for almost a week, he spoke to Mampane, and they agreed that I should take some of the young people away from Temeke to another place in Dar. This place was called Kinondoni. As I was preparing to leave Temeke I had another encounter with the Acting President-General, Oliver R Tambo.

After we were collected from around Temeke, we gathered under the shade of a big Kigelia, the sausage tree. All the new arrivals were making a meal out of OR's presence and bombarding him with so many questions about the struggle. Questions such as what have you been doing in the past) 16 years since the banning of the organisation? Where was the ANC when the Boers were shooting and killing us? What were you doing in Tanzania when the struggle was being fought at home? The youth accused him and the rest of the 'Mgwenyas' (the veterans) of neglecting their duties. Though it was in the afternoon, the heat was still strong as OR sat in the middle of an arch, emotionless and looking at these people throwing blow after blow at him. One of those confronting President Tambo was Isaac (Saki) Kekana (MK Tilly Isaacson) from Rockville. I knew Saki very well. He was my junior at Sekano.

Looking up into the empty sky, OR seemed to be momentarily lost in thought, then with a sharp move of his head he would turn his face towards us, eyes flashing. This went on for almost an hour before he responded. He saluted all those who spoke, as though he agreed with everything that was directed at him and his comrades in the leadership. OR was a teacher by profession and over the years he had mastered the art of engaging with people in various situations. The gravity of the prevailing atmosphere was matched by his, calm and collected demeanour. Once he had finished untangling the complex conditions existing both inside South Africa and on the international platform, he had won over everyone present and silence prevailed.

I left Temeke convinced that I had made the right decision to look for the 'Uncle' as Koli and John had advised. Because of the many ups and downs we had been through since leaving South Africa, Sakie and Norman decided to settle for military training. Phetho needed special care and had to stay. We parted in a somewhat happy and more relaxed mood, knowing we made good choices for ourselves without pressures from leadership and our peers. I arrived in Kinondoni, and with the Chief Rep we managed to get more of the young students from the hotels to join the ANC so that they could go to school. But the majority of those that I had made the journey with remained with the PAC. These were the first recruits into the PAC after the 1976 uprising. Some, like Bongani, Lungi's friend, left and joined the UNHCR in Dar and were taken to different countries in Africa and Europe.

After this long and thrilling journey from South Africa, full of exhilarating escapades – especially in Swaziland – through to Mozambique, finally I settled in Tanzania. I was pleased that I reconnected with friends I was separated from when that first kombi came to collect us to take us into exile. I re-united with Stan. Lungi, who had left Bongani with us in Swaziland, was also there. As I tried to understand my journey thus far, I was immediately assigned more responsibilities.

Within a short space of time from around October 1976 to June 1977 Dar, was flooded by hundreds of the 'June 16' youth. Many of them had already dropped out of school and were either working or without jobs at the time of the uprisings in South Africa. These large numbers were a test for both the ANC and the PAC.

The PAC chose to send everyone for military training. However, few countries were prepared to offer training. Among these were China, Kampuchea (present day Cambodia) and Libya. A few were sent for aviation studies (which was interpreted as military training by the leadership of the PAC, although it wasn't) in Nigeria, many remained grounded in Tanzania, and this remained a source of disappointment and caused serious problems within the PAC in the course of time. On the other hand, the ANC had far larger numbers than the PAC and the youth had the choice of either going to Angola to do military training or furthering their education.

Given that peer pressure was extraordinarily strong and was biased towards military training, this choice was not an easy one to make. There was anger against the white racist regime and the youth wanted to go and fight. Undeniably, the majority in the ANC also decided to go for military training, although in this case, there was no pressure from leadership. Everyone wanted to take revenge against the killers of their friends and family members. I too had lost family members because of the reckless killings by the trigger-happy racist police. A few days after arriving in Swaziland, one of my uncles,

A frosty beginning

Enoch 'School Boy' Nhlapo from Dlamini Number One, who had recently graduated from the University of Zululand, and was teaching at Mncube Secondary School, was shot dead by a stray bullet from a police gun at Avalon Cemetery. He was attending the funeral of Jacob 'Jackie' Mashabane, a 22-year-old university student who was killed by police whilst in prison. The anger in me, while still in Swaziland, was telling me to go back home. 'School Boy' was my hero and I pursued education partly because of his influence as I admired him. I was following in his footsteps when I went to Zululand.

Among these youth, there were hundreds that wanted to go back to school. I was fortunate that I was given the responsibility to help with the supervision of these students. In Dar, the number of youth arriving from South Africa, kept on increasing at a fast rate and the majority were from Soweto, the Pretoria surroundings, East and West Rand. The situation became unmanageable, and incidents of ill-discipline increased because there was nothing to do but wait. Many years later, reflecting on this situation OR said,

> *This uprising of 1976-77 was, of course, the historic watershed ... Within a short period of time, it propelled into the forefront of our struggle millions of young people. That process of course resulted in increasing the relative proportion of the youth and students within our ranks. It brought into our midst comrades many of whom had very little contact with the ANC, if any. It put at the immediate disposal of our movement militant cadres who were ready and yearning to carry out even the most difficult missions that the movement wished to give them. It increased many times over the responsibility we had to maintain large numbers of people outside our country.*[3]

To address the situation in Dar, after the Tanzanian government had raised its concerns with both the ANC and PAC, the ANC decided to send some of the youth inland to a camp located in a place called Magadu, in Morogoro, which is about 195km from Dar.

This town in which Magadu was situated, had been home to a large ANC community long before the 1976 uprisings. It is where one of the significant conferences of the ANC, the Morogoro Conference of 1969, was held and where the first comprehensive strategy and tactics document of the ANC was produced. The Magadu Camp was occupied by MK veterans, fondly referred to as the 'Mgwenyas', the veterans with a lot of experience.

Bringing the students here did not help to improve the conditions in Dar. But then again, a similar situation arose in Morogoro. After consultations, it was decided to organise teaching classes during the day in the Magadu Camp. In early January I left Dar for Morogoro and arrived at the time when this solution was being implemented. I joined the team that was tasked with the responsibility to look after the welfare, education and discipline of the students. This is where I found Stan; he was the camp commander.

On my arrival a group of about 20 students had left for Festac '77 (the Second World Black and African Festival of Arts and Culture – the first one was held in Dakar in 1966) taking place in Lagos from 15 January 1977 to 12 February 1977. At any given time, there were about 60 to 80 young people there. When the numbers increased, girls were moved out of the camp and accommodated in houses in town, one of them named after Charlotte Maxeke. They were transported to the camp on a daily basis. We organised classes and shared all other responsibilities so that no one escaped camp tasks such as cooking for everyone and other chores, like cleaning. We were equal irrespective of age and gender. The majority were still at primary or high school level at home when the uprisings started. We taught subjects like mathematics, geography, history and the like. Senior students became teachers and we rotated and allocated tasks according to individual strengths. Everything was done on a voluntary basis. Due to my educational background, my main task was to co-ordinate classes and teach political education.

I encountered men and women who would further shape my thinking, my life and my future. Among the first people I had to work with was Hosea Maruping Seperepere who became my mentor because he oversaw Magadu. It was my first encounter with a Marxist intellectual. He introduced me to Marxist theory and shared teaching methodologies with me. Some days I would take classes with him and I in turn gave classes to the students in the camp. 'Ntate Seperepere', as we called him, handled every subject with painstaking detail and elucidated such complex concepts as the difference between the mode of production and the means of production, and many other theories.

I tried to emulate 'Ntate Seperepere' in my own classes. My forte was political education, and I made sure these classes were properly organised as they were strongly encouraged by the movement. I had remarkably interesting political discussions, especially among my peers.

We started our discussions with current affairs. I conducted political classes in such a way that we had to apply the theories I was teaching to the concrete situation in South Africa. I had to simplify South Africa's political economy, especially for those who were 16 years old and younger, so that there was an easy connection to our struggle to bring about social change. Lindi Zikalala (younger sister to Snuki Zikalala), Thabisile 'Thabi' Zikalala, Mzwandile Themba Masondo, Dee Mashinini (younger brother to Tsietsi Mashinini, the student leader who led the 1976 uprisings in Soweto), Mjapan Chauke, Joseph 'Joe Small' Lebooa, Dannyboy Lingwathi, Mandla 'Corombi' Ncala (the younger brother to Edward 'Eddy' Spear Ncala who was with me at Sekano Ntoana), Themba 'Spear' Ndebele, Glory Dudla Sekete and Victor Makgale Modise were some of the students there.

We dealt with the history of struggle, the history of the ANC, the struggle of the people of southern Africa and the rest of Africa among other subjects. Other tutors taught subjects such as mathematics and

Chapter Two

physical science. On certain days, senior members of the ANC led the political discussions. These were the Chief Rep – Mabuse Mampane, Professor Keorapetsi 'Bra Kgosi' Kgositsile, who remained throughout our stay in Magadu, a brother, a father to the youth, and a mentor. Other senior leaders were the Secretary-General, Alfred Nzo, Mme Gertrude and Mark Shope, Kate Molale, Johny Makatini, 'Mendi' Msimang, Mme Mittah Seperepere, Bra Max Sisulu, Sis Jackie Modise (nee Mofokeng), Ntate John Nkadimeng, and many others.

'Bra Kgosi' as I used to call him, was one of the few elder comrades, who from time to time would leave Dar and come and spend time with us. Another was Max Sisulu. The two remained true friends to the youth of the June 16 generation, providing guidance until a Youth Section of the ANC was formed in the early 1980s. I remember how some of the youth, after being impressed by how Bra Max answered their robust questions, would pose questions to him, like: 'Why are you not in the NEC?' In those days the NEC was very small – less than 20. He had a standard answer too. He responded this way: 'My father on Robben Island is a member of the NEC, and I am fine as an ordinary member of the ANC'. There was also Ndabakayipheli Wilson Macozoma (MK 'Bra Phiri' Nkosi of the 'Ball of Fire'), who was our dedicated and trusted driver, who ferried everyone between Dar and Morogoro.

On certain days, some students reported that they were not well and needed medical assistance. Whenever Manto 'Sis Manto' Tshabalala (former minister of health, known as Tshabalala-Msimang) a medical doctor, was in the camp, everyone wanted her attention. They always felt better after they had seen her. I realised that many of the young girls and boys sometimes felt homesick and pretended they were ill, until 'Sis Manto' arrived, and everybody was fine afterwards,

It is while fulfilling this assignment that I came to grasp the overall mission of the ANC structures in exile. Life in the camp was totally different from the townships we came from. Here, there were MK veterans who had participated in the Wankie and Sipolilo campaigns, who lived with us, and others stayed in the neighbourhood. (The campaigns were military undertakings by MK and ZIPRA to try and infiltrate cadres into Rhodesia and South Africa.)

During the day, when we had finished with formal duties and classes, or in the evenings when thick darkness forced us to gather around a fire made up of dry wood from the bushes around the camp, the veterans recounted remarkable stories about the skirmishes they encountered with the Boers in Wankie.

The campaigns, which were launched between August and September 1967, involved about 80 cadres who had crossed the border into Rhodesia. The incursion was countered by the Rhodesian police and army (assisted by South African forces) and left casualties on both sides. On the side of MK cadres, 29 were killed and 17 captured within Rhodesia and 29 were arrested in Botswana, where one died. Only one cadre reached South Africa and was arrested in Durban, and one escaped back to Zambia. Although these were the only real encounters between MK and the enemy forces since MK was founded in 1961, these were stories of great valour and a living inspiration to the Qiniselanis – the June 16 generation. Qiniselani is a Zulu word which means 'be strong'. There was a popular song, *Qiniselani,* loved by the youth that was translated as, 'don't be afraid, be strong, victory is not far away, the cowards are afraid; they are saying it is better to go back home'.

The veterans also related to us what they had been through since leaving South Africa in the early and mid-1960s. The African terrain was quite different compared to the period when we arrived in the second half of the 1970s. They were surprised to hear about the changes that had taken place back in South Africa. Above and beyond politics, some had left South Africa when the currency was still pounds, shillings and pence or when rands and cents were being introduced.

It is in these dealings with the leadership of the ANC, the South African Congress of Trade Unions (SACTU) and the veterans of Umkhonto we Sizwe (MK) that one came to understand what it meant to serve the interests of the liberation struggle in a manner befitting the expectations of those back in South Africa. The ANC employed a trial and error approach to its assignments. All told, and with all the challenges encountered at that stage, the organisation was able to give the youth direction on the struggle for liberation.

A new dawn fell for the erstwhile stone throwers. We were confronted by other challenges here in the first years of exile. Sometimes there was no rice, the next day no meat. All the meat we bought at the marketplace in town and ate was from wild animals. You never asked which animal it was because nobody was going to give you an answer. All you had to do was to buy quickly before the meat got finished, otherwise comrades in the camp were going to suffer. One day the students noticed that meat was brought in a box that had worms and the camp decided not to cook and eat such meat. Leadership was summoned to the camp for the wrong reasons, because 'the Mgwenya' delivering the meat reported that the students were boycotting food that the ANC was providing.

The Magadu camp was in the bush. In this crude camp in the wilderness, the new enemies became malaria, the tsetse fly, the African bee and dangerous snakes which we had not encountered before. We had never imagined we would also hunt for snakes and eat them. There were those among us who became specialists in killing, skinning and removing the insides in a very meticulous way, using only a razor blade. There were various lizards that visited our place and would either perform a fierce fight with the dogs we had in the camp or be killed by them. On occasions when our dogs were successful, and they had killed lizards, the African monitor lizard would end up in our pots. This became part of our new daily life.

There were fewer women than men in the camp. As would happen given these circumstances, there would be fights among the boys over the girls. Some girls left South Africa at a very tender age and had not reached the age of puberty or were going through it. Given the conditions that were prevalent in South Africa at the time, in most cases the girls were not sexually active. I remember well that Cynthia Phefo (not her real name), realised that there was something wrong with her body and she could not explain what was happening to her. After some time, she was taken to meet elderly comrades to look for an explanation. She met with Mam'Kate (Kate Molale), MaSeperepere (Mittah Seperepere) and Bab' uMabhida (Moses Mabhida) and she was told that she was pregnant.

Pregnant? She was stunned! She was told that she had slept with a boy. For this she received the dressing-down of her life from three of them, with Mabhida being the severest of them all, as if she were his own daughter who was pregnant. He said, 'I want to see you strong because there are vultures out there!' Many years later, Cynthia remembers, that is what made her strong. From that day on, Cynthia withdrew herself from most activities in the camp as she was now afraid of boys. She thought if she came nearer to boys, she would get another baby in addition to the one she was already carrying.

One of the ways in which we were provided with clothing was through a process called 'mphando' (donations of clothing, mainly from the Scandinavian countries – Denmark, Norway, and Sweden). I hated the scramble that used to take place to claim these items. So, for over six months I wore one pair of trousers and had only two shirts to my name. When they were dirty, I washed them and while they got dry, which was very quick because of the heat in this region, I stayed naked under the blankets in the tent reading books. One day I got a terrible fright. After drying my shirt in the sun, I put it on as I usually did. The following day the skin on my left hip was itching and I kept scratching without paying attention. In the afternoon after repeatedly scratching myself, I pulled my shirt off and looked at my hip. I couldn't believe it when I saw a big white worm protruding from my skin. Out of shock, I screamed and threw away whatever I had in my hands.

Maurice Olehile Bada, our medic, came to my rescue. We squeezed the worm out of my skin, and I was cautioned that I should always use a hot iron – the iron charcoal rooster – on every washed item before putting it on. Because of the heat in Tanzania, flies laid eggs on every wet surface they came across and clothes were the easiest place for this to happen. That day I learned a valuable lesson. Later I understood that it was not actually a fly that laid eggs on my clothes, but that my skin could have been penetrated by a jigger flea, called a funza in Kiswahili, which deposits worms under the skin.

We also learned that every time one moved from one camp to another, and from one country to another, the writing of personal biographies was the norm. Pseudonyms and noms de guerre were often adopted. You arrived at a place being Dennis Hlatshwayo or Agnes Tlou and the next thing someone you had never met in your life would give you a name, Che Guevara Baloyi or Sophie Khuzwayo. Among the students in the Magadu camp, we did not enforce this practice but by the time one reached Magadu, one would have passed through places where this was practised. .

There was a large group of students that left for Nigeria that included, Sydney 'Nqaphi' Mophuting, Magang Mmereki Phologane (Dr, ambassador), Sello Pule, Moss Mothupi Malaka, Napoleon Jacob Mothopeng, Peige Amerie Boikanyo, Martin Dombo, William Sugar Mlangeni, Walter Themba Thabethe (ambassador), Godfrey Pantoki Pholoholo, Aubrey Matlole, Glory Dudla Sekete and Cecil Lucky Mabasa (Dr).

Months after this group left, Stan went to study in Bulgaria together with Chris Manduba (Dr), Desmond Shangase, Kenneth 'Bra Chris' Msengana, Martin Khahliso 'Mal Fra' Francis Monyane Maphisa, Maurice Olehile Bada Pharasi and Leornard Shego, among others. After this the leadership of the camp fell on me.

Trip to West Germany

In May 1977, the ANC received an invitation from the Anti-Apartheid Bewegung (AAB), the Anti-Apartheid Movement in West Germany to send someone for a road show for the commemoration of the first anniversary of June 16. I was summoned to leave Morogoro for Dar. In the ANC, sometimes you were never told what the mission was all about until you reached the place and someone informed you. This was the new life we had to adjust to quickly.

I arrived in Dar, and had to have photos taken for my passport, which had already been issued and was waiting for me. That was how things worked in those days, no fingerprints were taken. I discovered that my names were correctly spelt on my passport, but date of birth was incorrect. I was stuck with this error for all the years I spent in exile; and it caused me much distress to have to explain what had happened at the institutions of learning I was attending.

I was only informed of the trip and what was expected of me once I had received my passport. No one asked you if you were ready or not; if you were sick, or if you had suffered aerophobia. Anyway I was very glad to have been given this opportunity and the trust of the organisation. This was a major trip, my first trip overseas. Poor me, without a suitcase but a small bag carrying all my essentials; I was thrown into the deep end but this trip opened my eyes in many ways.

The Secretary-General of the AAB was Ingeborg Wick, a hard-working woman who had endured and withstood numerous dirty tricks from the apartheid regime and was also harassed by the local German police. The AAB was one of the strongest anti-apartheid movements in Europe. It was founded in 1974 and quickly established itself, with about 70 active branches in all the major cities of West Germany. Its support came from youth, student and church groups, members of parliament (the Bundestag), and with time support also came from the trade unions, and various political groups and parties, depending on the theme of their campaigns.

Starting on June 15 in Hannover, my itinerary took me to several towns, like Bielefeld, Münster, Dortmund, Düsseldorf, Köln (Cologne), Bonn and Aachen. By the end of four weeks, I had addressed throngs and throngs of students, youth, church groups and activists at tertiary institutions and universities, in small and large halls, in open spaces and closed sessions, at special events, conferences and marches. For the first time I personally experienced the outrage caused throughout the world by the June 16, 1976 events, when heavily armed police pushed and kicked black school children, beating them with clubs and shooting at them with live ammunition. These disturbing images of the Soweto uprising had shocked the world. For me it was a matter of educating German citizens about the situation in South Africa and how it affected us.

I explained what they already knew about the strong economic, cultural and political ties between the Federal Republic of Germany and the apartheid regime, especially the military and nuclear cooperation with the apartheid state. I called for action against their own government, explained the connections between this relationship and our oppression, and called for the intensification of sanctions and boycotts.

This being my first trip, at the end of it I was eager to fly back to Tanzania so that I could share these experiences with my comrades in Magadu. The excitement was giving me sleepless nights. I had to stay a week longer than was planned by my host because of the war over the Ogaden region between Somalia and Ethiopia. I was flying with KLM via Nairobi. At the time no flights over Eastern Africa were allowed.

I was staying at Dr Wolff Geisler's place. Dr Geisler was a medical doctor by profession, and he divided his work between his surgery and the AAB cause of supporting the liberation struggles in southern Africa. In the 1970s Geisler was the managing director of the German Committee for Angola, Guinea-Bissau and Mozambique. With the June 16 uprisings he dedicated most of his time to South Africa. He became an expert on many fronts, among others on the military cooperation between the FRG (Federal Republic of Germany) and South Africa in the nuclear and conventional sectors arms. He condemned corporate companies like Siemens, Daimler-Benz, Rheinmetall and Messerschmitt-Bölkow-Blohm in supporting the apartheid regime. He produced several books and literature, as a specialist, on these themes.[4]

I had turned 23 years old on June 20 during this visit and while talking about medical matters with Wolff, we ended up talking about circumcision. He told me it is such a quick process, and I should consider doing it. He took me to a private clinic where his surgery was situated. After they had finished, and because it was such a fast and painless procedure, I was still asking him, when is the operation happening? He laughed and said check your time, 'I said two minutes! It is long over, get dressed and go to the car'. This was my first encounter with German precision.

I really enjoyed my stay in Bonn with Wolff, Christa, and their colleagues in the movement – Clemens and Angela. I also got to know a very energetic anti-apartheid campaigner by the name of Ursula Schmidt, an elderly woman living in West Berlin. I also met Frene Ginwala for the first time. She was visiting at the time I was there and had come from London, to do research.

While I was waiting for my flight to Africa, I reflected on my trip to Germany. On the day of my arrival in Hannover, there was a big surprise waiting for me. The driver who collected me from the airport, asked me if I was related to the Mbatha sisters. This being my first trip to Europe, I responded quickly by saying 'no'. He then told me, two girls named Nomsa and Charlotte, had arrived and their surname was Mbatha. My heart skipped a beat and I asked myself, whether I had come to the right place or even the right country? Had I been lured to Germany to be handed over to the Boers? He suggested that maybe we pass by their place before he showed me where I was going to stay. Out of interest, and to see for myself who these Mbatha sisters in Germany were, I agreed.

As the car stopped I saw Nomsa and Charlotte standing outside. My disturbed reaction did not escape the driver's attention. He looked a bit confused because I told him I didn't know the girls. I had last seen them on the day when I visited their home desperately looking for transport to get out of the country. There was no goodbye, after this, I just left. I would never have thought of meeting them in Europe or West Germany for that matter. They were assisted by church organisations based in Germany and they safely escaped to Swaziland and then to Germany. They had arrived two days previously. Their parents, Khosi and Alex, were in detention under the Terrorism Act. The whereabouts of five other children in the family was unknown. We later met after my first engagement, and I left Hannover for the next town.

In one of the closed meetings in the towns I toured, at the end of my presentation, two gentlemen stood up and told the audience, one after the other, that I was being abused by the ANC leadership because I was from Soweto. What? They asserted that the ANC was not leading a liberation struggle against the white regime, and was working with the communists and Russians to protect the interests of whites. I was shocked and asked Ingeborg who these people were. She whispered that they were the Group of Eight.⁵ 'Group of Eight', it did not ring a bell as I had not heard of them since being in exile. Ingeborg said I should ignore them. I responded that there were many interpretations of our struggle, which were informed by the Freedom Charter and not by the communists or Russians. I said the fact that white comrades were members of our movement didn't detract from the fact that our struggle was about the liberation of black people. The audience applauded loudly and the gentlemen were silenced.

Finally, I left Bonn, the capital of West Germany, for Dar. As was the norm, on arrival I had to write a report on my trip before I proceeded to Morogoro. When I met the Secretary-General of the ANC, Alfred Nzo, for the first time in Dar, I asked him about the Group of Eight and why I had never heard anyone speak about them. He laughed and referred me to a statement made in 1976 explaining the expulsion of the eight members from the ANC. He said, 'if you met those comrades (he still called them comrades) then you can represent the ANC anywhere'.

It was the first time while in exile I had left a place and returned to unite with my comrades. Magadu was our home away from home, and this was my new family. I shared my experiences and engagements in Germany with them. I told them that at some places I addressed hundreds of youths, who were keen to listen and find ways to contribute towards our struggle.

Preparations for the GDR

At the end of August, word came that I was one of three students who had been awarded a scholarship to study in the German Democratic Republic (GDR). Scholarships at tertiary level were not easily available and many were disappointed. I was dealing with political education and had made it clear to my senior comrades that I was interested in German philosophy and wanted to study it nowhere else but in Germany, East or West. Going back to my days at Sekano-Ntoane High and the narratives about Germany, and my philosophy studies at the University of Zululand under Prof van der Merwe, I was now convinced this is what I wanted to study. The dialectical methods and reasoning of German philosophers, Fichte, Kant, Hegel and Marx, were further acknowledged by Ntate Seperepere, the first Marxist disciple I met. Everybody used to laugh when I said I didn't want second-hand information on German philosophy after coming so far.

There was another reason too. It was something that had bothered me since my childhood days in Western, the story of the notorious Vera 'the ghost'. The real Vera's family was my immediate neighbour in Western before the relocation to Rockville. I understood she was incredibly beautiful and was fond of me as a child. Allegedly, she was murdered by a jealous boyfriend and her spirit terrorised men in those old Public Utility Transport Company (PUTCO) buses with big engines besides the driver, next to the entrance. This happened along specific routes in the evenings. I was fascinated by the story, and wished to see a ghost personally. I convinced myself that the possibility of seeing a ghost in Germany was extremely high, given the millions of people that were killed there during the First and Second World Wars. There must surely be ghosts in Germany I told myself, However, although my wish to study philosophy in Germany was fulfilled, my wish to see a ghost remained just that – a wish.

The idea of separating from my new family in Magadu was difficult to bear. Every day I spent in the camp, the clock was ticking. I was not the first to feel like this. Every month since I arrived, there were new arrivals from home while others were leaving for different countries when scholarships became available.

The life we were living was simple but full of determination.

We got to know one another better and cemented our comradeship. There were many things we learned from the cultural activities we participated in. Thando Dlula, Dee Mashini (younger brother to Tsietsi Mashinini), Lindi Zikalala, Victor Makgale, Wandile Kabane, Nhlanhla 'Paradise' Mashinini (whose family home I knew very well in Dlamini Number Two), Moses 'Moss' Nkrumah Mazibuko (who was from Dlamini Number One and was my junior at Sekano-Ntoana), Madoda Makhanya (Dr) and others composed songs: and wrote and produced plays in which they also performed. There was Mmabatho Nlanhla (nee Molefe) and Ben Mokoena who had silver and golden voices respectively, and could sing melodies and compositions by great artists like Miriam Makeba and Gibson Kente. After being inspired by the poetry and writings of Professor Keorapetse Kgositsile, some among us wrote poetry.

I, like most of the youth, who were from Soweto and Johannesburg, was conversant in all the South African languages. There were people from the Eastern Cape, Transkei, Bophuthatswana, who spoke very deep isiXhosa, Sesotho and Setswana and so on, which used to fascinate me as I enjoyed the uniqueness of these languages. A few among us, like Bonner Seakhoa and Oupa Mophete Sekamane, were from Lesotho and Jeff Thamsanqa Radebe (former minister), Bheki Langa (Dr, ambassador) and Mphakama Oscar Mbete (ambassador) were from Durban.

I was now more than convinced that my encounter with Ciko Mbatha at the University of Zululand, was helpful in many ways. It proved to me that my claims of being Zulu were unconvincing. It is from Magadu that I started identifying myself as more Sowetan than Zulu. While I knew the origins of my parents, especially of my father, I told myself that I would no longer define myself through them or allow them to impose their identity on me. In the camp all 'Sowetans' understood each other because we mixed all the languages. In other words, Magadu, like the City of Gold was for South Africa, became a melting pot of South African cultures in exile.

We also mingled with people from all over the continent as well as those from Europe. The UN was openly supportive of the South African liberation struggle. African embassies invited us to their residences on their national days, espousing unequivocal support for our struggle. In a true sense, we left Tanzania well-armed to face the world both in the East and West as we found ourselves deep in the Cold War.

It was during this time – when I was about to leave Magadu – that negotiations started regarding Mazimbu, the farmland that the Tanzanian government had identified and offered to the ANC to develop a school. The ever-growing youth and student body in Tanzania presented a serious challenge to the ANC, especially in Dar. The Tanzanian Prime Minister's office raised their concerns with the ANC about the disruption of the general life of citizens and more importantly, the security situation in the country. The Chief Rep, Mampane, reported this to Secretary-General Nzo in Lusaka, who responded by requesting Mampane to approach the Tanzanian government and ask for a piece of land outside the city where the students could be accommodated, and possibly a school could be erected for them.

Armed with this request, Mampane returned to the Tanzanian government and was told to engage with General Muhidini Kimario of home affairs (later he became Major General of the Tanzania People's Defence Forces – TPDF, and Minister of Home Affairs). This is when Mampane was told to go back to Morogoro. With General Kimario's people, they visited the office of the regional commissioner in Morogoro and met Anna Margareth Abdallah, known as 'Mama Anna', a Chama Cha Mapinduzi (CCM) politician and the first female district commissioner in Tanzania.

Mama Anna is the one who proposed the 200-hectare abandoned sisal estate in a village called Mazimbu. Without delay, Mampane sent a report to Lusaka together with a letter from the ministry offering the land to the ANC. The Secretary-General replied sending a directive that the offer be taken. Mazimbu was actually founded by Mazimba (the MK name of Reddy Mazimba) and the idea was Alfred Nzo's. Before my departure I was given the responsibility to take some of the students to clear the land where a school would be built. Two years after my departure, the Solomon Mahlangu Freedom College (SOMAFCO) was inaugurated by President OR Tambo on the firm foundations laid down in Magadu. The establishment of SOMAFCO has been hailed as the best investment that the ANC made in youth that fled South Africa, and in the children of those already in exile. An alternative to Bantu Education, it was an academic and vocational institution with a nursery school, garment making factories and farmlands that supplied food to the institution. It included a modern hospital.

An affectionate relationship developed between me and Esme Molale, a gorgeous girl with sparkling eyes, who was the daughter of the archbishop of Gaborone. On the eve of my departure, she cried uncontrollably and nearly delayed my departure from Magadu to Dar. We flew out of Dar, Humphrey Quinton Magula (Dr), Mandla Pule and I, with an Aeroflot aircraft on the evening of Sunday, September 25, 1977, bound for Moscow, the capital of the Soviet Union, and arrived there early on the morning of Monday, 26 September. Within an hour or two, we flew to Berlin with Interflug, the national airline of the GDR.

After we left Tanzania, other students departed for the Soviet Union, among them were Nomasonto Mpho Thoabala-Motjope (nee Thoabala), Bheki Langa, Maminze Abe (Dr), Edison Eddy Maphumulo, Joseph Mlungisi 'Lungi' Daweti, Mandla Tshabalala (the last-born son of the famous tycoon and businessman in Mofolo who owned Eyethu cinema in Soweto) and Experience Zikalala. They were together with a larger group from Lesotho, among them, Jeff Moitsupedi Letsei, Mary Mafekeng, Uhuru Zikalala (nee Mafekeng), James Lefa Makgetha, McGregor Mosoeu and Bonner Seakhoa. Others from Lesotho, like James Lefa Makhetha went to study in Poland and Sefadi Makgetha and Bataung Mohapeloa went to Bulgaria. Over the next couple of years, Ndumiso Ntshinga left for Bulgaria.Leah Lulu Mabena (now Madalane), Mmabatho Nhlanhla, Mophete Oupa Sekamane (Lesotho) and Jeff Radebe joined me in the GDR.

Another group of 15 students left at the end of 1977 for Cairo, to obtain university entrances, they included Dee Mashinini, Victor Modise, Ntombi Mashigo, Mirriam Mbhele, Pitso (surname forgotten), Letta Rankoe, Spear Ndebele, Lucky Mogoai, Madoda Makhanya (Dr), Thando Dlula, Wandile Kabane, Thabisile Zikalala, Lindi Zikalala, George (surname forgotten) and Jerry (surname forgotten). Wandile 'Boss' Kallipa and Mark Chelepe Monare went to study in Romania. Leslie Mbangambi Gumbi (ambassador) went to Poland. The group that left for Cuba included Mzwandile Themba Masondo. During the commemoration of the 30th anniversary of June 16, in 2006 I wrote this prose dedicated to Magadu.

> *Magadu is about me*
> *Magadu is how I want to introduce you to what I am today*
> *Magadu is a symbol of my spirit of hope and despair*
> *Magadu was mother and father at the same time*
> *Magadu cared and never cared*
> *Magadu moved and yet she lay quiet among the thick*
> *bush of natural and unnatural surroundings*
> *We came to live, not knowing what we were doing in Magadu*
> *but we moved on, passed and left Magadu in peace*

*We interacted with her and her surroundings but disappeared
into many paths that carried us to many countries of the world*
Sometimes without saying good-bye to Magadu
Sometimes with happy experiences and
Sometimes with bitter and very bitter experiences
But Magadu remained Magadu
Magadu is a story about stories
Magadu is June 16 stories told against Magadu's background
Magadu is about what we thought then
when we found ourselves so far away from home
*when we thought we were going to come
back after six months or so*
Magadu is about the first experiences of exile
is about the first home away from home
is about the first experience of eating snakes
is about the first experiences with real politics of struggle
is about the first experience with malaria and tsetse fly
is about the first experience with being nowhere in the map
*is about the first experience of living without money, no
flushing toilet, no bathroom, no privacy, no nothing*
Magadu is about me after 30 years

Chapter Three
MY ENLIGHTENMENT

THE GDR – MY SECOND HOME (1977 – 1987)

Language Course in Leipzig (1977 – 1978)

I believed that more and better education of our people was critical to free of our country from apartheid oppression and economic exploitation

It was September and the weather in Germany was fantastic as we landed at the Berlin-Schönefeld Airport in East-Berlin, the capital of East Germany. I had no idea that this would become my second home. We were met by officials, who were our guides. This time I carried a suitcase which I had bought on my visit to West Germany. We were taken straight to the train station with the same name, Berlin-Schönefeld Airport, which was about a kilometre away. From here we took a Schnellzug (fast train) for a three-hour trip to our destination, Leipzig. The students' hostels were located southeast of Leipzig at the famous 'Straße des 18. Oktober 23-33' (October 18th Street). There were eleven residential towers, eight and nine floors high, with accommodation for just over a thousand students in shared and single apartments. The buildings also included students' clubs.

October 18th Street leads directly to the Völkerschlachtdenkmal (the Battle of the Nations monument). The name signifies the day of the vital victory of the Allied troops over Napoleon, in the Battle of the Nations near Leipzig on October 18, 1813. The monument, inaugurated on October 18, 1913 with a height of 91m, is one of the largest in Europe and one of the best known landmarks of Leipzig. It brought to mind my high school lessons and memories. The Voortrekker Monument in Pretoria, which was inaugurated on 16 December 1949 by DF Malan, the Prime Minister, is only 40m high, and its architecture resembles that of the Battle of the Nations monument. Around October 18th

Street, there were many other students' hostels. These were on Philipp-Rosenthalstraße and Tarostraße (Philipp Rosenthal and Taro Streets) and others were located about five kilometres outside town.

On Monday we were taken for registration at the German language school, the Herder Institute, which was part of the University of Leipzig. When we studied there it was called the 'Karl Marx' University of Leipzig. We also took photos for our new student identity documents which would allow us to collect our stipend every month. We were escorted in groups for shopping, mainly for winter wear. The authorities warned us to choose very warm clothes as the winter can be harsh. I got a winter overcoat, a pair of winter boots and winter socks, a scarf, winter hat and a pair of gloves. Long winter pants (called the Vasco da Gama undergarment in South Africa) was a must have.

Some students who were probably not well briefed and didn't take the advice of the teachers seriously. For instance a student from Madagascar, who was in my language class, refused to take a heavy winter coat saying it didn't look good on him. When winter arrived, he was one of the students who got terribly ill for many days because he wasn't dressed warmly enough for the bitterly cold weather.

The whole world was in Leipzig. Students came from Madagascar, Ethiopia, Angola, Tanzania, Benin, Somalia, Senegal, Laos, Vietnam, South Yemen, Iraq, Syria and Nigeria. Liberation movements were well represented too – from ZAPU, the South-West Africa People's Organisation (SWAPO), the Palestine Liberation Organisation (PLO) and the Popular Front for the Liberation of Saguia el-Hamra and Río de Oro (Polisario Front).

Leipzig was full of life and cultural activities, and forging relationships with people from all over the world was part of daily life. It was as if the youth of the world had gathered here. There were also students from communist parties in Western Europe, among others from Greece, Portugal, Spain, and the USA. Most of the youth belonged to either a political organisation, a developing country, a liberation movement, a country at war, or a country that had won independence or had just been freed from colonialism, fascism and oppression. Countries represented included Angola, Mozambique, Guinea Bissau and Cape Verde, Greece, Portugal, Spain and Vietnam. It seemed everyone knew of the June 16 uprisings in South Africa.

We were all here to study, but we all had to learn the German language first. I slowly learned to say, *Ich heiße Khulu und Ich komme aus Südafrika* (My name is Khulu, and I come from South Africa).

Breakfast, lunch and dinner were served at the students' main dining hall in the centre of town during the week. On weekends we could afford to eat at either a restaurant or we cooked for ourselves in the common kitchens provided on each floor of the students' hostel. We could also afford to take a bus or train and visit friends in other cities. Food and travel were unbelievably cheap in the GDR.

In the second week of December we went for our first excursion by train to Oberhof, a town in the Schmalkalden-Meiningen district of Thuringia, which was a famous winter sports centre and health resort. The intention was to introduce us to the marvels of nature, especially the topography and snow in Oberhof and its surroundings.

Before the train reached its destination, the warm carriages started getting cold and by the time we reached the last station, it was freezing inside the train. It was so cold stepping out of the train that some even thought of remaining in the train, but unfortunately everyone had to get off. I had never seen so much snow in my life.

This was an experience of a lifetime. We were taken to see part of the resort, but by the time we were taken for our hot meals, everybody wished to leave the area and go back to Leipzig. The cold was so unbearable that I told myself that I would never see that place again. Later in life I learned never to say 'never' because with time, living in the GDR, winter became the loveliest time ever. I became a winter person.

Over the weekends, trams – the main means of transport from town to the hostels – were available at intervals of half-an-hour after midnight. When returning from functions or events, instead of waiting for the trams, we would walk back to the hostels, especially in summer. The path through to the hostel cut across a big old cemetery called Friedenspark (Freedom Park). I thought I might see a ghost there. The Wehrmacht (the 'defence power', the armed forces of the Third Reich) lost 4.3 million men during the World War Two and I was optimistic that my aspiration to see a ghost was going to be fulfilled there. But to my great disappointment, I never came across a single ghost.

After completing my language course at the Herder Institute in June 1978, it was time to enjoy a vacation. Some students from independent countries and free nations went back to their home countries and returned at the beginning of the new semester in September.

For the rest, those mainly from Africa and the liberation movements, like me, there was nowhere to go. Considering that it was my first year, there was not much to do except visit other comrades studying in Leipzig or other cities. However, there were also a lot of summer activities in town where we enjoyed ourselves and we organised student gatherings and parties.

Studying in Jena (1978 – 1907)

At the beginning of September, I took a train to a small but famous town called Jena where I was to enrol as a student of philosophy at the Friedrich Schiller University (FSU). The FSU was founded in 1558. Johann Gottlieb Fichte (1762–1814) who was greatly influenced by Immanuel Kant, was an extraordinary professor at the university who was joined by Friedrich Wilhelm Joseph Schelling (1775–1854). Schelling in turn invited Friedrich Hegel (1770–1831), who was a close friend of Johann Wolfgang von Goethe (1749–1832), to join the illustrious group in Jena. To cap it all, Karl Marx (5 May 1818–14 March 1883), who was a student at the University of Berlin wrote a very controversial dissertation, 'The Difference between the Democritean and Epicurean Philosophy of Nature'. It was on the materialism and atheism of the Greek atomists and in those days considered very revolutionary. The conservative professors in Berlin were never going to pass it, so Marx decided instead to submit his thesis to the more liberal University of Jena. He was conferred with his doctorate with lively acclaim in 1841. This paved the way for Marx to pursue his radical ideas which later led to great works in the sciences. I found myself walking on the same paths that these remarkable personalities had traversed. I prepared myself to go into every detail of their lives to make sure I understood the challenges of their era, but I had no idea what awaited me.

Jena was a world centre of the optical industry with such companies as Carl Zeiss and Otto Schott Glasswerk. The town lies on a hilly landscape in the eastern part of the Federal State of Thuringia (Province). It rests next to the Saale River between the Harz Mountains in the north, the Thuringian Forest in the southwest, and the Ore Mountains in the southeast. It is the second largest city after Erfurt, the capital of the State of Thuringia, and with Weimar, the three form the central metropolitan area of this state. The town is much smaller than Leipzig and seemed to be much quieter.

I was met at the train station, and directed to the students' hostels seven kilometres out of town. I arrived at the Salvador Allende buildings, on Karl Marx Allee 1 – 3, in the suburb of Neulobeda Ost (New Lobeda East). Neulobeda, which is divided into Neulobeda Ost and Neulobeda West, is the largest district of Jena. It was founded in 1966 and completed while I was there in 1986. The hostels, located next to the bus end-station coming from town, became my second home for the next nine years. After spending a few days settling in,

I started attending classes. In the first year of my five-year course in philosophy, I still had to take the German language lessons, firstly, to perfect my German in general and secondly to orientate myself to the language of philosophy.

The five-year course in Germany was called a Diplomarbeit (diploma thesis or degree dissertation) which is equal to a master's degree. At the end of the period, one was required to complete a dissertation to earn a degree. My dream was becoming a reality. That year (1978/1979) there was no intake of German students in the faculty of philosophy, so my group was the first that was made up of foreign students only.

Louis Phillipe Da Silva, Auzenda Da Silva and Carlos Tavares were from Guinea Bissau & Cape Verde and members of the Partido Africano para a Independência da Guiné e Cabo Verde – PAIGC (African Party for the Independence of Guinea and Cape Verde). By then it was still one country as they shared a flag and a national anthem until 1980 when they separated after a coup on the mainland. Anna Koutoulogeni was a member of the Communist Youth of Greece (KNE), Gloria Bravo and Jorge came from Chile and Bolivia respectively, and lastly Humphrey Quinton Magula and I were from the ANC, South Africa. The eight of us belonged to revolutionary parties and had one thing in common, to delve into the terrain of philosophy. The journeys we had all travelled to be at FSU in 1978 were remarkably interesting.

The professors and lecturers never disappointed. They made it clear that they would apply the same standards to us that they applied to all German students. There were no favours. We had to read to be able to debate in class and for that matter we had to do it in German. If you had not read the required material for that month, you were easily discovered. All lectures were delivered in an engaging way. We were encouraged to sharpen our skills to master a position and be able to defend it with conviction and confidence. Our first year included among other subjects, Formal Logic, Aesthetics and Ethics, and Ancient Philosophy – Chinese, Greek, Roman and Indian, which we studied for two years.

Among my favourite subjects were Greek philosophy, the development of philosophy in the Middle Ages up to the rise of the bourgeoisie societies, the fall of the Roman Empire and the rise of the Ottoman Empire – the time of castles, guilds and peasants, monasteries and cathedrals.

I was intrigued by the contribution of French (e.g., René Descartes and Jean-Jacques Rousseau) and English (e.g., Adam Smith, David Ricardo, Thomas Hobbes and John Locke) philosophers to economic and political theories, and the development of philosophy in general.

The influence the German philosophers of the modern era like Kant, Fichte, Schelling, Hegel, Feuerbach, Marx and Friedrich Engels was fascinating. Marx's achievements with dialectics, historical materialism, the doctrine of the class struggle and the economic system of society, was best summarised by his comrade-in-arms, Friedrich Engels at his funeral:

> *Just as Darwin discovered the law of development or organic nature, so Marx discovered the law of development of human history: the simple fact, hitherto concealed by an overgrowth of ideology, that mankind must first of all eat, drink, have shelter and clothing, before it can pursue politics, science, art, religion, etc.; that therefore the production of the immediate material means, and consequently the degree of economic development attained by a given people or during a given epoch, form the foundation upon which the state institutions, the legal conceptions, art, and even the ideas on religion, of the people concerned have been evolved, and in the light of which they must, therefore, be explained, instead of vice versa, as had hitherto been the case.*

The study of philosophy is not complete without reading the writings of VI Lenin (Vladimir Ilyich Ulyanov) and the European Existentialism of the 19th and 20th century of people like Friedrich Wilhelm Nietzsche, Jean-Paul Charles Aymard Sartre and Martin Heidegger.

During my time in Jena, the university was one of the most cosmopolitan institutions of education in the GDR, with students from all over the world in various faculties and fields of study, especially linguistics, for students from the former socialist countries. Foreign students came from the Soviet Union, Hungary, Bulgaria, Poland, Czechoslovakia, Cyprus, Yemen, Iraq, Iran, Syria, Angola, Mozambique, Guinea Bissau and Cape Verde. Other countries represented were Nigeria, Egypt, Cuba, Mexico, Guatemala, Columbia, Greece, the UK, USA, Namibia and South Africa.

All intakes of students taking up philosophy after the 1978/1979 semesters included German students as well. In later years other students who joined our philosophy faculty were Leah Lulu Mabena (nee Madalane), Zandisile 'Keith' Pase and Zolile Nippy Magugu from South Africa. There was Salah Adameh (Palestine, lecturer at University of Jerusalem), Maritza (Cuba) and José Leitão (Angola, lecturer at Jean Piaget University of Angola and assistant professor at the Institute of Science in Higher Education in Luanda) and Carlos Cardoso (Guinea Bissau). Ahlam Adens, Samirah, Rashid and Alawi (Yemen), Sonbeto and Tsegae (Ethiopia), Faeq Zarif (Afghanistan), Jocho and Zoe (Mongolia) and Phay Phatavon (Laos) also became students of philosophy. Hugo Melgar from Guatemala studied medicine (and is now professor at the McGill University in Montreal, Quebec, Canada).

Coming from South Africa with its racial divisions, such a pluralistic, multinational and multicultural social environment combined with my studies of philosophy, was ideal to cultivate a new world outlook. At the end of my fifth year in 1982/1983 I submitted my dissertation for a master's degree entitled, 'The Analysis of the Social Structure in Africa Using the Example of Sub-Saharan Africa' and I was awarded my degree cum laude. The university was keen that I consider doing my doctorate in Jena.

At the beginning of 1983 I submitted a request to extend my studies in Jena to the Chief Representative of the ANC, Anthony Le Clerc Mongalo and I later received the necessary approval.

In the academic calendar-years 1983/1984 to 1986/1987, I proceeded with my research work and gave lectures on various topics, including South Africa, at schools and institutions in and around Jena. At the end of March 1987, I submitted my dissertation for a doctoral degree under the theme, 'The National Liberation Movement and the National Question in the Republic of South Africa'. In May, I defended my PhD thesis, earning magna cum laude. I was over the moon because I had followed in the footsteps of great scholars that passed through this university, and I could be counted as one of their disciples.

I was unable to celebrate this milestone with my parents, siblings, or the friends I grew up with. Nevertheless, I was happy that there were comrades who shared this joy with me. Nelson Miya, the Deputy Chief Representative of the ANC in Berlin, Zolile Magugu and Zolile 'Sello' Maqetuka (Dr) who was studying journalism in Leipzig, honoured this significant achievement with me.

It is in Jena that I became a staunch and proud Marxist scholar. Unfortunately, there were many people who took Marxists to be communists and vice versa. This stereotyping still exists today. The truth was that not all communists were Marxists, and not all Marxists were communists. Having stayed for ten years in the GDR I came to realise that the Socialist Unity Party of Germany (SED), had more communists than Marxists. Later, in a free South Africa, I discovered that the same was true for the South Africa Communist Party. There appeared to be many Marxist intellectuals and scholars in the Western world, especially at universities, both in Europe and the USA, than in the whole communist sphere of influence. The majority were not card caring communists and had never been associated with any communist party.

ANC Work and Students' Affairs

In the GDR I found that the ANC community consisted mainly of students and those who had completed their studies and were working or doing practical training. The community had a committee looking after their affairs as ANC members. At the time of the arrival of the Qiniselanis in the GDR, this structure was dysfunctional and there was petty rivalry between those stationed in Berlin and those in Leipzig. The rivalry was territorial as Leipzigers (those from Leipzig) believed Berliners (those from Berlin) wanted to 'control' them. Those in Leipzig, where most of the Qiniselanis were, also got involved in skirmishes with nationals from other countries. This was about trivial issues and girlfriends.

The situation worsened, and the GDR authorities were getting concerned. The responsibility to solve these issues fell into the hands of Ruth Segomotsi Mompati, an 'Mgwenya' and senior leader in the ANC. She had been seconded to the Women's International Democratic Federation (WIDF) headquartered in East-Berlin, as the ANC's representative. My arrival coincided with the time when Mompati – I called her 'Mme Ruth' – was in the process of dealing with some of the problems. While visiting her in Berlin, accompanied by Nomakhosazana Khosi Msimang and Mary Marutle, she spoke about the measures she intended to take. These included getting rid of the old defective structures and bringing in new blood to take charge of the situation. The new committee would then report to her and be guided by her.

On Saturday evening 7 January 1978, three months after my arrival, ANC cadres in the GDR assembled in a hall at a boarding school, connected to a company called VEB Bau- und Montagekombinat OST (BMK), in Potsdam, where Silas Shiburi was a student, to commemorate January 8, the 66th anniversary of the ANC. The following day, on a very cold morning, the members' general meeting was convened, and the agenda of the day was presided over by 'Mme Ruth'. She put forward her proposal and it won the day.

Khosi Msimang was elected as chairperson, Joy Rabotapi as secretary and I, as treasurer of the ANC's Students and Workers' Union (SWU) in the GDR. Among those present were Victor Moche, Obed T Motshabi, Temsy Motswenyane, Sylvia Neame, Hans Seatlholo, Paul Majwe, Mkhulu Radebe, Zephania 'Bra Zeph' Makgetla, Solly Makwakwa, Mary Marutle, Moeletsi Solly Leballo Dr), Barney Lebeloane, Olive Sindiswa Mthembu, Bassey Rakodi, Maria Nomathamsanqa Ndzanga, Kgosi Seatlholo, Gusta Nomkhosi Mvemve, Arnold Selby, Eric Singh, Sidney Themba Zola Skweyiya (Dr, minister and ambassador), Cynthia Poppy Nokwe, Vuyo Madida and Molwantwa Phasha (Victor Molotsi).

Khosi, Shaka Sisulu's mother and the eldest child and daughter to Mendi Msimang, arrived a year before me and was studying philosophy in Leipzig. Joy also came earlier than me and was at a technical school in Triptis. Joy, together with Hans Seatlholo, Moeletsi Solly Leballo (Dr), Barney Lebeloane, Olive Sindiswa Mthembu, Kgosi Seatlholo, Vuyo Madida, Molwantwa Phasha and Silas Shiburi left Magadu on 8 January 1977 for the GDR and arrived before me. About two or three months later, Anthony Mongalo, who we all referred to as 'Ntate Mongalo' (Father Mongalo), arrived as the first ANC Chief Representative. The mission in Berlin was the ANC's first to be accorded semi-diplomatic status in the world and was handed over to ANC President OR Tambo, in the presence of Pallo Jordan.

This elevated the ANC's bilateral relations with the GDR to a higher level. From the day Mongalo arrived, he made it clear that our presence in this country had to befit an organisation that truly represented the aspirations of South Africans. As the overall in-charge of the ANC bilateral relations with the GDR, Mongalo found the ground already well prepared by Mompati. While he dealt with the overall needs of the ANC, our committee was responsible for the welfare and affairs of all students.

From that day in 1978 in Potsdam, and for the remaining years I spent in the GDR, besides my studies, I also carried the responsibility of overseeing the affairs of the union as the treasurer (1978-1986). At all our annual member's meetings following the January 8th celebrations, the chief representative presented an analysis of the situation at home and what the NEC had been doing; the challenges met and the actions for the coming year.

The union's committee presented reports on its work of the past year and its programme for the coming year. Every second year we conducted elections to the committee. Because of the trust generated between the general membership and myself, I got re-elected unopposed as the treasurer until a year before my departure from the GDR.

Later I served the union with different comrades who led our committees as chairpersons, for example, Solomon Solly Theza Makwakwa, Joy Mojalefa Rathebe, Gershom Mxolisi Mbetse, Patricia Maqetuka and Wilson Mpalweni. Patricia was a student at the Technische Universität Dresden (Technical University of Dresden), a town in the State of Saxony and the second woman after Khosi who led the organisation. Others who served as secretaries were Jeff Radebe, Mophethe Oupa Sekamane and Zolile 'Sello' Maqetuka. We were accountable to both the ANC community and to our mission in Berlin under Mongalo, the longest serving chief representative in the GDR. Indirectly, our accountability was also in relation to the German authorities, for example, the Solidarity Committee. But this again was done through our mission.

Year after year, as the numbers of students increased, we improved our capacity to motivate and orientate everyone towards achieving success. We held enlightening and interesting political discussions during our annual meetings that involved the likes of Neva Makgetla, Themba Kubheka, Victor Moche and Joy Rathebe. From time to time, there were serious situations that we had to deal with. For example, during my time there was a case of stabbing and a rape case that involved ANC students. Prompt action had to be taken, and the students were sent packing back to Tanzania and Angola.

Nelson Miya, who came to deputise Mongalo, also weighed in very well in keeping cadres of the ANC organised and focused on the purpose of our mission to Germany, that is, studying and acquiring skills and knowledge. As the students' leadership, we maintained a good and friendly relationship with Nelson, who was always ready to consider matters in a positive way, whenever asked to intervene on behalf of the mission. Much of what we achieved was partly because of the political discussions held in the various cities and towns where ANC students were based.

Sechaba, the political publication of the ANC, was produced in the GDR and then shipped all over the world. For a long time Victor Moche was in charge of this project, before being replaced by Themba Kubheka (MK nom de guerre Aaron Mnisi). Kubheka came with his wife, Veronica Thandi, his daughter, Ntsiki Nonkululeko and his son Simo. After a few years Kubheka left for the Danish capital of Copenhagen to be the chief representative and Isaac Kekana replaced him.

We supplied *Sechaba* and other available material, like the News Briefings, which our London office compiled and distributed, to all members to keep them abreast about what was happening in the organisation and at home. Tshidiso Mahlomola Mokhoanatse (MK nom de guerre Alex Mashinini) was also posted to the Berlin office.

Beautiful weddings took place, one after another in Berlin in 1986, when Isaac 'Tilly' married Lilian Rose (nee Ndyanabangi) who was from Uganda, and Tshidiso married a German friend, Halima Iligen Hosh, known as Angee, from a town near Jena, called Hermsdorf. The next wedding was that of Patricia (nee Mbewe) and Zolile Maqetuka in August 1986 in Leipzig.

When members of the NEC were visiting the GDR, and whenever possible, we used the opportunity for them to address the general membership. If forewarned, we would send out notifications (telegrams in those days) so that institutions could release students to travel to Berlin. On one such occasion, President Tambo arrived in the GDR, and we organised such a gathering for the morning of Saturday, 20 May 1978. About thirty of us got together in a room at the offices of the Solidarity Committee in Berlin. The president, chaperoned by German authorities, joined us. After the Germans left, and with Comrade Mongalo in attendance and the formalities concluded, the President commenced his briefing.

About forty-five minutes into the session, the same Germans authorities walked in, whispered something to Comrade Mongalo, who in turn whispered something to the president. Tambo was rushed out and that was the end of the meeting. We were informed later of the sad news of the passing of Moses Kotane, the Secretary-General of the South African Communist Party (SACP) in Moscow, where the president was expected to fly that same afternoon.

Among other frequent visitors to the GDR were Tim Maseko, principal of SOMAFCO and Andrew Masondo, the National Commissar. We took advantage of their visits to deal with specific issues. We met twice a year as students, in January to commemorate

'January 8', and in June to celebrate 'June 26', which was called Freedom Day, the day on which the Freedom Charter was adopted in 1955. As treasurer I collected subscription fees from members and I also organised solidarity work to fundraise for SOMAFCO in Mazimbu, Tanzania. The union bought learning aids, sports equipment, toys and clothes for our comrades in Tanzania and Angola. We spent part of our holidays raising funds for the ANC.

All of us were highly active in the political mobilisation of public opinion in the GDR in support of our struggle. We asked our London mission to supply us with material to sell at solidarity bazaars. During my time, numerous conferences and symposia were held at institutions of education. We also sent delegations to participate in youth festivals taking place in Europe.

Summer School Hungary 1980

Summer school was an opportunity for ANC students to come together during long summer vacations to engage politically and also do some work as a way of contributing to the resources of the ANC. I was a delegate among 12 students from the GDR to the ANC Youth Summer School in Budapest from 27 July to 4 August 1980.[1] Joy Rathebe (chairperson) and Jeff Radebe (secretary) were in our delegation. There were about 60 delegates from 16 countries in Africa, Europe (east and west), the Americas and Canada made, up of a cross-section of youth from ANC structures, including MK. The majority were students. Max Sisulu played a key role as the representative of the ANC's Youth Section to the World Federation of Democratic Youth (WFDY) which was headquartered in Budapest. Andrew Masondo represented the NEC and opened the conference, which was attended by a Women's Section representative, Cynthia Thandi Ndlovu (Dr and MK nom de guerre Mavis Twala).

1980 was the year of the Charter, and the Free Mandela Campaign was gaining momentum on the international platform with, school boycotts increasing at home. We had fruitful discussions, among others, about the role played by the youth inside and outside South Africa; the role of women in the struggle; ANC education policy; the unity of the two fronts – military and academic – and the role of culture found meaning in Nelson Mandela's expression when he said, 'Between the anvil of united mass action and the hammer of the armed struggle we shall crush apartheid and white minority racist rule.' Participants went to a state farm to offer a day's work for solidarity.

After this we discussed international solidarity and how the liberation struggle connects with the anti-imperialist struggle. The victory of the Patriotic Front in Zimbabwe was hailed as a victory for all of us, and we vowed to continue with the struggle in Namibia and South Africa. All the campaigns we were involved in were to be intensified, especially the ones to save the life of James Mange, who was sentenced to death for treason in 1979 but later had his sentence commuted to life in prison, and to free Nelson Mandela. Both were freed in 1990. The declaration at the end of the summer school reaffirmed our resolve and dedication to reinforce and consolidate our efforts on all fronts in the struggle for liberation. It further called for the youth and students at home to fight side by side with the ANC youth.

Conference of the Youth and Students' Section, Tanzania 1982

Almost five years had passed since I had left Tanzania, the first place I called home after leaving South Africa. We were collected from the airport with other delegates that had arrived at about the same time as my delegation. There were about eight passengers in the kombi which made a stop at the offices of the ANC in Dar. As it came to a halt, I spotted the face of someone I had last seen in 1976 at home. He was about three meters away from the doors of the entrance. As soon as the doors of the kombi opened, our eyes met and I jumped out of the kombi. We hugged for a long time like twin brothers who had found each other. This was Koli (MK nom de guerre Ephraim Gazelle). My mind automatically flashed back to the day when he and Stan left me standing alone in our street in Rockville in 1976, because the car was full by the time it reached us.

After quick and very emotional greetings, Koli pulled me aside and away from the kombi. Looking at me with a serious face he said, 'Luister hier, daar's iets sleg wat by die huis gebeur het' (listen, there is something bad that has happened, back home). He told me that comrades from operations in the 'front' are sending reports that 'jou laitie' (your brother) was arrested and that the system is trying hard to turn him against the movement. Koli indicated that he had little information of the actual circumstances, but he was going to do his best to find out what happened. He told me that my brother was one of the best during the training and preparations for their special mission. Our chat was hardly more than five minutes.

For a while I was numb, Koli noticed that what he had said was tearing me apart emotionally. We hugged and parted, but not before I quickly scribbled my address on a piece of paper and gave it to him. I had arrived to attend the first ANC youth conference and Koli was leaving Tanzania on one of his assignments. He did not say which country he was going to, but I knew it was Mozambique. I returned to the kombi. With the people inside the kombi feeling happy to be in Dar again, I don't think anyone noticed my changed emotional state.

My mind quickly went back to all the letters and information I had received up to this moment. First, there was the letter I received from Bulgaria-based Sakie in December 1978,[2] who said he had read news briefings about Mandla 'Mendoza's fate. I had seen those reports too. Then there were the letters from my parents, also in December 1978,[3] indicating that Fana and Selby had also skipped the country following my departure. They also wrote that Mandla 'Mendoza' had returned to the country in the same year and had been arrested. The letters that reached me again from my parents in 1979[4] repeated the same news.

Then came a letter from Bransby 'Trizzer' Luke (MK David More) who was based in Lusaka, Zambia, dated June 9 1980,[5] in which he cautiously introduced himself to me, because he heard from 'Mme Ruth' that I was in the GDR. I responded quickly to Trizzer 'David' who was from Dube and was a frequent visitor to Rockville with another friend called Thami, a relative of Koli, that lived in Dube too, and was close to Koli's younger brother, Mxolisi. The letter that followed from Trizzer 'David', dated 30 June 1980,[6] indicated that this was the third letter, but I had not received the second one. In this letter he informed me that he was with Fana and Selby. He also mentioned that he had been with Sakie and Koli, and that Koli, who was with him for five months, had left for a mission in Maputo.

Arriving late in the afternoon in Morogoro, I had my very first encounter with Moses Mabhida (Bab' uMabhida), who had taken over as the Secretary-General of the SACP after Moses Kotane's death. He was with Andrew Masondo and Tim Maseko, who I had not seen since our adventurous encounter in Swaziland. The three were evidently angry that a fellow student and a comrade we were friends with, Nomalizo Kraai, had left the GDR to see her parents in Botswana without permission from the organisation. They were questioning us, Wilson Mpalweni (the chairperson) and I, on how this happened under our watch.

As a rule, students studying in socialist countries were not allowed to travel to the West or any other place, but only within these countries. This conformed to what pertained in these countries. The problem was, the ANC leadership never understood how this affected us as students. Of course, at that time, Wilson and I were not aware of Nomalizo's visit to Botswana, as this happened during the preparations for the trip to Tanzania. I explained to the leadership how this policy of not allowing families to see their children, where this was possible, was not correct.

They were obviously furious with me, and a long discussion ensued, with Mabhida, who had a striking handlebar moustache and was fond of caressingly touching it, listening intently to my argument. After two days of us discussing this matter, they finally agreed with me that these issues relating to visits outside the GDR could be addressed individually with the concerned students, without breaking the general rules.

At the conclusion of these discussions, our relations warmed and a close connection developed. When they came to visit the GDR, I was always called to Berlin to meet them. Unfortunately, our discussions took place after the fact. Nomalizo had been told not to come back to the GDR. I was not the only one who was depressed by this decision. It ruined her chances of qualifying in the medical sciences. Comrades in the cultural group who enjoyed Nomalizo's friendship were distraught by this news. I imagined it was the same with students at the University of Greifswald where she was an exemplary student.

Regarding the conference, the ANC's Youth and Students' Section, up to then loosely led by Comrade Eddie Funde, convened for the first time since 1976 to consolidate its structures. Wilson and I represented the GDR's union at this youth conference held in the 'Year of Unity in Action' on 17–23 August 1982 at SOMAFCO, Mazimbu in Morogoro where Welile Nhlapo (MK Andrew Mkhize) took over as the new leader of the youth. Since the banning of the ANC in 1960, the conference was the first of its kind and was of historical significance, as it involved all our youth structures; those serving in uMkhonto we

Sizwe, the working youth, and students. The main task was to map out a common programme geared towards the mobilisation of the youth in South Africa. The theme was 'The Role of the Youth in the Liberation Struggle'.[7]

After the conference, Wilson and I, stayed for another week in SOMAFCO and then Dar before we returned to the GDR. As expected, at our January 8th meeting the following year, I gave a full report about the youth conference to the union.

Cultural Voice of the Resistance Netherlands 1982

The Anti-Apartheid Beweging Nederland (AABN) which was one of the strongest in Europe, started making more contact with black South African artists in exile in the mid-1970s. While these connections were taking place, the Soweto uprising of 1976 and the death of Steve Biko in 1977 aroused anger in the world. A 1976 conference held in Amsterdam with the slogan 'Artists against apartheid' condemned ties with South Africa and in the same year the AABN published a critical report on the Cultural Accord with South Africa. The AABN accused the NZAV of being a pro-apartheid organisation and South African authorities of using the Cultural Accord to sell,' apartheid abroad.[8]

The progressive government of Prime Minister Joop den Uyl (1973-1977) came out in support of liberation movements in Southern Africa and offered to help victims of apartheid and racism. The government froze the Cultural Accord in 1977 and abandoned it in 1981. When the musical, Ipi Tombi, visited the Netherlands in 1981, there were protests and picket-lines at theatres naming the musical a product of apartheid. Over 40 organisations supported this boycott. This led to intense debates about the objectives of the cultural boycott in the Netherlands. Artists, sports people, writers and scientists got involved. For example, the Afrikaans author, André P. Brink and

Elisabeth Eybers (who had settled in Amsterdam in 1961) regarded the cultural boycott as being absolutely counter-productive, as they believed the idea of cultural contact was based on the conviction that ideas can persuade people, can change people.

It was then that the AABN consulted widely and decided to organise this conference. Mmabatho Nhlanhla (nee Molefe), Molwantwa Phasha, Zolile Maqetuka and I, together with members of the singing group from the GDR, participated in a conference themed 'The Cultural Voice of the Resistance: Dutch and South African Artists against Apartheid'. It was hosted by the Dutch Anti-Apartheid Movement in Amsterdam, Netherlands, from December 12–18, 1982.[9] For me it was an experience of a lifetime because there was a sizeable representation from South Africa, including many artists. Interacting with them and sharing the latest developments at home, gave me a sense of what was brewing on the ground.

There were South African artists that came from all over the world boosting the morale of delegates and strengthening the determination to bring down the apartheid regime. Moreover, they took to the stage as the Anti-Apartheid Riot Squad. They were Hugh Masekela (trumpeter), Jonas Gwangwa (trombonist), Dudu Pukwana (saxophonist), Peter Radise (saxophonist), Johnny Dyani (bassist), Gilbert Mathews (drummer), Lucky Ranku (guitarist), Pinise Saul (vocalist), Harriet Matiwane (vocalist), John Selolwane (guitarist) and Deez Dumayne (percussionist). From the ANC (Lusaka) there was Pallo Jordan, a member of the NEC and Barbara Masekela, the head of the department of arts and culture, Professor Keorapetse Kgositsile and Lindiwe Mabuza (chief representative to Sweden, poet and author).

The conference resolutions addressed issues such as the international cultural boycott and its practical implementation regarding South African artists' interaction and collaboration with foreign artists, especially those that visited South Africa. The ANC was at that stage in favour of total cultural isolation of South Africa. The conference favoured an alternative cultural agreement to serve the interests of all South Africans. The conference also acknowledged the role played by the citizens of the Netherlands in the fight against apartheid and in supporting the liberation struggle led by the ANC, and specifically the coordination of the cultural boycott strategy.

In 1987 another cultural conference was held in Amsterdam called 'Culture in Another South Africa' – CASA. The objective this time was to offer an environment to debate the future of South Africa and the role of culture. This was impossible to do within South Africa. The ANC referred to Amsterdam as 'the cultural capital of South Africa'. About 300 South African artists, the majority of them black, deliberated and debated the cultural future of a democratic South Africa. The conference decided that the cultural boycott of South Africa should be more selective, because some of the artists who visited South Africa contributed to the anti-apartheid struggle and they should be allowed to enter the country.

Summer Camp GDR 1983

I had engaged my comrades in the committee and our mission in Berlin about the idea of hosting a student summer camp in Jena. I received the go-ahead and started discussions with the authorities at my university about this. I had built a good rapport with the international department of the FSU and for the nine years I was in Jena, the university hosted six ANC AGMs around the June 26 Freedom Day period. My institution also paid for the celebrations, accommodation, food and the hiring of the hall for our AGM held after the celebrations.

The university was delighted to host the summer camp. It was held in 1983. The students, about 60 of them, came from Poland, the Soviet Union, Czechoslovakia, Bulgaria, Romania, Hungary and the GDR. We worked for a week in a forest around Jena, clearing it of dead wood, and the money we earned went to buy items for our comrades in Tanzania and Angola. After this we held a conference for two days to discuss developments at home and in the ANC, and how to intensify the struggle as youth. We also visited one of the well-known former concentration camps at Buchenwald, next to Weimar, and on one of the afternoons we played sports, including athletics and soccer.

Unfortunately, the summer camp was sullied by the death of a comrade, Sello Pule. His passing was heart-breaking. On one of the days we had dedicated to working in the forest, we had drinks at the reception area of the place where the students from outside Jena and the GDR were staying, after returning from work. Afterwards, students went to take showers and prepare for whatever event we had planned for the evening. When Wandile 'Boss' Kallipa, who had come with Sello from Romania, returned to their shared room, the door was locked from the inside and the key was in the door, Wandile went to the back of the room to check if Sello could see him so that he could ask him to open the door. The back window was slightly open and putting his hand through the window to move the curtain so he could see inside, he touched Sello's feet as his body was hanging from the ceiling very close to the window. He alerted the other students and they rushed to the back of the room and helped Wandile to climb into the room so he could open the door. Sello was pronounced dead by the healthcare personnel that came with an ambulance, and his body was removed by the police.

What was behind the suicide was never fully clear as Sello had left no note. According to Wandile, Sello was surprised to see the standard of living in the GDR compared to what they were experiencing in Romania. For example, as a medical student, he had no money to purchase instruments like stethoscopes and other appliances that were indispensable for a medical student. Unlike in most socialist countries, in Romania, students from liberation movements had to buy what they needed for themselves. Traveling for the first time and comparing his own situation to the conditions in the GDR, was apparently too much to absorb.

I had last seen Sello in Magadu before he left for Nigeria with many other students in 1977 to complete their studies so they could obtain their A level qualification. I had not spoken to him much on this visit to the GDR, but we were both excited to meet after so many years. He had indicated that he hoped to purchase some appliances that he could take with him as these were very scarce in Romania and one needed US dollars to get them. The suicide was devastating for all the students that were participating in the *subbotnik* (voluntary unpaid work).

National Consultative Conference Zambia 1985

Again, I was privileged to represent our union at the National Consultative Conference of the ANC, held from 16 – 23 June 1985 in Kabwe, Zambia, which I attended with Nelson Miya. The last such conference had been held in 1969 and had produced the famous 'strategy and tactics' document which so persuasively influenced ideological thinking within the ANC as well as the execution of political and military struggles. Since then, a lot had happened, including the youth uprisings of 1976. Back home, uMkhonto we Sizwe had registered relative success with its sabotage activities and propaganda. The people had 'unbanned' the ANC and the regime had warned about declaring a state of emergency, which was proclaimed after the Kabwe conference.

There were also negative developments in the ANC camps in

Angola that had to do with rebellions, that later became known as 'Mkatashinga', that took place in 1983 and 1984. At this juncture information about what really happened was very scant and mainly took the form of stories that were spread by individuals who were either there or heard others talking about the events. For me, faraway in the GDR, this was very disturbing news coming from our camps. At this conference, there were comrades, most of them based in Zambia, who were strongly mobilising delegates, especially those coming from abroad, to remove some of the leadership and elect new leaders. From my own reading, it appeared that these comrades were mobilising mainly along tribal lines, and targeting certain individuals to be voted out. Two days before the conference started on 14 June, the South African Defence Force raided and bombed houses in Gaborone, killing 12 people, including women and children. Only five of those killed were ANC members.

Despite this, the summit was able to display a revolutionary morality and practice which did not allow for personal ambition, factional conspiracies or cowardice and timidity in the face of an enemy counter-offensive. We resolved to intensify the struggle inside the country and to restore and reinforce unity within the organisation, to balance the internal and international demands of struggle and to strengthen the links between leadership and membership. We also resolved to ensure that the ANC enjoyed maximum political and organisational unity within its own ranks and that all members were to be involved in activities which contributed to the advance of the struggle.

With the masses of the people – Africans, coloureds, Indians and democratic whites – making their voices loud and clear in support of the Freedom Charter, the conference – by an overwhelming majority – opened its membership, including the NEC to all South Africans. Another positive outcome was that the ANC, in appreciation of the formation of the United Democratic Front (UDF) saw the need for the movement to continue its work and remain a front for all the people of South Africa.

Cultural Activities

By the time I had arrived in the GDR, ANC students had already made a name for themselves culturally, particularly in music. We had an ANC choir and cultural group that was extremely popular. It participated in many cultural activities to showcase some of our people's cultures, dance and songs. Cynthia Poppy Nokwe, gifted with a distinctive crystal voice, had been there in 1970 when the first 'Political Song Festival' was launched in Berlin. Founded by the Free German Youth's (FDJ) October Club and taking place every year in February since 1970, this festival was one of the major music events in the GDR. Our group worked with the FDJ in many aspects of our campaigns to mobilise solidarity for our struggle.

I had joined the cultural group during my days in Leipzig. The group was a founding member of an ensemble based at the University of Leipzig, known as the Karl Marx University's Ensemble 'Solidarity', a vibrant coming together of international students' cultural groups based in the city of Leipzig. They were from countries such as Hungary, Bulgaria, Czechoslovakia, Greece, Lebanon, Chile, Poland, Tanzania and Vietnam, among others. We performed on special national or international days such as the Workers' Day on May 1 or at international gatherings.

Again, culture was the single most unifying element in our struggle for liberation. In all the celebrations of our national days, people attended to enjoy the performances of our group. Sometimes we added poetry reading. Occasionally, the group performed jointly with the likes of Miriam Makeba, Letta Mbulu and Abdullah Ibrahim during the 'Political Song Festival' in Berlin. After Poppy left, Mmabatho took over as the lead singer of our group and she never disappointed. Among those who were active members at one or other stage, were: Hans and Kgosi Seatlholo, Jeff Radebe, Nomalizo Kraai, Patricia and Zolile Maqetuka, Temsy Motsoenyane, Olive Sindi Mthembu, Barney Lebeloane, Zandislie Pase, Zolile Magugu, Thuthukile Skweyiya, Sipho Njobe, Joy Rathebe, Timothy Motsoaledi, Joy Rabotapi, Tony Moloi, Vuyisile Vido Socikwa, Kid Sithole, Molwantwa Phasha, Cecil Ndzanga, Papi Moloto, Grace Lebowa and Lulu Mabena.

The Cold War and Living in a Divided Germany

Before coming to the GDR, I was privileged to have toured West Germany. This made it possible for me to talk about the country with some understanding of what life was like there. My knowledge of a divided Germany was extremely limited before leaving South Africa. I became familiar with the GDR during my time in Tanzania.. There were senior comrades who had been to the GDR before, and they spoke highly of it. Nonetheless, I didn't have enough information to be able to picture what a divided Germany was like. You needed to have been there or to have lived there to understand what a divided country was like and how a divided people lived, and what life was like in the GDR.

I am not sure if one can convey the full picture, especially in relation to Berlin, which remained the capital city of the GDR, while part of it became a city-state. I lived in a divided Germany for 10 years and 25 days, from September 1977 to October 1987. A divided Germany was part of my daily life and existence. The German Question, the 'divided Germany', the German 'National Question', or, the 'Question of Unification', was a live subject matter.

From the Prussia of 1451, that was dominated by the House of

Hohenzollern, to the German Empire of 1871 under Prussian rule; from the Weimar Republic of 1919, to the Third Reich of 1933; from the beginning of the Second World War to the division of that country into East and West Germany, and later the erection of the Berlin Wall, which starkly demonstrated this division, the 'National Question' in Germany was not a theoretical encounter but a live engagement.

The divisions were precise and well-defined, a reality that influenced every aspect of life from the time you woke up until the time you went to bed. Germany was the main centre of the division between the eastern and western worlds. What was called the 'arms race' was unmistakably a visible phenomenon and not a theoretical subject in boardrooms. The sight of huge carrier trucks moving the Pershing IIs and the SS20s missiles systems or nuclear warheads, from one city to another on both sides of the border, on both sides of the Wall and on both sides of the fence, with time, became normal. These demonstrations came to signify the show of power between the West and the Soviet bloc as part of the Cold War.

The 79th Guards Rifle Division, an infantry division of the Red Army, was based in Jena for the duration of the Cold War and became my daily experience as we shared the same public transport – buses, trams and trains – with some of its personnel. The Cold War was, so to say, a way of life here, and it kept the German 'National Question' alive. For many nations and individuals, the Cold War was an abstract issue, while for me it was a daily reality – I could feel it, see it and even touch it. After I left the GDR, the more I thought of it, the more terrified I felt. This experience remains embedded in my memory and flashes back as soon as I reflect on my stay in Germany. Whereas my coming to Germany was solely motivated by my wish to understand German thought and philosophy, the result is that Germany became part of me and the other way around.

As a South African, beside the gift of education I received in

Germany, I arrived during the depth of the Cold War and lived in the centre of the division – a divided Germany – among those who fought against the war, the anti-fascist forces, including those that were incarcerated in concentration camps on the one hand and on the other, I also lived among people who made the war, fought in the war, got scarred in the war, who – some of them – were prisoners of war. One of my professors had been a prisoner of war in the Soviet Union. I was astounded by his account of his experience.

It was exactly thirty-two years after the war when I arrived in 1977. Those that had been between the ages of 20 and 25 at the end of the war in 1945, were now between 52 and 57 years old. Because of the Cold War, all the happenings and the memories of the war were as fresh as though they happened yesterday for them.

There was also a new generation that had nothing to do with the war and had grown up in peace time. Growing up in the GDR, this generation was confronted with the results of the war, the divisions. Families were divided, with brothers and sisters living apart or parents separated from their children. We lived among these people. We became part of their lives while mobilising them for our cause.

Solomon 'Solly' Theza Makwakwa was a student at the Technische Universität Dresden, where he was taking an electrical engineering course. He found us work that earned us good pocket money in a small town called Riesa, which was not far from Dresden. It was at a steel factory and during the holidays we spent some weeks doing night and day shifts. It was in environments like this that we developed a better understanding and familiarity with the German people. This and other experiences gave me an appreciation of the hardworking citizens who contributed part of their monthly salaries to the solidarity fund that enabled people like me to study here and fight against oppression in my country.

International Solidarity

For my generation that came to study, work, or receive military training in the GDR, international solidarity became synonymous with the GDR, and the country was unwavering in its commitment to our liberation struggle. International solidarity was the quintessence of having a workers' and farmers' state that stood side-by-side with the workers of the world and all oppressed nations and people. The GDR, demonstrated solidarity by establishing relations with many Third World states, especially those in Africa. The GDR desired recognition from other states and the international community since its physical breakaway from post-war Germany. It represented the division of Europe and the world into east and west, the actual space where the Cold War was palpable, intense and humanly costly.

As a result, for many years the GDR was not recognised by West Germany (FRG), whose foreign policy professed to represent both Germanys. Many of the states in the west followed in West Germany's footsteps. Therefore, at the start of the Cold War, West Germany did not establish relations with states that recognised the GDR. With the UN giving recognition to both states in 1973, the tension between both states lessened, but the antagonism persisted.

Without a doubt, and perhaps it is too candid to state, the GDR, especially during my years there, became the jewel of all international solidarity the ANC received. The GDR provided the all-round support that was needed by the ANC. Acquiring military training and training in intelligence work, as well as skills in different sectors made insurgency or, what Mao Zedong called guerrilla-warfare possible. The state-owned Interflug airline fetched and flew military trainees from Luanda, Angola to Berlin in the GDR. While undergoing training, those who required medical assistance were accommodated in different military and public hospitals. They were attended to by the best qualified doctors and medical practitioners in the GDR. At the end of training, they were flown back to Angola.

The GDR also provided leadership training courses as requested by the ANC, the SACP and the South African Congress of Trade Unions (SACTU).

Cadres also received training in trade union leadership and in teaching methods for those dealing with revolutionary theory. Others received training in journalism. All other assistance considered, one of the greatest contributions the GDR provided to our struggle was in the education sector. Various scholarships, among these, from the governing Socialist Unity Party (SED) and the Trade Union Federation (FDGB) were offered. The GDR hosted the largest group of ANC students abroad. They were placed in various universities, vocational and technical training colleges, with full accommodation, stipends, and clothing and travel allowances. Those who were injured during training or in incursions by the racist regime's forces in the frontline states, were also sent to the GDR to receive medical treatment.

Khosi and Alex Mbatha, who I last saw in South Africa, were sent to the GDR after their long detention under the Terrorism Act, during which Khosi was given rat poison which nearly killed her. The GDR was the ANC's most dependable base outside Southern Africa.

This solidarity always had an international character. There were few nations and nationalities that were not represented in the GDR. It was fascinating just to get familiar with students from the 15 different republics that made up the former Soviet Union – Russia, Armenia, Belorussia, Estonia, Georgia, Kazakhstan, Lithuania, Ukraine, Uzbekistan, to mention just a few. Relations between the PLO, the Polisario Front and the ANC were at their best with a leadership that also coordinated their programmes and the mobilisation of the international community against oppression in their different territories. With this blend of people, all communicating in the

German language, I learned a lot about the struggles of other nations, and their cultures; literature, dance, music and food.

Homeboys: Sakie, Derrick, Trizzer, Koli and John

Since arriving in the GDR, I had been corresponding with Ingeborg and Wolff in West Germany. In one of the letters from Wolff he asked me if I wanted to inform my parents that I was alive and studying. There were many Germans from the Anti-Apartheid Movement who travelled to South Africa for work or leisure, and they always carried items with them when asked by the ANC or SWAPO members.

I had known Shimmin's work address by heart since I was a young boy. I sent a letter to Wolff and gave him my parents' address. I received the first letters from both my mom and dad that were sent to West Germany and posted to me by Wolff on November 2nd, 1978.[10] In the letter from my mother, she asked where I was and what I was doing. She wrote that my letter had been delivered by a white girl, who said she had studied with me in Europe and was now going to Cape Town.

My mother was extremely distressed since my younger brother, Fana, left the country. It was rumoured that someone from our street, Laurium Bhaba Ngcobo who lived directly opposite Sipho's – MK Themba Mlotshwa – home and who had left the country a year or two before the uprisings of 1976, had seen Fana and Selby (MK Larry Makhaya) in Dar-es-Salaam. My mother asked about Thiza (Themba Ntsibande) and Mandla (Mandla 'Mendoza', who came back to the country in May and was arrested in Daveyton. His trial had been set for November). 'Did you separate or what happened?' she asked. She wrote that the situation was very bad and that she would update me the next time she wrote. She urged me not to forget to pray, and to sing the choruses of salvation as they were doing the same every day back at home. 'Take care my child, it's me E.M.' My father's letter was short. He wanted to know when I would be paying back Mr Shimmin's money that I borrowed to go and study at university. At the end of the short letter he wrote, 'Please stay where you are, the situation is bad here. I wanted to write more but I am afraid. Don't forget us my son!'

The letters left me highly emotional and reminded me of the abnormality of the situation that we left back home, and that without us doing something from where we were, the fears, the oppression of our people would persist. With all that was happening in the country, my father was asking me 'to pay back the money!' I understood his frame of mind, and I felt deeply sorry for him. I was happy that at least they had received my letter without any danger to themselves and they knew that I was alive. I was extremely concerned that Fana had followed me. Again, this was unavoidable. Selby was supposed to have left with us, but at the last hour he had pulled out. Looking at what happened to me and other friends, I was convinced that there was no way he, and those we left behind, could remain in the country. I decided I wouldn't be writing home again. With Fana and Selby having followed me, our parents must be experiencing extreme stress, pain and difficulties. I did not want to add to their misery. Besides, writing too often might have put them in trouble with the police if my letters were intercepted or found at my home.

Out of the blue in December I received a letter from Sakie (MK Oupa Moloi), who was in Bulgaria.

> *Inocencio Dos Santos*
> *P.O. Box 405*
> *Sofia*
>
> *20/12/78*
>
> *Dear Comrade Khulu,*
>
> *I hereby wish to pass my revolutionary greetings to you and other comrades with which (sic) you study there. I am also happy*

to have this opportunity to write to you this letter, since it is a
long time not seeing you or even getting a word from you.

Khulu, well in connection with life it is promising and even
development inside the country. This situation inside the country
is hourly and day by day becoming ripe for the revolutionary
forces. The international situation and the balance of forces is
becoming also favourable in favour of the forces of progress.

I think you've seen in one of the news briefings (numbers
+- 30 – 35) that Mandla ['Mendoza', KM] has been
arrested. He was arrested in Daveyton. I've been trying
to follow his case, but I've got nothing so far.

Molefe's [Molefe Motsei (MK Ezra Makhosini)] younger brother
has also been detained. In a case involving four youths, who
burned a school in Kagiso, Krugersdorp. He's still on trial.

I met a lot of our comrades who were asking me about your
whereabouts. According to reliable sources I heard that you've
gone to GDR for furthering your studies. Well, I only came to
confirm this information when I arrived here in Sofia, coming
into contact with Mgadi (sic) [Stanley Mngadi, KM].

I am with Stanley. He said I must pass his greetings to you.
I also hope that you're working hard in your studies.

Khulu, I don't know if you can't buy me a suit of jeans or
wranglers. Since GDR is getting supply from FRG. Here in
Sofia they are difficult to get. You can only be able to get them
if you're in possession of DollarsI think you'll take this plea
into consideration please. I need it very much because it is
very rife or in fashion here in Sofia and it is in demand.

Khulu, I hope you won't disappoint me. Size is
of that corduroy you took from Mandla.

Mbatha ek het baie nodig vir die goed en wat ek dit kan kry ek
sal baie bly is. Wat jy twee kan kry, stuur maar die twee pakke.

Expecting reply very soon!

> *I won't be very long here in Sofia.*
>
> *Yours in the struggle,*
> *Sakie.*
>
> *P.T.O. Try to get lumbers and tekies. Bulgaria het nie so goed."* [11]

For the December holidays, Wolff Geisler had invited me for Christmas in Bonn. I got permission from Berlin and left by train across the border the day before Christmas Eve. I went with Christa to her family village on Christmas Eve. It was an unforgettable experience. On our return we spent a day or two in Bonn before taking the train to Jena.

The next letters from home were received in April 1979,[12] and had almost the same message, with my father still begging me to pay back the money. Again, they were repeating that Mandla 'Mendoza' had been arrested. I had parted with Mandla 'Mendoza' in Dar in 1976 when they decided, with Thiza and the rest, to stay in the PAC and wanted to go for military training, possibly in China. I had received the news briefings with some snippets of reports of how PAC guerrillas were arrested in a house in Daveyton. When I saw Mandla 'Mendoza's name, I was shocked. I knew he had relatives in Daveyton because during school holidays he used to visit them. I tried to follow the story in the next news briefings, but it just faded away. While I was still confused and getting frustrated by the absence of relevant news coming from home, I received another surprise letter from Morogoro.[13]

> *Box 680*
> *Morogoro*
> *Tanzania*
>
> *S.P. If I mention hot desert you shall remember who I am (S.D.P)*
>
> *Dear Cde Khulu,*
>
> *Revolutionary greetings.*
>
> *Well how is G.D.R. [?] with me Tanzania [,] I hope will be*

fine, congratulations on your good performance in all fields. You may wonder how I know but I must say I've met quite a number of cdes from that side and they all praise you, I shall always try not to disappoint you till we have won our Liberty.

Khulu I would like you to do me a few favours and I hope they won't be a burden, first I would like you to supply me with Sis Tsiki's address i.e. Sabelo's mother. I would also like you to send me blank tapes of course also some literature.

I shall try to keep in touch I shall be stationed here in Tanzania for a while. I have met quite a number of guys from our area though I may not say who they are for obvious reasons anyway keep in touch. Love

Yours in struggle –
Themba Mlotshwa

For a moment, this letter took me back home. The place we called 'hot desert' was a secret and special hide-out area that no more than six or seven of my friends had visited. No strangers were allowed. Covered by a bush and massive stones, the 'hot desert' was a well-protected den situated near our homes 'eziTandini' – in Rockville. The houses close to our den were known as 'emasotsheni' (soldiers' houses). The men in the families occupying these houses were former soldiers during World War Two. The 'hot desert' was the only place where the rules were different. We could drink, smoke cigarettes or dagga. Here you did what others were doing. This is where we discussed things in private. Anything that was discussed here was not passed on to outsiders.

Before I had finished reading the letter, I knew who it was. Only one person could remind me of this place. And I was happy to pass this message to Sakie in Sofia, Bulgaria and to tell him how excited I was to hear from Sipho Pewa. It did not take long for Sakie to respond with excitement.

Inocencio Dos Santos
P.O. Box 405
Sofia
Bulgaria

Hallo Khulu,

Hoping that you're still keeping up with your studies.
I'm still keeping too. Hoping all the best for you.

Man it is very difficult to write Phewa. But if you
write for (sic) him pass all my greetings to him
and tell him he's welcomed in the ANC.

Khulu ek dink om te se G.D.R. het jeans, so as jy kan
kry 'n een of twee. Die size kry my vier by die waist.
Ek het baie nodig vir daardie goed. Die plek het einklik
nie jeans en mooi broeke. So ek drink my geld uit.

Het ek jou vertel dat o'Koti en o' Hyman is moet
ons. Hulle het 1978 uitgegaan, en hulle is met ons by
A.N.C. Baie ander ouens is moet ons. Ek dink soos
jy nie vir my skryf ousies doen jou goed daar.

O'Koti het my vertel omdat Zodwa van by Sibongile 'n kind
vir my gekry. Ek was so bly maar ek kan nie my kind sien.

Molefi se sustergie [Mmabatho Motsei, MK Dorah
Modimala, KM] is ook buitekant hy [sic] het 1978 geskiep.

Khulu I will be leaving around the mid of August.
So you may write one or two letters, so that I
may know the developments about Phewa.

All the time I was on studying tourism of the
country, hence I could not write.

Greetings to all.

Oupa Moloi

Sakie

Answer very quickly.[14]

In the meantime, I responded to Sipho Pewa to tell him how pleased I was that we connected. I didn't know when he left home either, and what news he had from home. I asked him if he heard about Fana, Selby, and Mandla 'Mendoza' and jokingly told him that we could easily establish another 'hot desert' outside here. I forwarded him Stan's address in Bulgaria, and indicated that Sakie was there too. Sipho wrote back because he was now positive that I had received his letter and I was studying in the GDR.

> Box 2237
> DSM
>
> Dear Khulu,
>
> Well thanks for your letter, otherwise it came at a time when I was going to post the second one in which I was complaining as to why you don't reply after such long a time of separation, well that solved.
>
> Otherwise I am fine glad to hear that you studying to become a marxist leninist. Well before I can write anything in answer to the various questions you have asked, will you please send me information regarding the study on medical engineering i.e. find out what are the fields involved to that, e.g., maybe radiography or so – please this is urgent information that I need – since I'll be coming to study once it has been approved by the Headquarters – don't forget urgent.
>
> Now coming to your questions, I must say first, I left home a week after you left i.e. at the end of October 1976, 28/29, but me I left through Lesotho where I remained for the whole year until the end of 1977 – so that I really haven't been in touch with the situation at home. The whole of 1978 I was working for the organisation in Botswana – well other things are not allowed to be disclosed as you know, I then left Botswana for Lusaka then came over to this hot region of Africa – surely you'll understand why I am blank with the developments at home, otherwise I learned that Rufus [,] Seth's brother died,

quite a number of people especially in Rockville have died.

Concerning the whereabouts of Fana, I learned that he was with MK. Chivago [Selby, MK Larry Makhaya] really I have just learned from your letter that he also left home. Bucs is restricted to the Transkei – maybe he will make means to come out of it. I hope with Fana and Chivago they are safe and have not lost direction, really the question of Mandla ['Mendoza', KM] came as a shock and also as a disappointment, for instance, you remember that our aim at home was and has been to join MK. I don't really know what led to his decision – well it's all in the struggle as soon as I get information to the proceedings of his case I will let you know.

Please don't get disappointed about not receiving news from home as expected - well also Panas you remember him, he passed away whiles in Botswana, we were working together. Well I did a lot of work there although I still hope to contribute a lot, I am presently working with the scholarship dept of which I am a member of its committee and I am also secretary of the youth & students secretariat in Tanzania region – well this I know means hard work, dedication and selflessness.

So far I'll keep you in touch with whatever information that comes to my disposal concerning home. I'll also right (sic) to Stan – thanks for the address.

Amandla

Greetings on this year of the Spear

That's Sipho Pewa (Sika)

P/S Concerning musik (sic) I'll bring what I can.

P/S These are cancelled – Derrick, Sydney[15]

It was a great relief to at least have some idea of what happened after Mandla 'Mendoza' and I left the country. I realised now that many of our friends followed us. Some died at home as we left; others died on their way out while still trapped in Lesotho, Swaziland or Botswana, like Panas (Simon Mokgofe) who died in Gaborone.

Shortly after this I received a letter from John (Thabo Mkula), and I suspected that he must have gotten my address from Koli when we met in Dar. I remembered that in the rushed encounter with Koli in Dar, I had forgotten to ask about John.

The year of Unity in Action – 82
University of Camagüey,
Camagüey,
Cuba

82 – 9 – 5

Dear Khulu

I am definite this letter will come as a surprise to you, well always expect surprises in life. I am fine in life and yourself? It's very difficult for me to explain myself but I shall take a try. I will start by asking as to whether Derrick [MK Themba Mlotshwa] ever told you about Thabo Mkula. If not, then I am the bearer of that name or I go by that name. I am studying in Cuba (international law).

I am whispering to you since I have confidence in you and this goes between you and me, understood. Ek hoop jy verstaan my? Ne, kyk es maklik, ek dink jy weet hoe loop goete hierdie kant?

I have some requests to make to you, can you send me some clothing shirts, trousers, lumberjacket, it is difficult to get things this side, you must be a possessor of a 'tarjeta' which is a card possessed by workers, and to talk some workers into buying you something it is difficult, most of the clothing is sold in dollars which I do not have, needless to explain. Can you also send some philosophical books, political books etc of [sic] written in English.

> *Anything that you send should be by air or hand post directed to the mission whose address appears in the Sechaba, the Chief Rep is Alex La Guma. It should be by air since if it is by other means I shall not receive them, or they shall not reach their destination. If you happen to know the following which I believe you should Aron Mafaje, the daughter to comrade Maindy ['Mendi' Msimang, ambassador, KM] whose name I happen to forget which I regret, tell her, her cousin sends her millions of kisses who happens to be Thabo Mkula.*
>
> *Now the secret is, ek is Jannie, but this should go between me and you, please do not divulge it to anyone I am informing you with all the confidence.*
>
> *Always in struggle*
> *Thabo Mkula*
>
> *N.B. the daughter of Cde Maindy and happens to be Khosi I'm sorry I recalled the name later.* [16]

The letter brought so much excitement; I was over the moon. Finally, I could join the dots and reconnect to people who had changed the course of my life and who I hoped to connect with one day. There was a second letter dated January 17th, 1983[17] that John sent to me, almost repeating the same things he had written in the first letter. Because of the distance and the time it takes for a letter to reach its destination, he thought I did not receive his first letter. Nevertheless, he extended his greetings to the same people including Mafa Sicelo Ngeleza, who was also in the GDR. From Cuba I received a third letter from John.

> *20.01.83.*
> *Camagüey*
>
> *Hi Khulu,*
>
> *In response to your letter just received, I would like to express my joy and further inform you that I am studying law and doing my second year...*

> *How is life that side? Gazelle has informed me about*
> *Fana but it is unbelievable and I am still waiting for*
> *more information and clarification from him...*
>
> *I have thinned down since I got sick, believe*
> *me when I say my waist is 30"...*
>
> *I write this note being in a very bad state, I am hit*
> *by this thing called low pressure. I had to be fed with*
> *oxygen in order to be able to breathe properly...*
>
> *Hold on firmer than when you started. Victory is ours.*
> *Yours in the cause*
> *Thabo Mkula."* [18]

At this stage, I did not know that he was one of the injured cadres during the SADF (South African Defence Force) attack of our camp in Novo Catengue, Angola. He did not mention it in this letter. I bought some clothing and sent it as he requested. I remained concerned about John's health, because of the way he ended his letter to me. Three months later, I was elated again when I received Koli's first letter since our fortuitous first meeting in Dar.

> *29.04.1983*
> *Box 4720*
> *Maputo*
>
> *Hi Khulu,*
>
> *I am greeting you in this year of United in [Action,*
> *KM]. Wish you good health in your studies.*
>
> *Well, Khulu after our first meeting in exile, I was really excited*
> *by the historic meeting though it was short, and I was rushing*
> *down to base for pressing matters. I made a promise to write to*
> *you about further matters in the family's affairs. Well, I can see in*
> *this light I am blank, I have not heard anything, the people I meet*
> *mostly are not from the same place with [us, KM], even though*
> *some are from there, they do not have information one needs.*

I have written several letters to my family to try to get what is actually happening. I am expecting replies, I do not know when, because my time is running out in this region. The region itself is a frontier, to be in the frontier, one has to be vigilant I think Maseru is clear in your mind this explain what type of enemy we are fighting. The situation is becoming more fluid, there is no day that goes without any confrontation between the regime and the people.

We are also running up and [down, KM] here because of the 4th Congress of the Frelimo, which is very important for us and the people of Mozambique, this also include the region itself. There are very serious problems faced by this country, there is internal reaction and the resistance backed by the South African regime.

Do you know Sindi [,] she's here. If you want to correspond with her do not state that you got this from me.

What are your future plans after your studies, do you have any plan so far. There are people I know Popi – Tily, he works in the [office in Berlin, KM]. That young man I met him for the first time in exile, he claims to [know] you and some [of, KM] your friends. I knew his girlfriend.

There are people I met in West-Germany from the Cape [who] I used to work with inside the country. I even took them as far as Lusaka and back home. I used to do this clandestinely.

I have met people who know [you, KM] from that region, they have respect [for you, KM] and your discipline. Well, I also said in addition that is your nature. This [is, KM] what I expected from you.

Greetings to all the comrades and friends / please keep in touch. Before I forget, could you please get a copy of 'Naked among the Wolves'. This is a book for our people, get more copies as you can.

Amandla!

Yours in the struggle
(E. Gazelle) Gazz [19]

A few months later there was another letter from John, which was the last I heard from him.

> *Camagüey*
> *83.11.27*
>
> *Khulu,*
>
> *I wish to acknowledge receipt of the goods you sent me they came in at an opportune moment. But I wish that you should confirm that what I received is really what you sent. I received 2 shirts. Is that all you sent [?] Perhaps this clarification I am requesting is unclear to you. In order that you may understand why it is [necessary KM], it is because at times people do not receive all the goods sent to them. I hope you now understand.*
>
> *I wish to express my gratitude for this gesture of goodwill on your part. But, in reality I believe words fail to express my gratitude fully it is rather indeed ineffable truly.*
>
> *What are you doing? How did you fair in your thesis? My advice is that you should continue, what you do think, how does it sound? Eh! I am now in my third year and hope to be completing very soon. I have heard nothing from Gazelle of late. Are you not in a position to establish contact between me and any ANC students studying law?*
>
> *I would like to exchange opinions with them. I wish to apologize for the note I wrote requesting that you claim the goods, it was because of the time that had elapsed. I wish you the best of luck in all tasks you undertake.*
>
> *Victory is in sight. Tambo leads.*
>
> *Revolutionarily*
> *Thabo Mkula* [20]

Chapter Three

I had sent more items to John in Cuba. Because of the shortage of smart clothes amongst us as ANC cadres, and depending on where you were posted, asking someone to deliver goods to other comrades in another country, always had the risk of that person removing items from the package. As for Sakie in Bulgaria, I was never sure if he received what I had bought him in the GDR and I never heard from him again. He had indicated that he was leaving soon.

From that year, 1983, I never heard again from Koli or John – they just disappeared. I had to accept this as part of our lives. I was happy we had re-established contact, and both had indicated that they would be leaving the places they were when they wrote to me. I wasn't worried about them because I knew we were together. I was worried with developments relating to my family and friends back at home, though. The next letter from my mother arrived in mid-1983[21] informing me among other things, that Fana had certainly been arrested, that the police were threatening to arrest my uncle and his wife and the whole family in Pretoria, and that the situation was very bad.

Furthermore, the letter indicated that, there were rumours of Selby (MK Larry Makhaya) being seen by some people at John Vorster Square and that he was severely injured. When his family rushed to the police station, they were told that he had been released. She wrote that Selby had never come back home and his family was not sure whether he returned to exile or whether he had been killed. They were praying and that was all they could do! This was bad news.

Then in October 1983, a month into the new semester and starting with my research work for my dissertation, one afternoon I came back to my hostel and as usual checked my post downstairs. There was an envelope from West Germany, and I put my bag down in my room and sat on my bed. I opened the envelope and was happy that I had received another letter from home. I was hoping for more clarification about the whereabouts of Fana, Selby and Mandla 'Mendoza'.

The letter was from my mother. It was short this time, only half a page.

> *My Dear Son,*
>
> *Ngempilo enginifisela yona thina sisaphila emseni wenkosi yethu, ngaphandle kwamfowenu uJotham wasishiya June 1980 kwathi Feb 1981 kwashona ubaba wakho, babegula kakulu ngingajabula ukuzwa uthi wena ukuphi unjani wenzani ngokuxoxela kakhulu mangithole impendulo amade anginawo, nabodade wenu basaphila ngombuliso lapho ukhona.*
>
> *Yimi Ozithobileyo*
> *E Mbatha* [22]

Translation:

> *My Dear Son,*
>
> *Wishing you good health, at the mercy of our lord we are still alive. Apart from your brother Jotham who left us in June 1980, your father too passed away in Feb 1981. They were both terribly ill. I would be happy to hear where you are, how you are, what you are doing. I will be able to tell more once I get an answer. I do not have much to say, your sisters are still well. Wherever you are, greetings.*
>
> *Yours sincerely,*
> *E Mbatha*

For the first time my mother put her full signature on the letter. I fell backwards on my bed as if something heavy had knocked me over. I lay there with my eyes closed, then after about 15 minutes I opened my eyes and stared blankly at the ceiling until the tears flowed. I do not know how long I stayed in my room. When I regained my strength, I stood up and recollected myself. I felt lonelier than I had ever felt before in my life.

I took some money and invited my classmates for a drink at the students' club downstairs. When everyone had taken a seat around the table, I fetched the drinks I had ordered from the bar. Most of us were drinking Vodka-Cola, our favourite drink at that time. Before we raised our glasses, I divulged to my colleagues the sad news I had received from home; the death of my brother and father in 1980 and 1981 respectively. They comforted me and we tossed back our glasses, followed by me downing my whole glass at once. It took the edge off my grief.

The second and last letter I wrote to my mother was two years later in 1985, to tell her I intended to marry Anna. She wrote back, wanting to know whether Anna was African or white. She added, 'Siyabonga intonje uma usaphila naleyo mizamo eniyizamayo inkosi engathi ingabanani'. (Thank you, if you are well and whatever efforts you are making, may the Lord be with you.)

Marriage to Anna

Anna was the only one in our group from Europe. She and Louis' wife Auzenda were the only women in our class. This was a group of revolutionary youth that was invested in bringing about change in their own countries. With time our group jelled, and we found that we were pursuing the same goals, albeit in different environments. Anna was a member of the Communist Youth of Greece (KNE), the youth wing of the Communist Party of Greece (KKE) and had participated in anti-fascist activities back in Greece, a country which, like Portugal and Spain, was under fascist rule and a military junta from 1967 to 1974. My class and I learned a lot from her about the activities and challenges of the Communist Parties in Western Europe, which were new to us. Anna also had the advantage of being familiar with some of the philosophical trends that were dominant in Europe, including ancient Greek philosophy and the new modern trends. She was a

Birth certificate

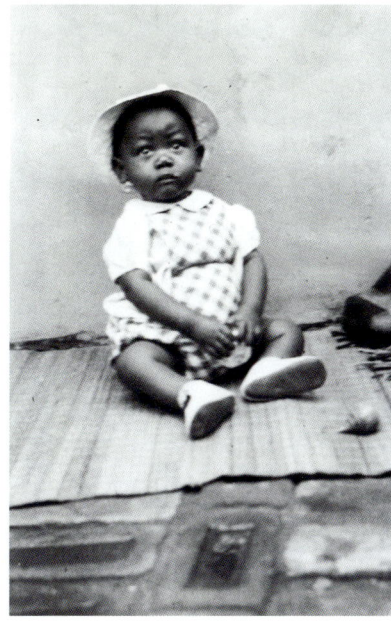

Six months old

My parents' wedding day

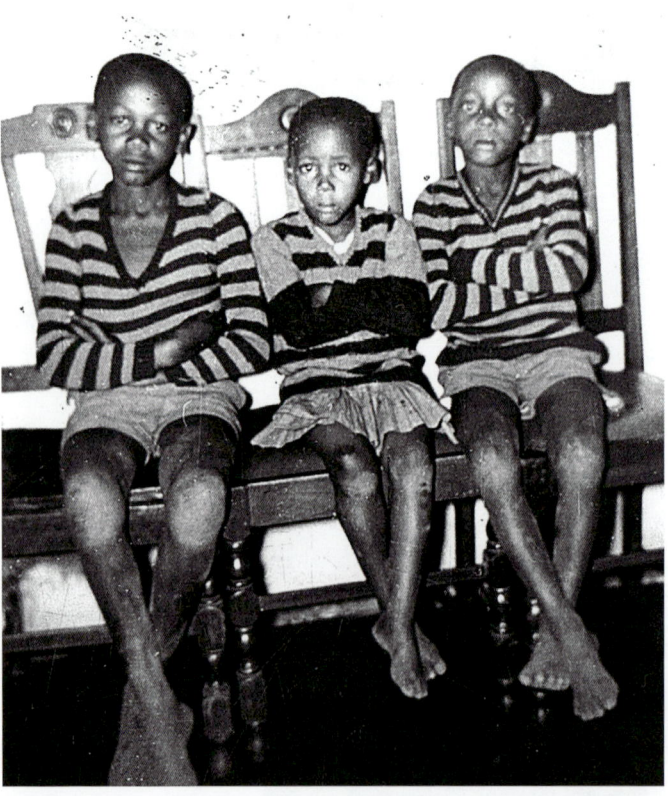
Left to right: Khulu, Maggie 'Nini' (sister) and Moses 'Fana' (brother).

Outside the yard of my home in Rockville.

Chriselda Refilwe Tshabalala at Senaoane Secondary School in 1973.

Mirriam Duduzile 'Dudu' Zondo in 1982 in New York.

Back, left to right: Dede Sondlo, Selby Vuyani 'Svari' Mavuso (MK Larry 'Bab' Makhaya, partial face) **Middle row, left to right:** Mandla 'Mendoza' Mtselu, Dennis Mxolisi 'Bucs' Ngqase, Fiki Gumbi and Derrick Sipho Pewa (MK Themba Mlotshwa); **Seated:** Khulu with baby.

John 'Jan' Magwegwe Vilakazi
(MK Thabo Mkula).

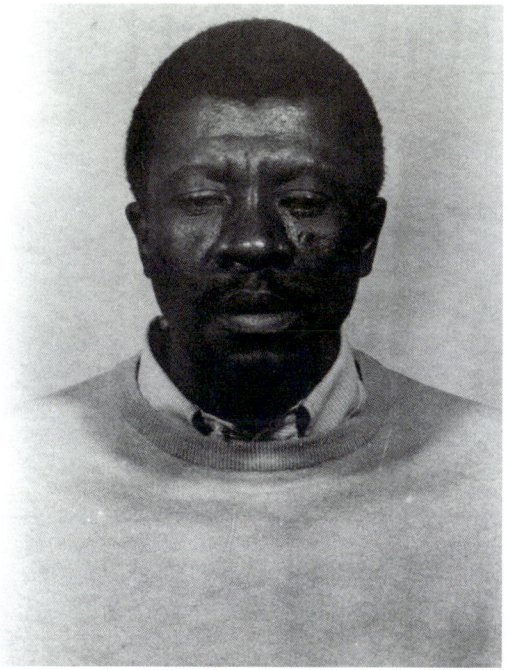

Kolisile 'Koli' Ngqase
(MK Ephraim 'Gaz' Gazelle).

Above: Reading a *Sunday World* newspaper.

Left: With the Wauchope children
Left to right: Jenny Ngwenya (nee Kaloate), Khulu (middle) and Kuku Wauchope Seated: Natalia 'Nat' Sifuba (nee Kaloate).

Left to right: Selby Vuyani 'Svari' Mavuso (MK Larry 'Bab' Makhaya), Khulu, Theophilus Mandla Bongani Nyembe and Dennis Mxolisi 'Bucs' Ngqase.

Left to right: Khulu, Mandla 'Mendoza' Mtselu, Derrick Sipho Pewa (MK Themba Mlotshwa) and Dennis Mxolisi 'Bucs' Ngqase (front).

School mates at Sekano-Ntoane High School
Back (left to right): David Mavuku, Khulu and Michael 'Mike' Mashinini. Front (left to right): Fiki Gumbi, Mandla 'Mendoza' Mtselu and Derrick Sipho Pewa (MK Themba Mlotshwa).

School mates at Sekano-Ntoane High School
Standing (left to right): Abednego 'Niko' Nkula and Khulu; Seated (left to right): Stanley 'Steyn' Radebe and Andrew Ndzonga.

Matric class at Sekano-Ntoane High School
Standing (left to right): Brutus Molefe, William Mukwevho (partially hidden), Moses 'Moss' Tholoane (white hat), Michael 'Mike' Mashinini, Lordwish 'Otis' Letsoalo (the tallest and behind Michael) and Khulu (seated).

With some of the best soccer players at Sekano-Ntoane High School at the back of the bus from a sports trip to the University of the North, Turfloop. Left to right: Bongani 'Manline' Sibiya, Khulu, Perry Basil Fana 'Pele' Mavuso (MK Jomo Sono), Enoch 'Skhebereshe' Mhlongo, Vicky 'Sister Nora' Mdlalose, Isaac 'Reason' Letsoalo and Stanley 'Steyn' Radebe (half face).

Group picture at the Rockville dam (now called Thokoza Park) before departing for the Munsieville picnic spot in Krugersdorp.

18 June 1977 on the occasion of the 1st Anniversary of 'June 16 1976': Khulu addressing hundreds of youth and students at the "Forum Aachen 77" of the KJG (Katholische Jugend Gemeinde/Catholic Youth Association) in Aachen, Germany.

Above, left to right: Zolani Mtshotshisa (ambassador), Wilson Mpalweni, Khulu and Makhosazana 'Khosi' Msimang.

Left: My classmates and lecturers at the Friedrich-Schiller University in Jena, Germany in 1983 after graduating and obtaining the master's degree (I am at the top right).

ANC Cultural Group during a recording of their songs at the Leipzig Museum of Ethnography in Leipzig (Museum für Völkerkunde zu Leipzig) in the summer of 1978, (left to right): 1. Oupa Mophete Sekamane (Lesotho), 2. Khulu 3. Molwantwa Phasha 4. Pule Nchee (Lesotho) 5. Mmabatho Nhlanhla 6. Kgosi Seatlholo 7. Jeff Radebe (former Minister) 8. Angelo de Bruyn and 9. Peter Modise.

ANC Cultural Group (left to right): 1. Felix 2. Johnny 3. Khulu 4. Barney Lebeloane 5. Thabo Mosupye 6. Temsy Motsoenyane 7. Olive Sindi Mthembu 8. Mmabatho Nhlanhla (nee Molefe) 9. Nomalizo Kraai 10. Timothy Motsoaledi and 11. Tsholofelo Moneedi.

Top, left to right: 1. Zandisile 'Keith' Pase, 2. Wilson Mpalweni, 3. Khulu and 4. James Mdlathi doing a Zulu dance. **Above, left to right:** 1. Khulu, 2. Vuyisile 'Vido' Socikwa, 3. Zandisile 'Keith' Pase doing a gumboot dance.

During the seminar at the Summer Camp in Jena 1984, left to right: 1. Wilson Mpalweni, 2. Jackie Selebi, 3. Patricia Maqetuka, 4. Jabu Radebe and Zolile 'Sello' Maqetuka.

Skiing during one of the snowy days in Jena.

Top, left to right: Khulu, Edward Thupi Mabusela (MK Edwin Mabitse) and Vusi Tshabalala in SOMAFCO, Morogoro, Tanzania 1982.

Left: Anna and Khulu – on our wedding day in Jena, 5 July 1985.

With Happy Bhembe in Athens, Greece.

With Zukile Nomvete in Munich, Germany.

At the Acropolis during my first visit to Athens in 1986.

Taking a swim and a dive in Athens, 1986.

Javier Pérez de Cuéllar (UN Secretary-General) shaking hands with Khulu Mbatha (ANC Chief Representative to Athens), City Hall of Athens, Greece, Thursday, 5th April 1990.

Khulu Mbatha, Oliver Tambo, Themba Kubheka and Nelson Mandela in Stockholm, Sweden, 1990.

Top: With Dimitra in Athens, Greece.
Left: With Nelson in Rockville, Soweto.

Maggie (my younger sister), Khulu and Siza (my elder sister) at Maggie's 60th birthday in 2019.

Dimitra and my mother during Christmas in 2007 at home.

Nelson and my mother in 2000 at home.

Khulu, Nelson and Dimitra in Athens, October 2021

revolutionary in her own right and very outspoken.

Most Greek girls I had seen in Leipzig had black hair, but hers was chocolate brown, which added to her stunning beauty. We started dating some time during the second year, for almost a year, but nothing came of it. It was my fault because I began to enjoy the extramural activities, which meant travelling to Leipzig for rehearsals and performances with the ANC cultural group over weekends. Sometimes Anna travelled to Leipzig too, because there were many Greek students there, and many activities. My traveling on the other hand, took me all over the place: Leipzig, Berlin, Halle, Dresden and Chemnitz (Karl Marx Stadt during GDR times). Towards the end of the fourth year our affair was rekindled, and we courted again. This time we did things together and when I travelled, we went together. This went on until our last year of the five-year course, in 1983.

She went back to Greece but we kept our communication alive, although at that time there were no cell phones. If I was not writing to her, I went to the telephone box in our building and called from there, provided it was working! Otherwise, I had to walk to the post office, which was a kilometre or so away. Towards the end of 1984 we spoke about taking our relationship to the next level. For me to get married, I had to get permission from Lusaka via the mission in Berlin. A positive response came back, and we started planning for our special day. Anna was already employed back home, so we waited for July when she could travel during the summer holidays.

On Friday, 5 July 1985, we were married at the City's Registry in Jena. It was a very emotional moment for the two of us. Anna was the only child in her family and her mother, Dimitra, had died when she was nine years old. She was raised by her father, Dionysios Koutoulogeni. Popi Kutsuku, her mother's sister and only aunt, and Stathis Koutologeni, her father's brother and only uncle were her only other relatives in Greece, and none of the three were with us for the wedding. Anna had brought an elderly lady from Greece, who was her colleague at work and very fond of her. She acted like a mother figure in Anna's life. As for me, I was there on my own, as I had been since I left home. Again, I had my comrades, Nelson, Pat and Sello. Present too were Zandisile 'Keith', Lulu and Zolile Magugu, comrades that had joined me in Jena and a few others that were at a technical school in Jena. Anna and I invited our friends, teachers and professors to celebrate our marriage at a restaurant in Neulobeda-Ost.

After a few days with Anna, she had to fly back to Athens. It was difficult to part, and I promised her that I would work hard on my dissertation so that the following year during holiday times I would be able to travel to Greece to be with her. In July 1986, during my summer vacation, I flew to Athens to visit Anna and I met her family – her father, her uncle and her lovely aunt, and they were all happy to see me. I had a good time and enjoyed my vacation and for the second time in my life I swam in the ocean (the Mediterranean Sea). My last swim was almost ten years ago in the Indian Ocean in Dar. With the help of Anna, a seamless swimmer, I perfected my swimming skills at the age of thirty-two. The professional swimming lessons I had taken on my arrival in Jena had prepared me. There was an indoor swimming pool next to our hostels and Anna and I liked going to the pool and the sauna. That is how I developed my love for the winter season. I stayed for a good six weeks in Athens before I returned to the GDR.

Birth of Dimitra

Towards the end of 1986, after my visit to Greece, Anna called and told me that she had suspected she was pregnant. A pregnancy test confirmed this. From that day I felt different. The possibility of being with Anna when the baby was born filled me with anticipation. . This would only be possible if I submitted my thesis on time in early 1987. I made it! In May I defended my dissertation and then flew to Greece on my second important visit. On 1 June our beautiful daughter, Dimitra Aretha, was born. From that day on, every day, was special.

Before my daughter's birth, we had agreed that if the baby was a girl, I would have the first choice to name her, and if it was a boy, she had the first choice. The music of Aretha Franklin, had been a constant presence in my life from childhood days growing up in Soweto until I left for exile. She had a 'one of its kind' voice that touched my senses in a special way. Her 1972 album, 'Amazing Grace' – recorded live at the New Temple Missionary Baptist Church in Los Angeles with Reverend James Cleveland and the Southern California Community Choir, was the best food for my spiritual togetherness and kept my hope of one day being a free man alive for my whole stay in exile, especially in the GDR. During the cold winter days, the Christmas holidays, when we as stateless citizens were left alone in hostels, the music of Aretha Franklin kept me company. When our baby was born, I discovered that the law required that the baby's first name should be a Greek name, so Dimitra was to be her first name and Aretha her second. 'Dimitra' was her grandmother's name, Anna's mother.

I had gone through all available English literature that I was able to buy at the time, and prepared myself on how to raise a baby, I did not regret the investment. I monitored Anna on everything she was doing, how many times she had to breastfeed and when she had to take a break. I helped with changing Dimitra's napkins and kept track on how long she slept and if she took more time than it was written in the book, I woke her up. By the time we had a rhythm for everything, all went smoothly. This was a most enjoyable time for me.

A pleasantly fortuitous incident took place during my visit to Greece. One day, on my way to the bus terminus before the shops closed for the siesta, I decided to pop in the Telcom Offices to cool down, because the afternoon heat in the streets of Athens was overwhelming. All buildings in Greece have cooling systems and at that time of the year they function at full blast. As I entered, the cool air engulfed me, and it felt so good. On my right, there were two queues with about ten people each and on my left, there was a wide-open booth with shelves holding telephone directories from all over the world. As I had no specific reason for entering this place other than cooling myself, I moved closer towards the directories, which were arranged in alphabetical order, and quickly checked if South Africa was included. I saw directories for Cape Town, Durban and Johannesburg. Next to Johannesburg there was one for Soweto. I felt my heart skipping. What, a telephone directory for Soweto?

I opened it and saw African names in alphabetical order and as I went through it and reached the 'Ms', I checked for the Mbatha surname. The list of the Mbathas was long and I went through it slowly until I saw Mbatha Elizabeth, my mother's name. Next to her name, our home address was confirmed. Then there was the telephone number. I felt cold and I wanted to tear out the page with my mother's name on it, because I felt like I would never see these numbers again. Yet something niggled me. At that moment, I felt as if all the people in the queues behind me were watching what I was doing. This made me extremely uncomfortable, as though I had voluntarily walked into a trap.

I put back the directory and felt very anxious that whoever was following me from outside, must have concluded by now who I was.

The 'system' (the Boers) must have followed me and placed this directory to see if I was the person they were looking for. I dashed out of the building, walked a few steps, and took some deep breaths. Now I was watching to see if anyone was following me. Was I dreaming, did someone put those directories there intentionally so that they could find out who I was? I quickly told myself, this was probably impossible. How would they know I would enter that specific building on that day and at that time? This calmed me down and gave me the strength to go back, so that I could write down the telephone numbers.

This time, I was on alert for any abnormal reaction on the faces of the people in the queues. I picked up one of the forms you usually find in places like a post office, reached up and pulled out the Soweto directory, this time with self-confidence. I quickly glanced at the queues just to be sure no one was looking in my direction. Using a pen attached to string on the shelves, I quickly wrote down the telephone number of my home in Rockville, Soweto. I put the directory back in its original place and left. With such 'gold' in my possession. I was full of smiles on my way to the terminal to take a bus to Voula, our suburb.

When I arrived at home, I told Anna about my discovery of the day and waited for the early evening to try and call the number. At around 6pm I went to the bedroom to make the call. I dialled and the phone rang as if I were calling Anna's neighbour. In a few seconds someone picked it up.

'Hello!' a child's voice on the other side came through.

I responded, 'Hello, ngicela ukukhuluma no-Ma!' (May I speak to my mother!).

'Oh, you want to speak to Gogo (grandmother).'

For a split second I paused, and then quickly responded, 'Yes!'

'Hello', my mother's voice that I had not heard for many years came through as clear as if we spoke yesterday.

I responded, 'Hello Ma!'

'Ah, who is it?' my mother enquired softly.

'Ma, its Khulu!'.

'Ah!', she calmly said, 'U Oupa wakwa Nyathi?' ('Ah, it's Oupa from the Nyathi family?')

Khulu, which is in isiZulu the same as 'Oupa' in Afrikaans, is the same name of the eldest son, Mangedwa Oupa Nyathi, of our neighbours, the Nyathis, who were two houses away from my home. I quickly interjected, and said:

'No, Ma! It is Khulu, your son!'

There was silence for a few seconds, and I feared she she may drop the phone in shock. Instantly, I interjected again.

'Ma! Yes, it's Khulu. How is Josefa (Joseph), Jotham, uncle Skhiya (Hezekiel), uGogo wase Pitoli (my grandmother in Pretoria)?'

I rattled through several family names that came to my mind so that my mother was reassured that it was not a hoax. I heard her taking a deep breath that was so clear as if she was standing next to me.

'Hawu, Khehla (that's how she called me, and it also means Khulu in isiZulu) my son, where are you?'

I had prepared for this, and I was quick to respond by telling her I was in Lusaka, Zambia.

'How is that place and how are you living?'

I told her it was fine, and we have food, and everything is okay. For obvious reasons, I had made up my mind before the call. I was not going to dwell on politics. I told her I called because we were the parents of a baby girl.

'Ha, your wife, what nationality is she?'

I remembered the question she had asked in her last letter to me, and I told her that she was Greek.

'Hawu!', she replied.

I was not going to hang up before asking Anna to come and greet my mother. I whispered into her ear, 'We are in Zambia'. She exchanged greetings with my mother. Probably my mother asked Anna about the baby's health.

'The baby is fine and healthy', answered Anna.

'Do you still want to speak to Khulu?', asked Anna.

My mother must have said, 'Yes'. Anna gave back the handset to me. My mother was laughing intensely on the other side. I waited politely for her to finish laughing. I had not heard that voice and laughter for almost eleven years.

'What's wrong, Ma?' I enquired.

'Hawu, m'ntanami, ukubiza ngegama?' (Hey, my child, she calls you by your name?).

I understood her very well. Straightaway I felt the effect of the eleven years of absence from my people and our culture, because over the years I had adopted new cultures. A woman, in this case my wife, never calls her husband by name. It is taboo.

'Ma, this side things are a bit different', I said trying to protect Anna, who never understood what she had done. We spoke about the family. My mother reminded me that Jotham and my grandmother had passed away, as I had also enquired about them when I was identifying myself. For the first time I realised that when death – something with such a grave impact on us as human beings – happens in one's absence, for example, as was the case of those of us who were in exile, it doesn't register in one's psyche in the same way. My mother once more informed me of the many people who had passed away and hearing the list of names she was reciting, was unbelievable and heart - breaking. We wished each other well and I promised to call her soon. For a few minutes I lay on the bed and ran through everything we had spoken about in my head. I felt as if I was dreaming. I never asked my mother who the little one was who answered the phone. I got up to check on Anna if she was okay with the baby.

She asked, 'Why was your mother laughing, when I asked her if she still wanted to talk to you?' I took my time to explain the customs of our people back at home. After a couple gets married, the wife stops calling her husband by his name – especially in the presence of her in-laws or strangers - and only uses his surname to address him. In this case I was 'Mbatha' to her. When there are children, like in my case, I was 'Baba ka Dimitra!' (Dimitra's father) to her and never 'Khulu'. Even today, I am not sure if it made sense to her. Nevertheless, she laughed and enquired if my mother was offended or not. I told her, not at all. That is the reason she was laughing.

It is the duty of mothers to guide their daughters-in-law. In our African tradition, the bride marries into her husband's family and with time she takes over the running of all household affairs. It is here that her skills in managing domestic affairs are tested. In this case, domestic means all the affairs of her new family. It is a very powerful position for anyone to influence household affairs.

Time was flying in Greece, and it was time to leave for the GDR. As a married man, I had explained to Anna that I wanted us to live together. At the same time, it was my duty to first report back to Lusaka after my studies were completed. That was what was expected of all ANC cadres after completing their studies. At the end of September, I flew back to the GDR a happy father.

My Departure from the GDR

While I was in Greece and before I left the GDR, Jacob 'Jackie' Sello Selebi had been elected as head of the Youth Section at a Youth Conference held in SOMAFCO, replacing Welile Nhlapo. The conference was opened by President OR Tambo in July that year.

During my stay in the GDR, I had received numerous awards and decorations as a student and political and cultural activist. I was awarded the university prize – the Salvador Allende scholarship, and a certificate from the Minister of Culture, as recognition for my contribution as a member of the ANC cultural group. I was also presented with the Arthur Becker medal from the Free German Youth (FDJ) organisation, and in 1986, Anthony Mongalo, the chief representative (as head of ANC Mission) endowed me with the ANC prize for my excellent educational, organisational and political work. These plaudits made life easy, not only for me but for many of my country people, comrades and friends. In Tanzania and in the GDR, there were comrades who could not take the stress and tribulations that we went through as stateless South Africans. A few comrades suffered from various forms of depression and others committed suicide. I lost dear comrades in this way.

After staying in the GDR for a full ten years, it was time to prepare for my departure, which was not going to be easy. At the Kabwe conference in 1985, Mongalo was elected to the NEC, and on 12 March 1986, the President of the Solidarity Committee of the GDR, Kurt Seibt, honoured him with a farewell celebration in Berlin. After this he left the GDR. When my studies were extended, and before he left, he had informed me that when I completed my studies, I would be joining the Secretary-General's office, as instructed by Alfred Nzo. Sindiso Mfenyana was the next chief representative in Berlin.

I reminisced about all the things I went through while in this country. I remembered the beautiful summer months, the harsh winter months, and some years that were without summer at all. One would wait and wait for summer days, only to be confronted by another winter. Some winters were more severe than others.

I reminisced, how when I came back from West-Germany after Christmas in December 1978, I decided to go and spend New Year's Eve with Phetho 'Edmund' in Stralsund, a coastal city in the north. He had since married a Tanzanian, Agnes, whom he left behind in Dar after their marriage, and joined us in the GDR. He arrived in

Chapter Three

April 1978 to do a course in motor engineering. I sent him a telegram asking if I could visit him. He responded that this would make him happy because he was feeling lonely in that town.

I took a train to Berlin on 29 December, and by the time it reached the city, it was clear the weather conditions were extreme. A four-hour trip lasted five and half hours. Instead of changing to the next train to Stralsund, I waited two and half hours before the train pulled off. By this time, it was getting very cold. The journey was supposed to take just over three hours, but on the way there was so much snow that it had to be removed from the tracks before we could continue with the journey. I reached Stralsund the next day at around three in the morning in a freezing train and, since this was my first time here, I did not know, which direction I was supposed to take. The snow outside the station was piled above my knees, all I could see were the streetlights.

I looked for a telephone booth and called Edmund. He told me that he had given up and then gave me directions to reach his place on foot. Did I get lost! I was nearly beaten up by a German family that I woke up at some unholy hour, only to find that it was the wrong place. I could not go back to the station. From the street, I called out Phetho's name, which is unusual in Germany, but there was no response. Just as I was giving up, by sheer luck, I found his place. He opened the door and immediately went to fetch more firewood from the cellar to rekindle the fire so that I could get warm. He put a bottle of brandy next to me and I knew I had to drink it neat if I wanted to survive. He had prepared a sleeping place for himself next to the fireplace and he gave me a duvet and I created my space opposite him so that we faced each other, in front of the fire. We spoke for the rest of the night without sleeping. This was 30 December!

We got out of our makeshift beds next to the fireplace around midday, dressed and rushed to a shop next to the station. It had not stopped snowing. We bought meat (pork is the favourite meat in Germany) and came back to prepare pap – GDR pap took only five minutes to prepare. We ate and thereafter went straight to our makeshift beds with another full brandy bottle. This was the only way to survive in this cold. We discussed everything about life, the friends we left at home, Ntate Mashego and his marriage. He showed me an album of family pictures. When he got married Agnes, was pregnant with Aletta Masechaba, the first born. He had left before Aletta was born and was now too far away to even play with her. He thought about them daily and worried about how they were coping in Dar. We talked about the road we had travelled thus far and asked endless questions. Did we know we were going to end up in Germany?

When I was warm enough and enjoying the heat, both from the fire and the brandy, I told Phetho, I would not stay another day because the following day was New Year's Eve. We were both convinced that the weather was only this bad in the northern part of Germany. Of course, that was naïve of us. Were there trains operating? We were not sure, but I told him we would find out the following day, 31 December, at the station. There was a train leaving at eleven in the morning and arriving in Berlin-Lichtenberg around three in the afternoon. From there I could rush to Berlin Schöneweide to get my train to Jena.

The following day came, and I was still wearing the same clothes I had worn on arrival. The snow had stopped but the temperatures remained far below minus zero. The train was there, and I parted with Phetho. He wished me well and I did the same to him, hoping the weather in Stralsund would improve.

The train left an hour late and only arrived at around six in the evening in Berlin. By this time ice had built-up on the inside of the windows of the train. The train's restaurant ran out of food and drinks. The passengers felt miserable and whatever people carried with them as drinks to take home for New Year's Eve, was shared with strangers on the train.

I had missed my train at the other station and this train was meant to continue to Leipzig, where I could connect to Jena. The train remained at the station in Berlin until after midnight. By this time, I was standing outside the train with other passengers because the inside of the train had turned into a freezer.

The fireworks in West-Berlin (there were no fireworks in East-Berlin) were exploding into the sky turning it into a beautiful colourful garden full of flowers in the sky. With nothing to drink or eat, the spectacle was not as enjoyable as it might have been.

The train only departed at around four in the morning and arrived in Leipzig at eight since it was moving so slowly. I took the train to Jena at around eleven and arrived at around four in the afternoon. When I got to my room I went straight to bed as I was not feeling well. On the third day of the New Year, I had to go to the clinic and see a doctor. I was told I had pneumonia and should stay in bed for the whole week. One thing I should never have done, was to have left Phetho's place, because the inclement weather was not confined to Stralsund but affected the whole of Europe. The weather stations on the Baltic Sea showed that this was the coldest winter in over 60 years. By the time I recovered, winter and I had become good friends.

I managed to put my things together and bid farewell to my German friends and the families that had become part of my life. Barbara and Dr Hubert Brühl and their children Sascha and Tania had welcomed me as part of their family.

Hubert who was born Bechstädt, was the first man I had ever met who had adopted his wife's surname through marriage. He was very much in love. He was also addicted to sports, and loved skiing. For 14 years he was at the FSU teaching and training sports students in the art of skiing. After German unification, he became the director of the best skiing institution in Germany, the Deutscher Skiverband (DSV – German Ski Association), the national governing body for skiing in Germany, which is based in Munich, in the Free State of Bavaria.

I had become a lover of German cuisine, especially the varieties of pork meats and potatoes, and had come to understand that Germans love beer. Hubert always had a different type of beer with meals. All cities and villages have their own brand of beer and so wherever he travelled around Germany, he bought beer from that place. Barbara was a German language teacher and expert who helped me a lot with the editing of my doctoral thesis, especially some of the translations I had to do from English to German. We did so many things together; braais in their parents' villages in Kayna and Lumpzig; put coal in the storage for the cold winter, and spending Christmas together eating sumptuous rabbit meat from the family stock.

Petra and Wolfgang Fried, with their two beautiful girls, Andrea and Jana, were another family in Jena that made my stay a genuine home away from home. I met the family with Anna, when we were on vacation together in 1982 at the Rügen Island, Germany's largest island, located off the Pomeranian coast in the Baltic Sea and in part of the state of Mecklenburg-Western Pomerania.

On this island, we watched the 1982 FIFA World Cup Final football match between Italy and West Germany together. The match was played on 11 July 1982 at the Santiago Bernabéu Stadium in Madrid.

In Jena, the family had all types of berries in their garden and during the summer we enjoyed varieties of berry-cakes. Petra and Wolfgang attended our wedding in Jena.

Another friend who was helpful during the writing of my doctoral thesis was Barbara Kirschnek, a student studying philosophy and in the same class as Lulu and Zandisile. She gave me treasured assistance during the translation of my work. Barbara Kirschnek married Professor Dr Klaus Vieweg, who was my senior as a student, and is now a professor of classical German philosophy at the FSU in Jena, and one of the world's leading experts on the philosopher Hegel.

Chapter Three

There were many friends and families I had to bid farewell to. All my lecturers and professors, among them Dr Frank Lindner and Dr Walter Berg, who were remarkable people individually and collectively. I took the train for the last time from Jena to Berlin. I spent the night at Nelson's place and the following day, 20 October 1987, exactly ten years and 25 days since my arrival, I left Berlin for Moscow, and from there on to Luanda, and finally I landed in Lusaka.

Chapter Four
CONQUERING THE WORLD

ZAMBIA (1987-1988)

Lusaka

It was ten years since I had stayed on African soil and I didn't know what to expect. Questions ran through my mind: Would I be received well and be able to integrate with ease? Did I know someone I could rely on to guide me?

As the plane touched down on Zambian soil on 21 October I realised that I was a completely changed person and I was confident of the person I had become. Uncertainty was not new to me. When I landed in Swaziland in 1976, I didn't know what to expect. I was on foreign territory for the first time in my life and everything was unfamiliar. Again, when I left Swaziland for Tanzania, I didn't know what awaited me in Tanzania, a place that became my first home away from home. When I left for West-Germany, my maiden trip out of Africa, and headed to Europe for the first time, I didn't know what type of a country I would find. When I finally left for East-Germany, I had no picture of the country that would be receiving me for my studies, and the people I was going to live with. The GDR, which became my second home away from home, certainly steeled me to be the person I had become. When I left the GDR for the continent, it felt totally different from all my previous travels, which were for me to get something from the countries I was visiting. This time I was traveling back to give to my new family – the ANC – what I had learned all these years that I had been away.

Although I had not lived in Zambia and had been here only once for the Consultative Conference held in Kabwe back in 1985, as the plane landed, I felt as though I had been here many times. The other reason, of course, for feeling like this, was because I was now in charge of myself, and my destiny depended on what I wanted to do. I knew exactly what was expected of me and I also wanted to show how much I had learned in my studies abroad.

I was not prepared for my first wake-up call, which was that no one had come to fetch me from the airport. Communication about my arrival had been done as was normally the case, through our offices. I was from Germany, and planning was the ABC in matters like this. Nelson Miya was very professional in his work and before my flight to Moscow, I had spent the last night at his place in Berlin. Headquarters was informed, and specifically the head of the education department, Mohammed Tikly, had been notified about my arrival. Secretary-General Alfred Nzo had given a directive that I was to come to the Secretary-General's office, and join the education department under his deputy, Henry Gordon Squire Makgothi. 'Ntate Makgothi', as we fondly called him, was a simple and down-to-earth person, almost the same as the Secretary-General, I last saw him at Kabwe. Tikly had previously been head of SOMAFCO and was seconded to head-office to be responsible for the education department.

Did something go wrong? It transpired that both Makgothi and Tikly were out of the country. I knew no one else in Lusaka. Someone in the department, should have made arrangements. Since nobody knew where I was supposed to go,, I was driven to the Andrews Motel in Lusaka, which is 36 kilometres away from the airport, and because of the traffic, it was about an hour's drive. This was routine practice when there was no instruction from those responsible, and I had no choice. What I did not foresee, was that this motel would become my permanent residence for the next two months, until two or three days before Christmas in 1987.

On Sundays, lunch at the motel was served outside in the yard as a buffet, which included braaied meat. On one Sunday, after two weeks had passed, someone I knew very well from home, came with some comrades to have lunch at the motel. This was a welcomed surprise. The person was Jomo (Perry Basil Fana 'Pele' Mavuso, MK Jomo Sono). He was my junior at both Ndondo and Sekano-Ntoane, and a cousin to one of my best friends, Selby Vuyani Mavuso (MK Larry 'Bab' Makhaya). He played beautiful soccer, like the famous Pele of Brazil. He was in the company of his wife, Thoko, Thabo Mohlala (MK Klaas Masemola) and his wife Dorothy, and Johnny Sexwale, among others. Jomo was also suprised to meet me at the motel. I told him that I had been calling the education department's offices, and someone had promised to come and see me, but I was still waiting.

Jomo informed me that Stanley, Thiza and Mandla Mangethe were also in Lusaka. My spirits lifted for the first time since I had arrived. I asked him to inform them that I was stuck at the motel. Another week passed with no news from the department or from my friends who were in Lusaka. What kind of place was Lusaka, I wondered. Again, Jomo came with the same comrades to have lunch at the motel. This time I sent a message with him to ask Thiza, if they had a spare room. I wanted to leave this place; I was sick and tired of eating the same breakfast, lunch and dinner and doing nothing. I had re-read the books and magazines I had with me for the hundredth time. I was now reading the Bible that is always provided in hotel rooms. This was the first time I had read the Bible since I left high school in Soweto. I finished reading it in a week and was now repeating certain chapters out of interest in the philosophy of certain teachings.

A few days before Christmas, Mandla Mangethe organised for transport to fetch me from the motel. I signed myself out in the same way I had checked myself in when I was dropped there. The motel was used to this as they never asked me to pay or asked who was going to pay for my stay. The comrades who fetched me told me not to worry, the movement will pay. I told myself I would never return to this place again. This is how I came to stay in Chilenje, one of the suburbs in Lusaka.

Many things had taken place since we parted with Thiza and Mandla Mangethe in Dar in December 1976. Stanley, who stayed a short distance from where the two lived, had left me in Magadu in 1977, when he went to Sofia, Bulgaria. He wrote me a letter once in 1979 and for almost a decade I had heard nothing from him.

There would be a lot of catching up to be done. To begin with the parents of Mandla Mangethe, Thiza and Stan had been to Lusaka for a visit, and I was stunned to hear of this. How was this possible? Mandla Mangethe told me that since arriving from Angola, they had seen some parents of comrades coming to visit them in Lusaka. They also raised their hands and arrangements were made for their parents to visit too. Apparently, an underground structure inside South Africa was responsible for those arrangements.

Thiza, who had recently married an Ethiopian woman, had remained in Addis Ababa, but he eventually joined us in Lusaka. They told me that his mother only learned on arrival there that his younger brother, Petrus Tuka Ntsibande, had been killed in an ambush in Angola in October, 1984. Angola was the first country in the frontline states to have made training camps available to the ANC. Preparations started towards the end of 1976, and the actual movement of cadres was early in 1977. This was in the middle of a civil war that started on the eve of the fall of the Portuguese colonial rule and the declaration of independence in November 1975.

The civil war would inevitably also affect our presence in Angola. There were several attacks on our camps by both the Union for the Total Independence of Angola (UNITA) and the South African Defence Force (SADF). Thiza, whose brother Tuka was responsible for logistics, explained that one day, while moving from one camp to another, a convoy of our cadres was ambushed and came under severe attack around Cacuso. In the skirmishes that ensued, Tuka and three other comrades were killed. The four were buried in the camp. As

Thiza narrated these events to me, I could see that that the memory was still alive and painful, as if it had happened the past week.

Among other news that came with the parents, was the confirmation that my brother, Fana, Mandla 'Mendoza' and many others had been arrested. No further details were available. All our parents had to report at the Protea police station on certain days of the week, where they were questioned about whether they had any news from their children who had left the country. Gilbert Mazibuko, who got arrested on the day we left the University of Zululand, had passed away. It was not clear how he had died. This was sad news for all of us, especially for me hearing this for the first time.

Over the time I was in Lusaka, I listened to more stories about what parents had related during their visits. We also talked about what had happened after we had separated in Dar in December 1976. I had heard little about the happenings in the PAC, except the killing of David Sibeko, which was well publicised in the international media. I got snippets of information from Thabo More, who was based in Rostock with Charlie 'Mingus' Mahlathi. Thabo was from Rockville and the cousin of George 'Best' More – the renowned soccer player. He had been with the PAC when Sibeko was shot. After these dramatic events he was one of the cadres that left the PAC and joined the ANC. He was then sent for studies to the GDR and that is how I got part of the news.

What had stayed with me since Swaziland, was that the PAC discouraged any talk about anyone pursuing studies. Those who aspired to go to school were denunciated as cowards. Thiza and Mandla Mangethe explained to me that the PAC managed to get scholarships for studies in Nigeria. These studies were in the field of aviation, deemed to be part of military training. This was not the case at all, however they were to be educated at the long-established Nigerian College of Aviation Technology, a higher education institute in Zaria, Kaduna State. That is how a group of 22 who were considered to have a foundation in mathematics from South Africa, were selected to go to Nigeria in early January 1977. They were:

1. Happy Bhembe
2. Rocks Boqwana
3. Siphiwe Cele (Dr)
4. Bongani Dlamini
5. Zero Goba
6. Raymond Mbulelo Fihla
7. Pule Gaelisiwe
8. Reggie Khumalo
9. Shaka Komani
10. Chris Kote
11. Gerald 'Gerry' Malinga
12. Mandla Mangethe
13. Maas Ngomesa
14. Lucky Nhlanhla Ngema (Ret Gen)
15. Nyamiso Njingana
16. Themba Nkenene
17. Willie Siyaya Nkonyeni (Ret Gen)
18. Themba Thiza Ntsibande
19. John Ranko
20. Themba Serote
21. Titus 'Titi' Sithole
22. Max (Surname unknown, had disappeared from Nigeria)

They arrived in Nigeria during the Festac '77. This month-long celebration of African culture in music, fine arts, literature, drama, dance and religion was attended by 16,000 participants, representing 56 African nations and countries of the African Diaspora.

South Africa's Miriam Makeba and Hugh Masekela, Stevie Wonder from the United States, Gilberto Gil from Brazil, Bembeya Jazz National from Guinea, Mighty Sparrow from Trinidad and Tobago, Les Ballets Africains from Guinea, and Franco Luambo Makiadi from the Democratic Republic of Congo participated in the festival, staging incredible performances. The festival, which aimed to ensure the revival, resurgence, propagation and promotion of black and African culture, values and civilisations, opened at the National Stadium, Surulere. A parade of participants marched past visiting dignitaries, diplomats and the Nigerian Head of State, Olusegun Obasanjo.

The PAC group was aware that the ANC had sent a big delegation from Morogoro, but the PAC and ANC delegations never met as they were separated by the host. The group stayed for a few days at the Festac Village before proceeding to the schools where they were going to take up aviation sciences – piloting, flight-engineering and air-controls. After they had left for Nigeria, a significant number of militant youths had remained in Tanzania. In March that year, the PAC's Potlako Leballo, announced that China had agreed to take bigger groups for military training. Apparently, China was training PAC cadres, but they were smaller groups compared to the influx of the June 16 generation. Even in this case, China was only taking a group of 78 people, who were then divided into three groups.

The first group left for China in the same month of March for a three-month training course and returned in June. This group of 26 included, among others, Richard Matwetwe Nyide, Fanie Mazibuko and Mandla 'Mendoza'. The second group, which left in August and came back in October 1977 included people like, Sabelo Victor Phama, who later became secretary for defence and commander of APLA. Teboho Josiah 'Tongogara' Lebakeng (Dr), Lucky Lidlanga Moeketsi, Clement Fana Hlongwane, Ingram Mazibuko, Steven Linda and others were in this group too. Twenty-five cadres, who were to proceed to Cambodia (also known as Kampuchea), were also part of this group, who after some special training in China, were to be further taught by the Khmer Rouge under Pol Pot, who had come to power in 1975.

The Khmer Rouge were to teach South Africans how to create an underground guerrilla army in the rural areas of South Africa. After their arrival in that country, Vietnam launched a full-scale invasion of Cambodia. This was at the height of the Cambodian-Vietnamese War. The PAC group had to retreat into the countryside and dense forests, drowned by the monsoon rains, with no food, eating spiders and frogs. After many months they reached Thailand in late 1980. They were rescued by the UN who flew them out of Thailand to Pakistan and from there to Tanzania, where they found a new leadership of the organisation had removed Leballo.

A third group had followed and gone to China. People like Joe Bhembe and Reuben Linda Zwane were part of this group. The whole of 1977 was spent doing training. Only a certain number could be accommodated for training. For those who received training, what followed was a long period of waiting in the camps in Tanzania without any further deployment. The cadres had had their training and were itching to go back home. With no sign of further movement, tensions arose from the waiting and dallying, and at the same time, the tussle for the leadership and control of the PAC also gained momentum.

Unbeknown to many of us, especially the June 16 generation, the PAC had been beset by infighting long before the 1976 uprisings. Potlako Leballo's leadership had been challenged before. After the uprisings, David Sibeko, the PAC representative at the UN, Vusi Make and Elias Ntloedibe, were allegedly at the centre of this contestation. It was reported that at this time, life in the camps had become hell for many because of clashes caused by tribal factions, cliques, and all sorts of divisions. The PAC's armed wing, the Azanian People's Liberation

Army (APLA) camps in Tanzania housed 178 Basotho belonging to the Lesotho Liberation Army (LLA). This group was connected to the Basutoland Congress Party under Matooane Mapefane. It is alleged that Templeton Ntantala, the deputy to Leballo, with his 70 APLA cadres, was threatened by the influx of new recruits, the Soweto generation, and he attempted a coup against Leballo in Dar. The LLA soldiers foiled this coup because they were loyal to Leballo, and Ntantala was frustrated.

APLA cadres who had left the country before the June 16 generation consisted of those who left in the 1960s and a group of 26 primarily former university students, who were influenced by the BCM, and had left during and after the Pro-Frelimo Rallies of 1974. Among these, there was Justice 'Majase' Nkonyane (Ret Gen Nkonyane) and Laurium Bhaba Ngcobo, who were both at Fort Hare University before they left separately for exile and met in Dar. Ngcobo came from my street and our parents were close; our mothers treated each other like sisters.

There was also January 'Ché' Masilela (who later became the secretary of the SANDF) and Mfundo Njikelane. The former university students had undergone training at different times in Libya before the arrival of the June 16 group in Tanzania. They were joined by former university students who had come from Botswana and were not members of the PAC, and they staunchly defended their independence.

The end of 1977 saw tensions rising in the camps because there was no activity. In January 1978 at a central committee meeting preparing for what was to be a Consultative Conference in April, in Arusha, Leballo deposed the entire High Command of the PAC and expelled Ntantala, his main rival, and others. He appointed Vusi Make to head a special Task Force, which took instructions from him and no one else. Following these developments, on 27 February Robert Mangaliso Sobukwe, the President of the PAC, died in South Africa, and Leballo became Chairman of the PAC. With pressure mounting for the PAC to hold its conference, it finally took place in Arusha in September 1978, and allegedly endorsed resolutions in favour of Leballo's faction.[1]

After Arusha, the PAC managed to send cadres back into South Africa in late 1978. This was not without some drama. Cadres had summoned the political and military leadership, or high command to come to the camps to address them about their plan or programme to send trained people home to South Africa. Those who participated in the meeting reported that interaction between the leadership and cadres was very tense.[2] Nevertheless, a compromise was reached to speed up the process of developing a home-going programme. From nowhere and overnight a directive was given to send cadres home with no details and plans as to how this was to be executed. Some suspected that they were being thrown into the lion's den because they were too outspoken, and the high command was clearing the camp of perceived troublemakers.[3] Nevertheless, for these cadres this was preferable to sitting in the camps doing nothing. A large group left Tanzania for Botswana:

1. Mbanya Dube
2. Prince Dubu
3. Steve Khumalo
4. Teboho Lebakeng
5. Shadow Mazibuko
6. Ernest Tshepiso Gumede
7. Kenny Mkhwanazi,
8. Philemon Nki Moema.
9. Dan Mohato Mofokeng 'Romero Daniels' (Ret. Gen Mofokeng)
10. Sello Mosikidi
11. Mandla 'Mendoza' Mtselu
12. Vusi 'Knox' Thusi
13. Mawethu Vitshima
14. Lolo Zobane [4]

Chapter Four

Their arrival in Botswana caused some uneasiness within the country's security sector. When another group of ten cadres followed, they were not allowed to enter the country and were sent back to Tanzania. Matwetwe and Fani Mazibuko were part of this second group.

Eddie Phiri 'Lancelot Dube' the commander, his deputy Justice, Mfundo Njikelane, Basie Sydney Mabusela, and Bobo Moerane formed a PAC structure that was already based in Botswana at the time. For this mission Justice and three others – Tshepiso, Mawethu and Sabelo – went into South Africa to do reconnaissance. They came back and gave a positive report, which then convinced those in charge to send cadres on a curtain raiser and homecoming campaign.

Among those in the first group to go into the country were Sabelo, Teboho, Tshepiso, Mawethu, Mandla 'Mendoza', Kenneth Mkhwanazi and Mthunzi 'Shadow' Mazibuko. It is alleged that the late Philemon Nki Moema insisted on entering South Africa alone. Later, this turned out to have been a disguise for his double role as an agent for the South African police.[5] Others would follow, including Dan Mofokeng, Prince Dubu and Vusi Knox Thusi. The plan was that the cadres were going to spread out in small groups throughout the country to mobilise people and recruit them to leave the country to train as guerrillas. Justice and Tshepiso managed to come back to Gaborone to report on the challenges inside the country, and to organise for more cadres to go into the country. They found the situation in Botswana was getting uneasy as the authorities wanted to send South Africans that were involved in military activities back to Dar or Lusaka.

Justice and Tshepiso were determined that they were not going anywhere but South Africa. This was how they got involved in taking Miriam Duduzile 'Dudu' Zondo[6] and her 11-month-old baby, named Sizwe, back to South Africa. Dudu Zondo was from Rockville and had been my classmate at Ndondo Higher Primary.

They made their way across the border by crossing a river and travelled by buses until they reached Potchefstroom. They had intended to take a train to Johannesburg but panicked because of the movement of police. They got a lift with a truck driver, who was heading for Johannesburg. They told the driver that Justice and Dudu were a married couple and Tshepiso was Dudu's brother.

The trip was safe, and the driver even dropped them in Phefeni, Soweto, not far from Dudu's father's place (her mother stayed in Rockville after separating from her husband). Justice and Tshepiso left Dudu at her father's place, promising to come back for her and take her back to Botswana, which is what she wanted. This was supposed to happen as soon as they got a car that was promised to them by someone, named Stanley Zobani, with whom they had spoken during their reconnaissance mission in South Africa. Dudu had been very brave to return home. Drama erupted because her parents did not want her to risk her life by leaving South Africa a second time. Days passed without news from Justice and Tshepiso, then the media reported that the two PAC 'terrorists' had been arrested at a Soweto house.

'Mendoza' was arrested in Daveyton, while Sabelo, Mawethu and others got caught in the Transkei. Kenneth Mkhwanazi was ambushed and killed by the police at his hiding place, which was his cousin's place in Zone 6, Diepkloof, Soweto. More reports, which could possibly be propaganda by the regime's police, advised that the government had arrested more 'terrorists' throughout the country. Dudu panicked and with her parents failing to persuade her to hide inside the country, somewhere in Natal, her father had to assist her with the second escape into exile through Botswana, which was successful. From Botswana, she managed to get back to Tanzania by January 1979. She found the PAC in disarray in Dar and was accused of having sold out Justice and Tshepiso to the police in South Africa. Some PAC cadres wanted her dead. Fearing for her life, she left the PAC residence and declared herself a refugee after registering with the UNHCR.

Back in South Africa, the person who had promised to organise a car for Justice and Tshepiso, turned out to be working for the police. They were arrested in a trap at Stanley's home in Naledi, Soweto, taken for interrogation, and tortured at Protea police station. After some days without being broken down, they were taken to Jeppe police station and held in different cells. Some prominent leaders like Sally Motlana had also been detained. It was not long that Justice and Tshepiso, through Motlana, befriended a police warden. The situation in the country among black people was slowly changing, and support for the guerrillas who were being arrested was growing as people realised these were the students that had run away into the neighbouring states not so long ago.

Attitudes within the police force were also changing. The friendship with Sgt Samuel Ngubeni, the warden at Jeppe Police Station, resulted in Justice and Tshepiso making a spectacular escape that made headlines and led to one of the greatest manhunts for the fugitives. The police searched along the border to Botswana since they knew this was the way they had entered the country. This gave them an opening to escape through the Swaziland border. It was too dangerous for them to stay in Swaziland so they were assisted by Swazi policemen to cross into Mozambique, where they handed themselves over to the police and found sanctuary.

Following a plea from the PAC headquarters in Dar, Samora Machel's Frelimo government was happy to fly them to Tanzania, in defiance of the South African government, which threatened Mozambique with reprisals if it did not return these 'terrorists.' In Dar, they received a heroes' welcome. When Justice and Tshepiso became aware that Dudu had been falsely accused of selling them out, they put the record straight, but the allegations against her severely affected her emotionally and she resolved that she would not return to the PAC.

After Kenneth Mkhwanazi was killed, things became difficult for Teboho who was in the first group to return. He tried to hide in Zastron, where his parents originated from, but the police were hot on his heels, and eventually he escaped safely back to Botswana. This was not without challenges, as he nearly became a meal for lions after getting lost in the bushes of Botswana. He was saved by an old man who had seen the lions heading in the direction that Teboho was following.

He found Dan Mofokeng had already returned from South Africa. Others who joined them later were Mbanya Dube and Sello Mosikidi. They admitted later that the mission was good propaganda for the PAC, but the ramifications were disastrous.[7]

Lucky Moeketsi and Paul Carlie Mohohlo, who had followed in another group in 1979, both came from Rockville. I knew them well. We were together in the first group that landed in Dar. Carlie trained in Cambodia. They were both arrested in 1980 and detained without trial, interrogated and tortured with electric shocks. Their trial began in April 1980 and on 30 May, Lucky was sentenced to five years. When he was taken to Robben Island in July, he was shocked to see other PAC comrades there.

Meanwhile in Tanzania, by 1979 the battles and divisions within the PAC had escalated. When Leballo left for England to receive medical attention, the triumvirate of Sibeko, Make and Ntloedibe took over and announced Leballo's resignation on 1 May. They had finally succeeded in toppling him. A Presidential Council came into being with more powers than previous structures, like the Revolutionary Council. These developments did not sit well with those who were loyal to Leballo's leadership, the young APLA commanders, who felt they were being outmanoeuvred by Sibeko and others. They left the Itumbi Camp, in Chunya near Mbeya and rushed to Dar-es-Salaam to confront the new leadership. This led to the shooting and killing of

Sibeko at Sea View Flats on 1 June, with Make, who was also present, escaping death by inches. Make was declared by his faction as the new PAC leader (chairman) but APLA commanders rejected him. In the end though, he became the new chairman of the PAC.

In the same month, August, Templeton Ntantala and other expelled military members, formed a rival organisation, the Azanian People's Revolutionary Party (APRP). By 1980 the APLA forces finally accepted the leadership of Make, on condition that he dropped some people from his leadership team. Those involved in the shooting of Sibeko were given heavy sentences of 15 years each, which were reduced to 10 years.[8] Leballo was declared a persona non grata in Tanzania. Vusi Make's authority continued to be undermined though, especially in the camps. On 11 March 1980, the Tanzanian army intervened to prevent a deteriorating situation. This led to the killing of four APLA combatants, including Paulos Poki Mgqwati from Dlamini Number Two, Joe 'Big Joe', Mbuso and Javas from Orlando West, and the injury of countless others.[9] Many escaped to neighbouring countries, like Kenya. About 40 APLA soldiers were considered extremely dangerous and were sent to a detention camp in Mgagau, Iringa.

The return of Justice, Tshepiso and Dudu was accompanied by these developments. Justice and Tshepiso, as well as others, like Matwetwe, joined those in the camp. They were mainly the youth that came from Soweto and other parts of the country, including Free State and other places. The feuds were mainly with those from the Eastern Cape, who had been under the influence of people like Ntantala. Those wishing to leave the camp had to be taken by a specific country and offered refugee status and study opportunities. That's how Matwetwe and Justice, among others, left for Canada while Tshepiso remained in Tanzania.

Dudu had remained with the UNHCR. Before Sibeko was killed, he tried to convince her to come back to the PAC. Having worked within the SSRC mobilising for 'June 16' at Orlando High, she was a political asset, strong and mature for her age. As it happened on the fateful day that Sibeko was killed, she had just left Sibeko's place with her then boyfriend, Godfrey Muntu Molemohi. In fact, on their way out they met the cadres that had attacked Sibeko. For the second time, Dudu was accused of being part of the conspiracy. She was interrogated by the Tanzanian police. Fortunately, the UNHCR supported her throughout this. This episode sealed her separation from the PAC forever. She accepted a scholarship to study in the USA, as did others.

All these events marked the end of Leballo's leadership and influence in the PAC. He tried to work his way back through Zambia, Zimbabwe and Uganda but ended up being expelled from these countries. He would spend his last days in Libya and Ghana. At the time of my arrival in Lusaka, he had died in London, in 1986, a lonely man. In February 1981, John Nyati Pokela, another PAC member, was released from detention in South Africa. He took over from Make. Many of the problems within the PAC, especially among the youth in APLA, had remained unresolved by 1983, Pokela's unexpected death in 1985 shocked many, but even before this, others in the organisation had made up their minds to hang up their gloves, Some joined the ANC. Others decided to go to countries like Australia, the USA and Canada, which had offered to take them.

I knew many of them and when Thiza and Mandla Mangethe mentioned some of their names, I shuddered because the dream of freedom that was the driving force behind the radical steps we took in leaving South Africa suddenly seemed to be evaporating. Questions about where people were and who had died took days and even weeks to assimilate. Many years later Dan Mofokeng had this to say about this period:

Putting the record straight. From 1978 to 1984, the PAC had an unstable existence, particularly in Tanzania. What we used to refer to as crisis. This is a period in which internal conflicts made a serious dent on the organisation's image and performance. As a result of this internal disputes a consultative conference of the PAC was held in Arusha, Tanzania in 1978. This conference resulted in the expulsion of over 60 members. The expelled members subsequently formed an organisation called the Azanian People's Revolutionary Party, APRP. Despite these expulsions the organisation continued to be unstable. Subsequently clear conflicts emerged and namely, the internal leadership squabble or conflicts, conflicts between the leadership and the cadres. The internal leadership conflicts resulted in the expulsion of the then and the late chairman of the central committee of the PAC, PK Leballo and a few other members who allegedly were his supporters.

The conflict between the cadres and the leadership on the other hand, resulted in the death of the members of the PAC triumvirate, David Mamumza Sebeko [sic] who was shot and killed by six APLA cadres who were expelled from the military camp in Itumbi, south of Tanzania. The six APLA cadres were arrested and subsequently sentenced to an effective 15 years in Tanzania, each, by the Tanzanian High Court and therefore cannot be made an issue any more as they were formally charged and sentenced.

Consequently, the remaining PAC leadership lost total control of the forces at Itumbi camp. Eventually the Tanzanian Defence Force intervened and in the operation to wrest control of the camp, four APLA cadres were killed by the Tanzanian Defence Force, TDF. [10]

When the group that went to Nigeria completed their studies; some at the end of 1979 and others in 1980, they were familiar with the events taking place in Tanzania. Many in the group were still loyal to the leadership of Leballo, and had no confidence in Make's leadership when he was based in Nigeria serving as the PAC representative. Make visited Nigeria to try and persuade the 22 disaffected students to return to the PAC in Dar, but they flatly refused. They split into three groups with Happy, Siphiwe, Reggie and Gerry deciding to return to their first country of exile, Swaziland, and the second group consisting of Pule, Rocks and Themba Nkenene choosing to go to Zimbabwe, while the rest elected to go back to Tanzania, but not as PAC members.

The group that left for Swaziland arrived there two or three days before Christmas Day in 1980. Armed with UN passports but with no residence in Swaziland, they were to report at the Mbabane police station to register for their stay in the country. After registering with the police and being advised to return to the police station in the New Year to assess their future in Swaziland, they had nowhere to go. The festive season had already begun and Reggie decided to go and look for a Khumalo family that didn't live far from the police station to see if they could provide accommodation for them. While Reggie was away, a detective arrived at the police station and seeing the three outside the police station building with their bags on the ground, he asked the other police who they were. On finding out that they were South Africans, the detective who was obviously drunk, summoned Happy and Siphiwe to come inside the building and explain what was their mission in Swaziland. This was after finding out that Happy was a trained aircraft engineer, Reggie a radio and radar electronics engineer, and Siphiwe and Gerald were pilots. Gerry, who had remained outside to look after the bags, was also beckoned inside and the drunk detective told them they were highly dangerous persons to be let loose in Swaziland. He ordered that they be imprisoned at the police station. When Reggie returned from his unsuccessful mission, he was also shown the prison cell doors.

The mission to Swaziland had become a nightmare. Looking back at what was happening in Swaziland during this period, it was highly possible that this detective collaborated with the South African police. There were ANC and PAC people who had recently been arrested and some had been deported to Mozambique and Tanzania. Kidnappings of cadres by South African police from Swaziland were occurring without any explanations from local authorities. The prison rooms at the police station were appalling. The windows had steel rods instead of glass. The four refused to tolerate the place so they were escorted by police vans and scooters with flashing blue lights to another police station which was no improvement on the place they had come from. Feeling desolate and exhausted by this stage, all they wanted to do was sleep.

With glassless windows, the rooms were a playground for mosquitos. They asked for the lights not be switched off to keep the parasites away. The food they were given was the worst they had seen. They limited themselves to the porridge and ate as little as possible of whatever was provided to survive.

Swazi citizens had trained with the four at the same college in Nigeria. One of their fellow students was King Sobhuza's son, Richard Dlamini, who was a pilot. On arrival at the airport in Mbabane they had made enquiries about the whereabouts of other fellow students from Swaziland: Pa Khumalo and Sam Mnisi, who had trained as air traffic controllers. The airport staff knew them, but they were not there. They befriended a Swazi policewoman at the police station, and through her, made further enquiries about Khumalo and Mnisi. A few days later, they received a surprise visit from Pa Khumalo and Vernon Mokate, a South African who was living in Swaziland and had also trained in Nigeria. They told them they had been searching for them and had almost given up. The four were elated to see the men and asked them to please bring some decent food. The two men never returned. Many years later it emerged that the food was delivered but the authorities warned the two never to set foot again at the police station and never to inform anyone of having seen these people if they wanted to live in peace. The authorities must have enjoyed a sumptuous meal that day.

One night, the four were visited by the head of intelligence in Swaziland, wanting to know how and why they returned to Swaziland and what their intention was. The head of intelligence got nothing from them and was furious. It became obvious that the Swazi authorities intended handing them over to South Africa.

Perhaps what saved them, was the fact that they had been seen by some people so their presence was not a secret. Godfrey Sabiti, the UNHCR representative in Mbabane, acted quickly after he became aware of their presence and alerted the authorities that the four should be allowed to be sent back to where they came from. The UNHCR acted immediately and arranged for the police to buy them food from an eatery next to the police station. The policemen who had mocked them, now envied them. The day of their deportation, 2 January, 1981, arrived and for the first time in almost two weeks, they were given water to wash themselves. Thereafter, pictures and fingerprints were taken and they were whisked off to the airport, again, under heavy police guard on motorbikes with blue lights flashing, and sent back to Nigeria via Kenya. They remained in Nigeria until Pokela replaced Make in 1981 and they returned to the PAC.

At first, things were not that difficult for the second group that chose Harare as their destination as they landed safely. When the old white security personnel, which was loyal to the former Ian Smith's regime, came to know that they were actually PAC members, they were harassed to the point that Pule and Rocks were forced to leave

Zimbabwe once the UN intervened and got them scholarships to study in Canada. Themba Nkenene, who had remained, eventually found employment with Air Zimbabwe.

The last group was the worst off. It consisted of Mandla Mangethe, Thiza Ntsibande, Maas Ngomesa, Lucky Ngema, Titi Sithole, Mbulelo Fihla, Shaka Komani, Nyamiso Njingana, Willie Nkonyeni and John Ranko, among others.

They flew to Dar where they were detained at the airport and refused entry into Tanzania unless they joined the PAC or the ANC. They were determined to engage the leadership of the PAC before deciding whether to return to the PAC or not. This was not accepted by the Tanzanian authorities. They were now stuck at the airport, where they were visited by ANC people who informed them that they were welcome to join the ANC. They were resolute that they wanted to deal with the PAC first. Having reached a stalemate, the authorities took them away from the airport and dropped them off at a place in town where the PAC could engage them.

The PAC was able to divide the group, and some re-joined the organisation, while some like Mandla Mangethe, Thiza, Maas, amongst others, were taken to a camp near Mbeya until they had made up their minds. Once the security people relaxed their guard, they escaped and went back to Dar. Because they went to stay in houses where PAC people lived, they were easily arrested again and taken to a prison outside Dar. Again, they escaped and went to hide at a place called, Kariakoo, where there was a bazaar market that was popular and densely crowded. Here they lived like Tanzanians and could not be easily identified. They managed to dodge the authorities and members of the PAC. After some time, the net began closing on them, when a Tanzanian citizen who was sympathetic to them arranged for them to be relocated to another part of Dar, some distance from the busy town.

The same citizen thrashed out a plan for them to escape from

Tanzania to Kenya. In the dark of night eight of them got into two fishing boats and rowed towards Mombasa, Kenya. From Mombasa they found their way to Nairobi where they came across some South Africans who were refugees, some of whom had also left both the ANC and the PAC. On their advice, they handed themselves over to the UNHCR authorities and sought refugee status. Once the UN authorities got to know how they landed in Nairobi, they were handed back to the Kenyan authorities. The Kenyans drove them to Maili Tisa town, in Namanga, where there is a border crossing to Tanzania, and they were kept there for more than a month. After this, they were given to the Tanzanian authorities who detained them in Arusha for another month before driving them back to the central prison in Dar.

They were taken to a camp in Iringa, then to another camp. Finally, they joined those who were presented with choices of countries they wanted to go to. Mandla Mangethe and a few others ultimately decided to join the ANC, because they still felt they wanted to fight. After meeting with Chris Hani in Dar, Mandla Mangethe, Thiza, Maas were first taken to Mazimbu, in Morogoro and later moved through the border to Lusaka. Within a week they flew to Angola for military training. It is here that they met friends who had left the PAC in Dar, after the Nigerian group had left for their aviation studies. This is how Thiza was re-united with his younger brother, Tuka. At the end of the training Thiza was sent to the Party school in Bulgaria and Mandla Mangethe went to the Lenin Party School in Moscow.

Both came back in 1982. Mandla Mangethe first worked for Radio Freedom, but it was not long before he was moved to work with Uriah Mokeba, the chief representative, at the office in Luanda. Around 1983 the civil war worsened in Angola and there was no way that MK would be spared. This is when the tragic events involving the ambush in Cacuso, where Tuka was killed, occurred. After this, one thing led to another, including two rebellions in the camps, one in 1983 and another in 1984. These rebellions or mutinies are popularly known as 'Mkatashinga', a name that in a way ridiculed the participants. Mkatashinga was a song that was sung in Kimbundu, one of the Angolan languages, by MK cadres and Angolans in the People's Armed Forces of Liberation of Angola (FAPLA),[11] especially after they had been on joint missions against the National Union for the Total Independence of Angola (UNITA). It goes:

> 1st group: Ngamkatambunda (my back is sore)
> 2nd group: Ngamkatashinga (my waist is sore)
> 1st group: Ngamkatashinga
> 2nd group: Ngamkatambunda
> 1st group: Malanje
> 2nd group: Malanje ishi yethu (Malanje is our place)
> 1st group: Luanda
> 2nd group: Luanda ishi yethu [12]

At the Kabwe Consultative Conference in 1985, where I had participated as a delegate, there were comrades who were directly involved in these mutinies. At that time, I knew little about who was involved and the details of what triggered the mutinies. These incidents were not discussed at Kabwe and it was difficult to make head or tail of what had taken place. The Stuart Commission Report of 1984 was never shared with the general membership until after the unbanning of the ANC. It was presented to the Truth and Reconciliation Commission (TRC), at which the pre-1994 human rights violations committed by all sides during the fight to end apartheid were exposed.

I learned from Thiza and Mangethe that Norman (Bongani Matwa) was one of the Committee of Ten.[13] I was shocked to the marrow. What else happened in Angola that was still to surprise me? In the GDR where I was stationed, new students who arrived from both Angola and Tanzania shared stories about apartheid spies who had infiltrated the organisation and had intended to kill the leadership. Although disturbed, I told myself that I was grateful that a catastrophe had been averted. Moreover, I already sensed that in terms of the administration of the military camps, the early 1980s were a big challenge for both the ANC and the PAC. There were disturbing reports of lack of discipline in Angola, corroborated by Thiza and Mangethe, who recounted the circumstances that led to the mutinies. There were genuine frustrations brought about by staying for a long time in the camps without any information as to when cadres were to be sent home to go and fight. These were trained soldiers, and they were not used to camp life and doing nothing for a prolonged period.

What made things worse was the lack of proper leadership, with young cadres staffing the security apparatus and having powers far exceeding their capabilities. The unrestrained behaviour of young administrators with no people skills and qualifications, resulted in them feeding on the camp livestock, like pigs and ducks, while the fighters – the rank and file – survived in misery. Tolerance and debate on matters affecting the cadres were fraught with problems as the securocrats scrutinised everything discussed and identified people as 'agent provocateurs'. For incomprehensible reasons, security concerns were used to silence critics of the leadership. All this led to serious animosity between the administrators and the security personnel, who lived a different and better life, and those who were restricted from speaking out.

There was genuine dissatisfaction and there were also real security issues that put the lives of ANC members in danger, like the poisoning of food in the camps. This was a sign that there was a network of enemy agents within the organisation, and this was not in the camps only, as evidence would later show. These agents were everywhere, including in the ANC offices in London.

The welfare of combatants in the ANC camps was in jeopardy, and the entire environment, including politics, training and relationships, deteriorated. The Pango camp, where Norman was in charge, was no exception. As a staff commissar, Norman bore the brunt of explaining what was happening to the rank and file. As head of political education, he was supposed to teach even the admin staff about ethical behaviour in a revolutionary organisation; for example, that you cannot live a lavish lifestyle whilst the soldiers are starving.

Around this time President Tambo called for discussions in all the camps on the way forward. At the Pango camp, Norman facilitated this process, organising workshops for discussions, suggestions and proposals. This made the Pango administration unhappy. They didn't want open and frank discussions on problems facing MK fighters.

Concomitant to this, there was also a general mobilisation of MK cadres to go and fight UNITA on the eastern front of Angola – in the Malanje province. Norman was deployed as a camp commissar at Camalundi camp. At the beginning, the drafting of MK cadres to assist FAPLA, indirectly the Angolan government, against UNITA, which was backed by the USA (CIA) and apartheid South Africa (SADF), was not a problem.

Our own cadres were being ambushed and killed by UNITA. This deployment was in a real war situation, and it was bound to affect MK cadres if the numbers of casualties increased. Remaining in Angola under these conditions meant that MK cadres had to secure their safety by being involved in the fight against UNITA. MK soldiers wanted to be deployed inside South Africa rather than fight an enemy far away from home. This was a genuine concern. It needed adequate political motivation from leadership. It was very evident that there was lack of such a leadership within MK Camps and by those who carried these responsibilities within the leadership of the ANC.

Once MK was committed to this peculiar situation, a strategic plan was needed to handle the matter. What I heard, and reports later confirmed this, was that there was negligence on the part of those who were in charge. Thiza and Mandla Mangethe painted a picture that, I for one, would never have tolerated. Many of our comrades lost their lives. I asked myself how we would explain this to our people if we became free one day. I was not sure who was still locked up in Angola Norman's bravery was mentioned often in connection with these events.

Many years later, when we were back in South Africa, I learned more from those who were directly involved and had been with Norman during this period. I also had an opportunity to have a discussion with Chris Hani at Shell House, and I appreciated his frank view on the mutinies. He was clear that at that time, we should concentrate on the negotiations taking place between various organisations and the South African government about the future of the country.

Norman himself, a quiet individual and a military man, spoke little about himself and the suffering he had endured at the hands of our security personnel.

In around 1982, Norman had been a staff commissar and head of the political education department at the Pango camp. He held political classes every Tuesday that dealt mainly with the ANC, its alliance partners, the SACP and SACTU, news analysis from home and the international situation. He also explored some Marxist concepts on societal knowledge and development. He proved to be a fountain of political knowledge and was a critical analyst. He became popular and was revered as a political instructor, while at the same time becoming one of the best field commissars in Angola. When the Mkatashinga started with MK soldiers demanding to fight in South Africa rather than die fighting UNITA in Angola, Norman was in the thick of it as a responsible leader and the commander in charge. After this episode, there were MK fighters that went to the Viana camp outside

Luanda, with the intention of meeting and discussing the concerns of the soldiers with the Regional Command.

The Regional Command suggested setting up a committee representing the troops in Viana. A Committee of Ten was elected like the Soweto Committee of Ten elected after the June 16 uprising. Norman was number one on the list, having been nominated by the troops at the Viana camp. He was followed by Ephraim Nkondo (MK Zaba Maledza), Jabu Mofolo (MK Shadrack Lebona Sepamla), Nomfanelo Ntlokwana (MK Kate Mhlongo), ...(MK Grace Mofokeng), Mbulelo Musi (MK Moses Thema), Khotso Morena (MK Mwezi Twala), Sindile Velem (MK Simon Botha), Vusi Mndebele (MK Sipho Mathebula) and Omry Mathabatha Makgoale (MK Sidwell 'Mhlongo' Moroka), who was elected in absentia.[14]

The committee decided that for tactical reasons, Norman should be the convenor rather than the chairperson, and Zaba was appointed secretary. Norman became a persuasive leader as convenor and the mutineers trusted him to convey to the leadership the genuine complains of the combatants.

No discussions took place; the Committee members were arrested at the Viana camp and sent to Luanda central prison where later they were interviewed by Stuart Commission members, consisting of Hermanus Gabriel Loots (MK James Stuart), Anthony Mongalo, Sizakele Sigxashe, Aziz Pahad and Daniel Oliphant (MK Mtu Jwili) from the June 16 detachment, while all the other members in the Commission were members of the Luthuli Detachment. The Commission's report stated:

> *Whilst it is true that these [spies in the ANC, KM] would have exploited every opportunity to achieve their reactionary and counter-revolutionary goals, the Committee of Ten could not be deemed to have been an organised act of conspiracy on the part of the enemy...*

> *The Commission found conditions in some camps shocking, to say the least. Extremely poor quality of food. no fresh meat, vegetables of fruits for months; hardly any recreation facilities, low level of cultural activities; poor tents, uniforms, boots, sports shoes if any; no medicaments, corruption and fear is omnipresent. This is what we found. Fear of the brutal punishment devised in the camps.*
>
> *The Commission feels that these conditions in the camps coupled with the insensitivity and the open abuse of authority on the part of some officers, have prepared the grounds for these disturbances.*
>
> *However, the Commission, while accepting that the cadres had many genuine grievances, strongly criticise the tactics adopted to solve these.* [15]

After the Stuart Commission left, the ten were badly tortured by the ANC security (also called Mbokodo – a grinding stone) in the Luanda state prison. For his 'sins' Norman suffered severe torture at the hands of the security personnel. It was the intervention of people like Gertrude Shope that saved his life and the lives of the others. They were taken to Quatro, where they spent almost five years in detention, being tortured daily.

Meanwhile, following the investigations by the Stuart Commission, and after the Kabwe conference that had produced a Code of Conduct, changes took place. In 1987, President Tambo directed that the security and intelligence department be restructured and new personnel were brought in, including members of the NEC. The department was then put under the supervision of the Secretary-General, Alfred Nzo.

The wish of the mutineers to have a consultative conference (Kabwe 1985) was fulfilled, though in their absence and without dealing with some of the issues they had wanted discussed.

When the ANC had to move out of Angola following the tripartite agreement on Namibia, most of the detainees were taken to Tanzania. Coincidentally – maybe ironically – they were released by the regional commander at the time, who happened to be Mbulelo (Ret. Gen. Phako), in November 1988, and taken to Dakawa in Tanzania via Lusaka. Mbulelo came from the same township as Bongani and was with us in Swaziland when we left for exile.

As for me, Christmas came and passed with nothing special happening in Lusaka. This was not Germany, and I had been in Tanzania before. It was the same with New Year's Eve, nothing special on offer. We cooked the same food we had every day. I lost track of why I had come to Zambia in the first place. I was even angry with myself for not joining Thiza and Mandla Mangethe immediately I knew that they were around. When we were together again, we continued talking about their stay in Angola.

They also stayed in Angola longer than was necessary after completing their training because fewer people were being trained and they could not leave the camps unmanned. In 1985, after the Kabwe conference and at the recommendation of Chris Hani, they were taken back to Zambia to revive their careers in aviation. They left for Addis Ababa with Maas, who had been with them throughout. They were joined by Thabo Mohlala, Themba McClain, Gilbert Zakhele 'Mpho' Thwala and Masango Khanye. When I arrived in Lusaka they had just come back from Ethiopia.

Among the many happenings the two related to me was the killing of Sakie (MK Oupa Moloi) in 1981 in Angola. He was killed by comrades in an ANC camp commanded by Muziwakhe Ngwenya (MK Thami Zulu) in Camalundi, Malanje.

> *Torture of Umkhonto soldiers in Camalundi camp in Malanje province and the death under torture of Oupa Moloi, head of the political department, took place in 1981 under his authority as camp commander. Zulu brazenly threatened others in the camp with the same treatment.* [16]

Thiza and Mangethe confirmed that Sakie's wrongdoing was smoking dagga and drinking locally brewed beer. I had come a long way with Sakie; growing up and playing together. I remember very well how in the late 1960s and early 1970s we spent many Christmas Eves or New Year Eves together. We slept the whole night on the green grass under the grape tree at my home, listening to Lourenço Marques Radio (Radio LM) pop music that was beamed from Mozambique. Besides Stan, he knew the details of our departure from home to exile. He was with me throughout in Swaziland and, together with Norman 'Bongani', we had made that mission to the ANC offices in Tanzania and bumped into OR Tambo that first day. We parted in Temeke knowing we had taken the best decisions together. Between 1978 and 1979 he was posted to the Party school in Bulgaria, most probably where Thiza was sent to later, and he had written me letters from there while I was in the GDR. Those letters had lifted my spirits knowing that we were still on the same course. The news of his killing shattered me and left me cold. How would this be explained to his family? This was a cruel crime!

According to the findings of the Stuart Commission, violence and physical punishment had become the norm in the ANC camps.[17] After listening to this, I decided that I would never associate myself with any security structure (Mbokodo), within my own organisation or with anyone working in these structures. I took this decision prematurely, and not knowing that some of the people working in these structures were close to me. I was informed that Jomo, who I had already met, and David 'Trizzer', were in fact employed in these structures and were also protectors of none other than, OR Tambo.

I was forced to retract my position and stated that I would make exceptions. As if Jomo had overheard me, not long after this, he invited me to his house for lunch. His wife, Thoko, prepared such a delicious meal for me that I felt like a king for the first time in Lusaka, downing my food with whisky. During the meal we went through some of the things I had already heard from Thiza and Mangethe. We concluded that it was part and parcel of the struggle. Now and then I thought of the whereabouts of Norman and felt very bad about what happened to Sakie.

With the new year having started, I asked for a lift to the department of education. What I found there made me understand why nobody had met me at the airport. The lines of communication were missing. It took me many days to understand how things worked in Zambia. I met with the Secretary-General, Alfred Nzo and thereafter with Ntate Makgothi. I got an idea of what they had in mind when they suggested I should come to Zambia. This was followed by a meeting with Mohammed Tikly who gave me a broader illustration of what was happening at headquarters and the links to SOMAFCO. In short it was up to me to decide where I could contribute.

I began participating in meetings of the ANC Education Council, in which there were, among others, Sophia De Bruyn (nee Williams), Billy Modise and Ivy Florence Matsepe-Casaburri. Aunt Sophia, as I fondly called Sophia De Bruyn, was a founding member of the council, which was formed in 1980, to set the curriculum for SOMAFCO. She was a teacher at the UN Institute for Namibia in Lusaka, whose director was Hage Gottfried Geingob, the current President of Namibia, since 2017, who was head of the institute until 1989. The Namibian institute was created to prepare and develop skilled personnel for a SWAPO government in the future, and Aunt Sophia trained young cadres in behavioural sciences and etiquette. She was well-liked and respected by all at the institute. I was happy to finally meet her and to work with her. A veteran and founding member of the South African Congress of Trade Unions (SACTU), she was a fulltime organiser of the Coloured People's Congress.

Above all, at 18 years-old, she was the youngest leader of 20 000 women who marched to the Union Buildings on 9 August 1956, to protest against the carrying of pass books by women. I had studied with her son, Angelo in the GDR, and became close friends with her daughters, Danielle Crady (nee De Bruyn) and Sonja Sebotsa (nee De Bruyn). I became her other son. Her husband, a down-to-earth father, Henry Benny Nato De Bruyn, was one of the first to work underground after the banning of the ANC, joining Umkhonto we Sizwe and leaving for exile in 1963. He served as our chief representative to Italy and later I joined him in the Department of International Affairs (DIA) in Lusaka.

Billy Modise was the Assistant Director to Hage Gottfried Geingob at the UN Institute for Namibia from 1976 to 1988. I also got along very well with him, and came to know his lovely wife, Yolisa too. Some of the meetings of the council were held either at Aunt Sophia's place or at Modise's. Later, together with Modise and Benny De Bruyn, we served in the diplomatic services of the ANC.

I was privileged to participate in another event of historical importance in Lusaka. The 'In-House Seminar on Constitutional Matters and Related Issues' met from 1–4 March 1988, to consider the Constitutional Guidelines for a Democratic South Africa. This was the culmination of work that started in 1986. As part of the 74th anniversary of the founding of the ANC in January that year, the ANC leadership, established a special committee of experts consisting of legal persons, lawyers, scholars and constitutional experts. Their unprecedented task was to develop a proposal for a constitutional framework for the future South Africa. Because the ANC was still committed to an armed revolutionary struggle, this showed remarkable foresight. The ANC felt that there were initiatives being taken inside South Africa by the regime and the west, involving think tanks, which may cause a problem if the ANC failed to address these developments.

The concern was for the protection of so-called minority rights.

Jack Simons was appointed to chair the committee and to work with the NEC's sub-committee on Constitutional Guidelines. He presented the finalised draft text for debate. Out of this lively and robust meeting the ANC's Constitutional Guidelines were published in 1988.[18]

I began to feel part of the ANC community in Zambia. After meeting Reginald 'Reggie' September, Ray Alexander and Jack Simons, who was Professor Emeritus of Political Science, at the University of Zambia, my stay in Lusaka became meaningful. I would spend the rest of my time in Zambia having interesting and sometimes heated debates on the national question in South Africa with the three of them. One day I arrived at the Simons' home and Comrade Jack handed me an official letter signed by September, the secretary of the Department of Political Education. It stated:

> *Comrade Khulu Mbatha,*
>
> *Dear comrade,*
>
> *Re: Your Thesis*
>
> *We understand that your thesis is on the National Question. Needless to say, our department is most interested. Comrade Jack informs us that you are presently working on a translation into English. Would you be good enough to favour us with a copy?*
>
> *Meanwhile, we are also hopeful that you will be prepared to help us in the preparation of lecture notes for our syllabus. Whenever you are near to our office please call.*
>
> *Amandla!*
>
> *Reg September (signed)*
>
> *Secretary* [19]

I had already started with the translation, but the letter gave me impetus to continue. In those days, it was the most challenging task.

There were no computers, no internet, and no cell phones, and so everything had to be done by hand. I found that the ANC library was not a conducive place to work. Only some of the literature that I needed was available, but what was even more disturbing was the attitude of the person assigned to look after the library, a political appointee who acted more like a security official, than a librarian. His name was Jeff Marishane. He refused to allow me to take a single book out of the library to read at home. The fact that he had befriended Stan and was allowing him to take books home, fuelled my discontent and I made up my mind to go back to my university in Germany and do the translation of my thesis there. It would be easier because of the availability of the literature I needed.

I wrote to my alma mater requesting them for sponsorship to return and work on the translation of my thesis. The director of international relations wrote back with an approval that I could go back. I was thrilled by this, but it never happened.

Five months passed and I was now getting well acquainted with the situation and happenings in Zambia. I was at headquarters one day when I met Mme Ritah Seperepere, who I last saw in the GDR. She had replaced Ruth Mompati as the ANC's representative at the WIDF in Berlin. She pulled me aside and asked me what I am doing in Zambia, which I easily explained to her.

She told me she had been approached and asked if she could go and open an ANC office in Athens. Athens is a hot place, and for health reason she did not want to go there. Knowing that my wife was Greek she thought I might be interested. I did not take her seriously, but the discussion left me torn apart. I was starting to connect with issues in Zambia. I asked her to let me think about it.

The next thing I heard was that Mfanafuthi Johnstone 'Johnny' Makatini, head of DIA, wanted to see me. When I entered his offices, he said to me, 'Comrade Mbatha, here is your letter of appointment,

I have informed the Secretary-General that you are going to Athens'. There was no chance to question Makatini about anything. The next thing I had to do was to see Treasury about the ticket and other logistics. That was it.

I waited for the Secretary-General to come back to Lusaka so that I could discuss this matter with him. When he came back, I found him with the Treasurer-General, Thomas Titus 'TT' Nkobi. I relayed the matter of Greece to them and with their approval, began preparing for my departure for Greece. Unlike when I left Germany for Zambia, there were not many people to bid farewell to. I had told Stan, Thiza and Mangethe about the new deployment. It was a difficult move as I knew we were separating again; but that was life in exile. After seven months in Zambia, I prepared to depart for Athens on the 25 May 1988.

There were many advantages of having been at headquarters, and one of them was the rare chance of meeting some people from Rockville and other parts of Soweto that I knew. The comrades were in operations and doing underground work inside South Africa. One of them, who had just come back from home or was preparing to go back home again was Tseko Nell (MK Steve Rantso). To get first-hand facts on what it meant to work among the people at home after undergoing training in Angola and places like in GDR was fascinating. What's more, Tseko, Stan and I reminisced about the few months and days at the University of Zululand before June 16, 1976, and what happened two days later on the morning of June 18. It felt as though these were recent events.

I met friends from Rockville, who attended school with me. We shared information that made me feel connected to my roots and to what was going on in exile. There was Ephraim 'Tata' Ngwenya, Joseph 'Poponi' Dube and his cousin Mathiyane 'bra Sam' Hlongwa, who informed me of the arrest, of their cousin, Ceasar Hlongwa (who was sentenced to five years on Robben Island). He was in my class at Ndondo Primary. They also told me about the arrest of Jabu 'Dubu' Masina (MK Jabu Gwamanda), who was also from Rockville and a friend to Jerry (my brother) and Caesar's brother, Taylor Hlongwa. Together with Frans 'Ting Ting' Masango, Neo Potsane and Joseph Makhura, 'Dubu' was arrested in September 1986 in Winterveld, Pretoria.

They belonged to the 'Icing Unit' or 'elimination unit,' a special entity set up to assassinate 'apartheid collaborators', which included members of the apartheid government's security forces and homeland leaders. They were placed in solitary confinement for nine months in terms of Section 29 of the Terrorism Act and were severely tortured. When their trial started in 1987, they faced multiple charges, including high treason, and came to be known as the 'Delmas Four'. During my stay in Lusaka in 1987/1988, the trial had already received a lot of publicity both locally and internationally because the four had elected not to participate in their trial. They refused to acknowledge the legitimacy of the apartheid government and demanded to be tried as soldiers.

Their stance was that they were soldiers of MK acting under orders and involved in a 'just war' to liberate the country from an illegitimate government. They faced the death penalty and were prepared to die for this ideal.

Through this trial, I came to know more about the deeds of 'Dubu'. He was the MK cadre that in June 1978 followed Orphan 'Hlubi' Chapi and killed him. Hlubi's house was opposite the Ndondo Primary School; his gate was opposite the main entrance to the school. He was my close neighbour. Wandile Kabane's family lived next door to Hlubi and I knew all his children. He was a well-respected police officer in our community in Rockville and was with the Brixton and Robbery Squad. During my days, this was the police unit most feared by criminals around the whole of the Johannesburg area. When there was a robbery – mostly in town – it was Hlubi who took over the role of tracking and arresting the perpetrators. If he was standing in his yard, no taxi driver or owner went past Hlubi's house without hooting the car's horn or shouting 'Lekgowa' – his other nickname; which means 'white man' – as a sign of recognising his authority. He knew all the owners, as there were no more than 50 taxis in the whole of Soweto at that time. Taxis only operated in the township and did not ferry people to town, and PUTCO buses and trains were the main means of transport. After June 16 1976, as the townships became ungovernable, especially Soweto, most security police were assigned to deal with the unrest. This is what made Hlubi notorious and the man most feared and talked about as the uprising was escalating. The ANC responded by creating the 'elimination' unit.

On 27th April 1989 the Delmas Four were sentenced to death and put on Death Row with other activists, such as Robert McBride, Sibusiso 'Mantolo' Masuku and Oupa Josiah Mbonani. The four refused to appeal their death sentence until the ANC intervened.

I found out that there were two Wauchope family members that had joined us in exile and were at some point in SOMACFO, Nat and Kuki. At the same time someone had reported the sad news of Kuki's death in Tanzania. I was left confused and miserable not knowing what to believe. I remembered how I used to collect them from their home and walk with them to the clubhouse in Dlamini Number One.

GREECE (1988-1990)

Athens, ANC Chief Representative

I had mixed feelings about returning to Greece, although I had communicated with Anna about my new assignment, and I was happy that I would be with my family again, especially our baby Dimitra. I landed in Athens a few days before her first birthday. It felt as though I had never left.

After a few days I contacted the offices of the Greek Committee for International Democratic Solidarity (EEDDA), which were in downtown Athens. EEDDA is a Greek non-governmental, non-profit and public organisation, established in 1981 with the objective of supporting and standing in solidarity with the struggling people in Asia, Africa and Latin America. The NGO, in supporting people fighting for their national independence and sovereignty, for peace and social justice, drew its members from trade union organs, civil servants and bank employees. It brought together women's associations, peace movements and prominent personalities in Greece. I was given a desk and space in the EEDDA offices to do my work.

It was time for me to familiarise myself with Greek politics. After Dimitra's birth, I had attended and successfully completed a Greek language course at the Athens Centre in 1987. I knew from experience how important it was when living in a foreign country, to learn the language in order to understand and be understood. The ANC's presence in Greece and my coming to set up this office was preceded and underpinned by the friendly and cordial relations between the SA Communist Party and its Greek counterpart, the KKE. Moreover, the ANC Youth Section had previously been invited to participate in the Greek Communist Youth (KNE) annual summer festival in Athens.

It was this cordiality and the nature of these interactions that led to the suggestion to establish our presence here.

It did not take me that long to hit the ground running. The Greek people did not shy away from supporting our struggle, and it was noteworthy that the Greek Government, under Andreas Papandreou of the Panhellenic Socialist Movement (PASOK), supported UN sanctions against the apartheid regime. Not long after my arrival, in August, I was invited by the mayor of Lefkada to a ceremony at which Nelson Mandela was awarded the Medal of Peace. This was followed by Greece hosting the United Nations' Symposium on Culture Against Apartheid in Athens from 2–4 September 1988.[20] It was organised by the Special Committee against Apartheid under its chairman, Joseph N Garba, in cooperation with the Ministry of Culture of Greece. Presided over by Melina Mercouri, the then Minister of Culture for Greece, this watershed conference was attended by 36 prominent artists, performers, film and theatre directors and writers from all over the world. They included South Africans from within the country as well as those in exile.

Among others from the US, Europe and Africa, participants included Harry Belafonte, Michael Cacoyannis, Glenda Jackson, Joseph Papp, Maximilian Schell, and Nobel Laureates Nadine Gordimer and Wole Soyinka. Also present were Pallo Jordan, Jules Dassin, Arja Saioimaa, Marilyn Bergman, Kader Asmal, Johnny Clegg and Little Steven. The symposium deliberated on the situation in South Africa and the international response to it, reviewed the role of artists and entertainers in the struggle against apartheid, and reflected on the cultural boycott of South Africa and its implications. The cultural boycott against the apartheid culture of South Africa and the Policy Guidelines for the boycott that had been adopted by the Special Committee were endorsed.

The Athens Appeal was adopted and all writers, artists, musicians, composers, entertainers, actors, producers, distributors and other cultural workers in the international community were called upon to refuse to perform or have their works performed in South Africa. The conference appealed for the monitoring of the boycott to be strengthened and expressed full support for the efforts of the United Nations to promote the isolation of South Africa. The Appeal recognised and called for the support of indigenous cultural expressions countering oppression in the country.

Another important resolution that was adopted called for the establishment of a trust fund for scholarships to be granted to young artists whose talents have been suppressed by apartheid.

During the symposium I organised a meeting with the foreign ministry of Greece and subsequently accompanied Pallo Jordan, who was an NEC member and head of the department of information and publicity of the ANC, to a meeting with the Deputy Minister of Foreign Affairs.

A month later, another event of historical importance took place in Athens. It was the Conference of the Association of West European Parliamentarians for Action Against Apartheid (AWEPAA) on 20–21 October 1988.[21] The theme of the conference, organised by the Ministry of Foreign Affairs of Greece under the umbrella of AWEPAA, was 'Frontline States, How to counter South African Destabilisation'.

Participants came from around Europe and Africa; Ministers of Foreign Affairs from Greece and Mozambique, Karolos Papoulias and Pascoal Mocumbi, and Zimbabwe's Speaker of Parliament from 1980 to 1990, Didymus Edwin Mutasa took part. Advocate George Bizos, who originated from Greece, and who had defended many South Africans against apartheid laws, notably in the famous Rivonia Trial, addressed the meeting. Others who participated were Sipho Mpofu from Botswana's Foreign Ministry, Saki Macozoma from the South African Council of Churches (SACC), the Dutch activist Klaas de Jonge, and Abdul Minty who led the World Campaign against Military and Nuclear Cooperation with South Africa, from Oslo. The conference applauded the message Bizos delivered and discussed how to intensify sanctions. I was able to get direct news about the situation at home from both Bizos and Macozoma. I accompanied visitors to the old Olympic village in Olympia which was four hours away by bus from Athens. We returned to Athens overnight by boat.

From 13–19 March 1989 the First Peace Olympiad was hosted in Athens with international participation. At a reception honouring the international guests, I met the Zimbabwean member of parliament, Che Chimutengwende. Also present was the Zambian Ambassador to Egypt, Kalenga Kangwa, who was accredited to Athens, and Rev Kofi Nkrumah-Young from Jamaica.

Greek artists and musicians answered the call for people around the world to unite against apartheid. I put together South African works of art – writings, poetry and songs – translated into Greek, and together we produced one of the biggest events ever organised, produced and performed in Athens. In honour of the struggle against apartheid, we used the 29th anniversary of the Sharpeville massacre on 21 March to launch the Africa Now Concert at the University of Athens. It was to take place on 6 May, 1989, at The Palace Theatre (Pallas) in central Athens. George Katsaros – the composer, conductor and saxophonist, Lakis Halkias – the legendary composer, producer and singer and Dimitris Iatropoulos – the splendid writer and poet, staged the musical concert. From this concert, in which I also performed, we produced an album that sold and raised funds to support the Anti-Apartheid movement in Greece. One song, about the 'shining light of Africa', which is about Nelson Mandela, captured the minds of Greeks around the globe and still touches many who listen to the song for the first time.[22]

This work found continuity through other Greek musicians,

including the famous Vassilis Papakonstantinou. Vassilis contributed funds from performances in clubs around Athens, specifically to support my office. These artists and the supporters of the ANC held the anti-apartheid momentum high when apartheid propaganda was being used to silence the true voices of South Africans. They helped to mobilise political support from other Greek political parties, trade unions, cultural organisations, musicians, artists, municipalities, universities and the civil society at large.

One unforgettable event that took place in Athens, was the holding of the Session of the World Peace Council from the 6–11 February 1990.[23] I was a participant. A few days earlier, on 2 February, President FW De Klerk unbanned the ANC, the PAC and other organisations. This was followed by another extraordinary statement on 10 February, a day before the closure of the World Peace Council meeting, when De Klerk announced that the most famous political prisoner in the world, Nelson Mandela, would be released the following day. The last day of this conference was marked by numerous interruptions, with the international media led by CNN, repeatedly informing the international community that the South African authorities had postponed the time of Nelson Mandela's release. It was remarkable how this interrupted with the proceedings of the WPC conference.

When Mandela finally walked out of the Victor Verster Prison in Paarl, the whole world had waited and waited, to see what he looked like after 27 years' incarceration. No pictures of him had been taken since his imprisonment. Instead of closing with a call for the release of Nelson Mandela and all political prisoners, the conference ended on a high note. I was thrilled when my organisation, within a month of his release, invited me to personally meet him in Europe. Other chief representatives were there too. Flying to Stockholm, on this occasion was a unique experience. On 16 March 1990, before all the chief representatives had met with him, I asked Jomo if he could arrange for me to greet the two leaders (Mandela and OR Tambo). He told me to wait and he would indicate when the timing was appropriate.

I waited until he came to fetch me. He took me to a room where the two leaders were meeting. Both gladly received me and my 'intruder,' comrade Themba Kubheka, who had been with me in the GDR during my stay there, and had overheard me asking Jomo to arrange the meeting. Meeting Nelson Mandela during his first visit to Europe, in Stockholm, was very meaningful for me. Later that afternoon, Mandela addressed a gathering of ANC members and that evening the Swedish government organised a cultural event to welcome Mandela, with none other than Miriam Makeba as guest artist. What a night to close that memorable day. I left Stockholm for Athens smelling freedom in the air and convinced that changes were coming our way.

The following month on 5 April 1990, I was given a rare opportunity to meet the UN Secretary-General, Javier Perez de Quellar on 5 April 1990 in the City Hall of Athens, during his visit to Greece. I extended the ANC's appreciation and recognition for, the UN's role in supporting our struggle and the role played by the international community.

The 'Welcome Concert for Nelson Mandela' at Wembley Stadium in London, on 16 April 1990 was something out of this world. Two years earlier on 11 June 1988, artists had gathered at the same venue for Mandela's 70th Birthday Tribute Concert, demanding his release. Now he was here in person. The event, featuring 60 musicians, comedians and actors, ran for 11 hours and was watched by around 600 million people in over 60 countries. Nelson Mandela's presence made it a universal celebration, with 72 000 people in the stadium. Mandela's charisma was immense.

Financial Challenges

I had come back to Greece mainly to do political work, but also to join my family. My political work had no financial backup. Under normal circumstances, the offices of the ANC chief representatives, were funded by the local host, either the government as in Sweden, or the Anti-apartheid movement, as was the case in the UK. In Greece this sort of support did not exist. While the EEDDA provided offices, it did not have funds to subsidise my private needs or support my family. I was not alone; I had a wife and a baby. I did not know that this would be the situation before I came to Greece, and the matter had not been raised between the ANC and EEDDA. It was out of the question for me to abandon the political work I was doing and my family and return to Zambia.

I decided to carry on with my work. This would prove to be detrimental to my private life. To address my financial situation, I flew back to Lusaka in 1989 to discuss my difficulties with the Secretary – General and the Treasurer-General. They understood the situation and agreed that the political support provided by the Greek government both in Greece and at the United Nations was extremely important. The fact that I was with my family was considered positively and the Treasurer- General asked me to fly back to Athens via London so that I could get some funds from the ANC treasury there.

I remember asking Ambassador Kangwa to issue me with a new travel document because the one I had used to come to Athens was either no longer valid or about to expire. I arrived in London carrying my Freedom Charter document, which is what we respectfully called our 'travelling document,' issued by the Zambian authorities to enable us to traverse the world. It gave us the freedom to move from one country to another, a privilege denied to our people back in South Africa. The passport officer pulled me aside and asked me pertinent questions: 'What is your nationality? What are you doing in Zambia? Why was the document issued in Cairo, and not in Zambia? Who will you stay with in London? What is your next destination? I explained that I was a South African, travelling from Lusaka, with a Zambian document and that from London I would travel to, Athens, where I lived.

Five countries were involved: South Africa, Egypt, Zambia, the UK and Greece. The perplexed expression on the passport control officer's face reminded me of the reality of my situation, and I was not unsympathetic. It was something of a riddle for both of us. Once the preliminary questions were dealt with, others ensued. He wanted to know about my mission in London; who I would be staying with and for how long, and who would carry the costs. I kept repeating that the ANC was responsible. I was saying this with confidence, but I had absolutely no proof that what I was saying was fact.

Finally he asked me whether I thought South Africa's problem would be resolved soon. I answered in the positive because of my conviction that our cause was just. I was pleased to be able to describe the daily lives of oppressed South Africans to an ordinary British citizen. My stay in London was only for two to three days, but I managed to meet with Pat and Sello Maqetuka again, who I last saw in Lusaka in 1987, and a few other comrades like Mafa Ngeleza, Sipho Derrick Phewa and Stanley Mngadi, before leaving for Athens.

OTHER SOUTH AFRICANS IN GREECE

The Embassy of South Africa

Since my arrival in Greece, I was conscious of my proximity to an institution that represented everything that I was fighting against, the South African regime's embassy. I was sure that my presence in the city as the ANC representative would not go unnoticed by the embassy. We represented two antagonistic and irreconcilable objectives. Atrocities perpetrated by the racist regime continued unabated. On 14 March 1982, a bomb exploded at the ANC offices in London and on 17 March, Ruth First was assassinated by a parcel bomb in Maputo. There were numerous intrusions and massacres of our people in neighbouring states. Just before my posting in Athens, there were several attempts to assassinate Godfrey Josiah Madileng Motsepe, our chief representative in the Benelux countries, based in Brussels. On 4 February 1988,[74] there was an armed attack on his offices. On 29 March 1988, Dulcie September was assassinated in Paris.

I was fully aware of the dangers and came to Greece psychologically prepared for any eventuality, but I kept this to myself so as not to cause concern. I was therefore not surprised that when things started happening in South Africa, the embassy and I were giving conflicting interpretations of agendas and events. For example, the agreement among the People's Republic of Angola, the Republic of Cuba, and the Republic of South Africa (Tripartite Accord) was signed in December 1988. This agreement, also known as the Three Powers Accord or New York Accords, granted Namibia independence from South Africa and ended the direct involvement of foreign troops in the Angolan Civil War. Then there were 'talks about talks' in South Africa, especially with regard to the regime engaging with Mandela. The embassy saw these overtures as an expression of goodwill by the Pretoria regime towards black people in South Africa.

Under the headline 'Mandela Visits Botha Secretly, Pretoria Guarded on Release Prospects,' the Athens News of 11 July, 1989, reported about the first ever meeting between Mandela and President Botha. The meeting had occurred on 5 July and I pointed out to the newspaper that the headline was misleading because readers might think that Mandela had escaped prison to see Botha. For a prisoner to meet a state president, proper arrangements needed to be in place, which I assumed was the case. I pointed out that Mandela remained a prisoner and prisoners can never negotiate. The embassy's response was that I didn't have a clue what I was talking about.

When Mandela was finally released in February 1990, the embassy, replying to a Greek anti-apartheid citizen who questioned why Mandela was jailed in the first place, stated:

> *It is futile, at this time, to argue the merits and demerits of the imprisonment of Nelson Mandela in 1964. The fact is, he was sentenced to life imprisonment for plotting the violent overthrow of the lawfully elected government of South Africa after a trial in open court in which he had pleaded guilty to three of the four charges levelled against him. The fact is that he has been released now.*[25]

I decided that no further exchanges with the embassy were necessary. The embassy was there to represent the government of the day and it was time to focus on what was unfolding back at home.

My Countrymen

Ethiopian Airlines and Air Zimbabwe were the few airlines from Africa, besides Egypt Air and other North African airlines, which flew to Athens. It was such a pleasant surprise to encounter a black South African who was also a pilot; in Athens. I was filled with joy and pride to meet with Zukile Nomvete who was with Ethiopian Airlines. In those days the ANC was still regarded by some in Europe as a terrorist organisation and here we had some of its cadres transporting hundreds of people with such great responsibility. I was excited to find out that there were more South African pilots who worked with Zukile and flew to Athens. I later met with Tunki Petje and Tshepo Peege. The greatest excitement was to see my cousin, Happy Bhembe, now a crew member with Air Zimbabwe. We had not seen one another since we separated in Dar 11 years ago, in 1976.

My interaction with my compatriots relieved the dreadful loneliness I experienced while I was in Athens and made life a bit more bearable. Each time they landed in Athens, they spent three or four days in town; enough time to apprise one another of what was being reported in the media about happenings inside South Africa, and what was going on in Zimbabwe and Ethiopia or in Africa in general.

They also brought me good news that 'Koli' (MK Gazelle) was now based in Ethiopia. On one occasion when Zukile was in Athens I introduced him to Saki Macozoma, who was representing the SACC, at the AWEPAA conference.

I would share information about the happenings in Greece and Europe and the challenges I was facing. At that time the upheavals in Eastern Europe were beginning to be a matter of concern. I remember saying that when the Berlin Wall came down, it would be the end of socialism in Eastern Europe. The socialism we knew in the GDR, was the main pillar of the socialist block. If the Berlin Wall collapsed, the entire system would disintegrate.

By the time I left the GDR in 1987, citizens were beginning to raise questions about the political direction the country was following. Student gatherings on Saturday mornings at the square of the cosmonauts (Kosmonautenplatz), now called the Eichplatz, were a weekly occurrence. Students wanted to know what directives were coming from authorities in Moscow.

After the death of Leonid Brezhnev in 1985, the situation changed dramatically in the Soviet Union. Within a short space of time new leaders positioned themselves. Yuri Andropov, Konstantin Chernenko and the Mikhail Gorbachev questioned the trajectory of the socialist state and proposed changes, sending shock waves, not only in socialist countries but throughout the world.

International news and world cameras focussed on what was happening, especially in Hungary, which bordered the West, and the GDR. In mid Europe, besides the GDR, Czechoslovakia (now Czechia and Slovakia), Hungary and Yugoslavia (now Slovenia, Croatia, Bosnia-Herzegovina, Serbia and North Macedonia) all bordered the West. East European refugees, mostly from East Germany, flocked to Hungary and exerted so much pressure there that the authorities yielded, and dismantled the electric fence along Hungary's border with Austria. Historically this was the first crack of the 'Iron Curtain' in June 1989.

We spent days and nights together, analysing the global situation and connecting it to what was happening in South Africa. My compatriots sometimes spent part of their holidays in Greece. For example, Zukile came to Athens on holiday with his wife Sibulelo and their daughter Phumla.

South African Students

Thessaloniki, in Northern Greece is the second main economic, industrial, commercial and political hub and is regarded as Greece's cultural capital. One day a Zimbabwean student, who called himself 'Mjozi' otherwise known as Evans Ndevu and a student in Thessaloniki, came to EEDDA's offices to see me. I was careful with such unsolicited encounters. During our conversation, he often switched from English to Ndebele, which he occasionally mixed with Zulu, to make an impression on me. He told me he had read about me in the *Athens News*, the only English daily newspapers available. After engaging with him I realised, that even if he had been sent to me with malicious intentions, I could handle him. He told me about South African students that were studying in Thessaloniki, and after he had visited Athens, I decided to visit Thessaloniki to meet with these students.

I waited for one of my compatriots who worked with Ethiopian Airlines to arrive in Athens and accompany me. Zukile arrived first and we travelled together by bus to Thessaloniki; a long seven-hour trip.

The first group of black students from South Africa that had arrived in Greece in September 1988 included Wonderful Mothiba and Steve Molapo. A year later, in September 1989, the second group arrived. Kaizer Makole (Dr) was in this group. The students in the group were aged between 18 and 24 years, with the majority coming from townships around Johannesburg and Pretoria, and a few from Bantustans like Bophuthatswana. They had scholarships from the Greek government issued by the Greek Embassy in South Africa.

They were studying courses ranging from English literature and international law to medical studies, at the Aristotle University of Thessaloniki. It was the first time since leaving South Africa in 1976 that I had met students of that age outside Africa and the socialist countries. All of them were in Europe for the first time. I could not help thinking about my own experiences when I left South Africa at that tender age. Unlike those of us who went into exile, the students knew they had safe homes to return to.

I had to be careful about how I introduced myself so that they didn't think I was there to recruit them into a banned organisation. I told them honestly that I was a member of the ANC and its chief representative in Greece. At the same time, I told them that I was not visiting them as the ANC chief representative, but simply as a fellow South African who had heard about their presence from Mjozi. I was interested to know who they were, how they were catered for, their well-being, and of course how things were back at home. I also wanted to tell them about what I had been doing outside South Africa. From our interaction it became clear that they had not been exposed to international politics, especially that of banned organisations like the ANC. A few among them were interested in knowing about the ANC as I expected they would be.

I decided that for this first meeting I was going to give them a general picture of the ANC objectives. In doing so I had to tell them that the ANC had been formed in reaction to the unjust conditions under which black South Africans lived. I briefly touched on the reasons that led to the banning of political parties, and I quickly moved on to the international arena and how the world is behind the majority of South Africans, who because of Apartheid laws, are not part of the political system. I emphasised the importance of education, and told them how pleased I was to see them here in Greece, an experience that only a few were exposed to, since South Africa had been isolated for so long.

Zukile spoke about how South Africa had not been able to realise its full potential because of the oppression of black people, and that their presence in Greece would expose them to things they didn't know about their own country. In Greece, they would realise that they were equal and would not be treated differently because they were Africans or belonged to other nationalities. He too stressed the importance of acquiring an education outside of South Africa and the opportunities that lay ahead of them if they did well in their studies. We left them in good spirits. I had brought with me a few copies of *Sechaba*, which I gave them so that they could be informed about what was happening in the organisation.

On my next visit to Thessaloniki, I was joined by Tunki. I took the liberty of briefing the students about developments in the Southern African region, especially the upcoming independence of Namibia. I gave a background of the Harare Declaration, adopted in August of that year, and its implications for South Africa. I explained the vital role of the ANC in all these developments. I sensed that some of the students were interested in hearing more. We spent more time answering their questions and making sure that we did not leave them in doubt about what was unfolding in South Africa. I met them again after the unbanning of the ANC, PAC and SACP and my trip to Sweden when Mandela held meetings with Tambo and the ANC leadership. I saw how they were moved by these developments and this time they wanted to hear more about what was likely to happen in the future.

I was informed that they had already established a South African Students Union (SASU). This was normal with foreign students in any country. The main focus was on ensuring that South African students found accommodation and that their living conditions were up to scratch, and most importantly that they received their monthly stipends on time. With time they realised they needed to augment their stipends by doing part-time jobs in restaurants or in the construction industry. During summer holidays, some students worked in restaurants and in the farming sector on Greek islands like

Halkidiki. In a bold move, SASU adopted a resolution to engage the Greek community and students, about the political discourse in South Africa.

This resulted in actions calling for the end of apartheid, the release of all political prisoners and the holding of elections for all South Africans to decide their future. There were a few students who rejected these activities for fear of being arrested when they returned home. Some of these were from the 'homelands' and had a negative attitude towards the ANC. Kaizer Makone and Steven Molapo were very keen to engage me more on the ANC and its work. They made sure that SASU remained organised, and a force to manage student's issues while at the same time raising political consciousness in the student body. They also established cultural activities to support their political work.

My Divorce

The funding I received from the ANC was not enough to sustain me and my family. Since I came to live in Greece, Anna and I had agreed that she should continue with her work at the GDR embassy in Athens. I would assist by caring for Dimitra in the mornings and go to the office in the afternoons, when she was back from work. During the summer season people worked from morning to midday and took a siesta before returning to work. At the embassy where Anna worked, staff worked in the mornings and knocked off just after the lunch hour.

This arrangement worked perfectly for me, and gave me an opportunity to bond well with Dimitra. I was going by the book – when to feed her and when to let her play alone and when I had to keep her busy. One day Anna took me by surprise and told me that our arrangement was being questioned by her family. I, as a man, staying at home and looking after Dimitra was traditionally not acceptable in Greek society. She proposed that I consider looking for a job in Greece. I was totally taken aback by this. Anna was a professional and a modern woman. However, I observed that the Greeks were very traditional and conservative people and I had accepted this. For example, when we went out for lunch or dinner at a restaurant, when finished, Anna would take out her purse from her handbag and give me the money under the table, so that it looked as if I was paying for the meal. In Greece it was taboo for a woman to pay the bill. The first time I experienced this I was shocked. I always hated this moment whenever we went out for a meal or a drink. However, I had to accept it as I had respect for Anna and the norms in Greece. I didn't anticipate that this tradition would have direct consequences for me and my relationship with my own child.

I asked her what work she thought I could do. Anything, she said, 'Even selling from a kiosk'. I pointed out that this would not suit the work that I was supposed to be doing. I could teach at the university but there was no way I could teach in English and learning professional Greek for this purpose would consume a lot of time and take me away from the mobilisation and solidarity work I was involved in. Speaking a language was different from teaching in that language. In Germany I did both, I learned the language and I could teach too, but this was not an option in Greece, We discussed this repeatedly and I could see that it was becoming stressful and troubling our relationship. Her family wanted me to consider doing any job, no matter what, but not stay at home and look after the baby.

I suspected her uncle was behind this. He had only visited us once after Dimitra was born in 1987, and Anna had never suggested that we pay him a visit. I told Anna I was committed to the liberation of my country. This was my main mission and the reason why I joined the ANC. If I could have found a paying job in Athens, and have time for my political work I would have done so. I gave examples of people like the professors Dennis Brutus and Kader Asmal, who were leading figures in the fight against apartheid while being employed as lecturers. I asked her if she would be prepared to come with me to Zambia because we would not have to worry about traditions and our welfare; the ANC would look after us. I would then be engaged politically to free my country. She made it clear that this would not work for her.

I tried to convince her that my commitment was for life and no compromise was possible. We did not see things the same way. She understood my point but her family did not. Eventually we talked about nothing else and it became evident that we would have to live separately for the sake of peace.

Anna insisted that living separately would not solve our problems and we should get divorced. We both agreed to the divorce, and that Anna would draft the divorce papers. There was one proviso; that I would have access to Dimitra.

This was the most difficult period since our marriage. I could never have imagined this situation. We were enlightened individuals in terms of our world views. From my perspective, the state of affairs had to do with how Anna's society, which by virtue of my living in Greece was my society too, expected us to live. We were not poor in the sense that we had no food at home; neither were we rich. I made no demand on Anna financially as she was the breadwinner, and there was Dimitra to look after.

I wanted to leave Greece immediately. The ANC would certainly keep me busy either in Lusaka or in another country. After assessing the situation and speaking to some Greek friends, I was persuaded I should not leave when the pressure on South Africa was intensifying. Christos and Anika, agreed to accommodate me at their flat in town. I left my family home in the second half of 1989, just over a year after arriving in Athens.

I saw Dimitra on weekends. I would fetch her on Saturdays in the morning and take her back in the afternoon. We went to the parks or children's playing grounds and spent some quality time together. A new life had begun for me in Greece, and I adjusted accordingly.

Lack of funds forced me to again fly to Zambia at the end of 1989. While waiting to engage with the leadership, I heard that Koli (Gazelle) was also around. I was excited at the prospect of reconnecting with him again, but this was not to be. I was told that he had been arrested by the Zambian police for shooting at local citizens. I learned that he was visiting Lusaka from Addis on work-related matters. He had fired shots at people that he suspected of breaking into his place where he was temporarily staying; and stealing some of his belongings. This happened at a time when such petty crimes of theft from ANC houses by Zambian citizens had become a daily occurrence. ANC people had been warned that the authorities intended to arrest anyone found to be involved in such incidents. Koli was detained.

The conditions in a prison in Zambia, as in many African countries, were far from ideal. When I visited Gazelle, accompanied by Brian (MK 'Scratch'), he was very emaciated, a sign of not eating properly. I did not like what I saw. Between us there was an iron grid marking the end of freedom for him. On his left and right, and behind him even skinnier bodies were cramped together in the confined space. They begged for attention, shouting to the friends or relatives who were visiting them. I was forced to shout so that Koli, could hear what I was saying. There were tears in my eyes as I touched his hands for a moment, at a loss about what was happening. Visiting time was over and we left with the sound of the iron gates clanging behind us. It was Brian who told me about the events that led to Koli's arrest. Brian and I visited Koli again before I left Zambia. I took some food with me this time. I was extremely worried about what would happen to Koli in the following days and months after I had left. Again, after so many years,

Chapter Four

I parted with Koli under miserable circumstances.

I returned to Greece in mid-January 1990. Koli was eventually released after a year or so. He went back to Addis, where he had been before he was detained.

Just before my departure, a major event took place in Lusaka. The recently freed ANC leaders, Govan Mbeki, Walter Sisulu, Ahmed Kathrada, Elias Motsoaledi, Raymond Mhlaba, Andrew Mlangeni, Wilton Mkwayi among others, arrived on 15 January. There was such jubilation and emotions were high when the leaders were welcomed at Mulungushi Hall by ANC members to thunderous applause. Later that evening, the red carpet was laid out at a state reception given by President Kenneth Kaunda. I came back to Athens rejuvenated. I went via London, so that I could get some funds. I was now convinced that my days of exile were numbered, but it was not yet clear how this would unfold.

As an ANC person in Greece, four times a year I was summoned to the main police headquarters to be questioned by the security branch of the Greek police. At some stage I suspected that they were collaborating with their South African counterparts but it never worried me. The bombing of our offices in places like London and the assassination of my comrade Dulcie September, in Paris, affected me badly, but I was consoled by my conviction that our cause for freedom and justice was right. Now that my marital status had changed. I wondered how the news would be received by the Greek police. When I reported to the police station I told them all was well. I am not sure if they knew I was now divorced.

With the unbanning of liberation movements and the release of Mandela in February 1990, I continued with my political work.

The Birth of Nelson

I wanted to make sure that what I had initiated in Greece didn't suffer because of my new living circumstances, and the challenge of having to squat with another family. Members of EEDDA and many other the people were always ready to assist me in whatever project I was involved with. I had support from the former director Nikos Fotiadis, and the secretary, Electra Georgula. Others like Evgenia Papamakariou, Maria Gazi, Eli Matezi and journalists like Dina Vagena and Constoula Sclavenitis were always of assistance. Chritos Theodoropoulos and Anika Theodoropoulos went all out to make my stay comfortable with them. There was Nikolas Voulelis from the United Nations and Olga Fachuridu in Thessaloniki who gave me support. Uta and Georgios Loumiotis – who studied in the GDR during our stay there remained friends with both Anna and I. Panagiotis Dimitropoulos, another friend from Greece, would check on me whenever he was in Athens from Germany. Vassilikis 'Vasso' Polymeridou was a staunch supporter of our struggle, and her sister Catherine (Tina), sometimes joined me after collecting Dimitra and we went to the park together.

I tried to make things as normal as possible for myself. It was always fun to be with Dimitra, especially when other people were around. She was an active and energetic child. Taking her on the bus, was always a mission as she engaged with everyone in the bus. When we reached our destination, and the bus was full, I had to tell the driver that I needed to retrieve my daughter from the rear of the bus. The bus driver would shout, 'Please give the daughter back!'

Lakis Halkias with his wonderful wife, Aleka, would on certain occasions invite me to their house for a delicious meal. Thereafter I would join Lakis at his performances in various clubs and restaurants in town.

Thekla Metaxa was a member of EEDDA and from time to time she assisted me with my solidarity projects, especially during the preparations for the Afrika Now Concert. We worked closely together and our closeness developed into an intimate relationship. During this period Thekla fell pregnant.

From the time of the unbanning of the ANC and the release of Mandela, things started moving faster at home. To wait for *Sechaba*, and other media to be informed of new developments and what was happening at home was no longer sufficient. I was eager to get back home. The Groote Schuur Minute of 4 May 1990, was followed by a meeting at which practical negotiations were discussed, including indemnity for returning exiles and the release of political prisoners.

Then came the Pretoria Minute of 6 August, 1990, that addressed the suspension of the armed struggle by the ANC. This was unexpected and went against what the ANC had pronounced in earlier statements. All these developments raised anxiety levels to unprecedented altitudes. The question of amnesty was very worrying.

I decided I had to move nearer to South Africa, and I decided I would fly to Zimbabwe to be closer to home when addressing the amnesty matter. In early November I packed up lock, stock and barrel and departed for Harare. Nelson, was born on 27 December 1990 just a month after I left Greece.

Chapter Five
MY RETURN HOME

ZIMBABWE (1990–1991)

One step closer to home!

Harare

As usual, I arrived in Harare and reported to the ANC offices. The chief representative at the time was Max Mlonyeni. I introduced myself and we talked about the happenings at home, including the amnesty issue. He informed me about the communication from our newly opened offices in Johannesburg, and the arrangements to inform all our external offices of the daily lists dispensed by the government of people who qualified for amnesty. At the time, this was a bizarre signal of things that were to come. The question everyone was asking was: Amnesty for what? Things began unfolding over the coming weeks and months.

I had hoped it would not take long before I crossed over to my homeland. I was mistaken. The amnesty issue became sticky, and I had to give up going to the office every day to check whether I was one of the lucky ones that day. I wrote to Thabo Mbeki, the head of the Department of International Affairs (DIA) in Johannesburg, informing him of my return from Athens and advising that I was in Zimbabwe waiting for the amnesty papers before returning home.

The Secretary-General, Alfred Nzo, passed through Harare in December and when we met, he asked me to attend a conference in Libya. The conference, held in Tripoli, turned out to be training on the teachings in the Green Book.[1] Muammar Gaddafi's people engaged us on the contents of the Green Book for a whole week, with a promise that we would get to meet Gaddafi himself. I had, during my studies of philosophy, come across the doctrines from the Green Book but this was the first time that I was engaging directly with these ideas. It was a thought-provoking gathering that helped me understand Gaddafi's philosophy. Sabelo Phama, who was now the commander of APLA, and Barney Muntu Norman Hlatshwayo (Ret. Gen. Hlatshwayo), who I last saw in Tanzania in 1976, were there on behalf of the PAC. We had flown together from Harare. This being my first visit to Libya, I learned a lot about the country and enjoyed the thick camel's milk which I was exposed to for the first time. There were people from a few African countries with us in the training. The promised meeting with Gaddafi never took place. I didn't know at the time that in my later life and career I was to meet him several times, and I was disappointed

I returned to Harare to find that there was still no amnesty clearance. The year ended and 1991 began. I was able to observe how Zimbabweans were faring ten years after independence. I was impressed by the school system and how the local television and other media produced educational programmes to augment teaching in the countryside. I even followed certain educational episodes myself.

Reports and news coming from home about various political and social developments in the country left me with many questions. There were incidents of arrests and kidnappings of people returning from exile. I was convinced that returning home was not going to be smooth sailing. I waited and waited. On some weekends, I visited my cousin Nomsa Mbatha in Bulawayo. She had married Tony Mumbengwegwi, a Zimbabwean medical doctor, who studied in Germany at the same time that she was there. They had three sons named Tapiwa, Tafara and Tatenda. I used to enjoy calling out their names one after the other since they sounded very melodic. I also enjoyed the five-hour trip by bus from Harare through the countryside. The roads were well-maintained then and despite general challenges, the countryside had potential for developmental projects.

In Harare I was able to reconnect with Tunki, Tshepo and my

cousin Happy again. I also befriended some Zimbabweans in the city who were part of the elite running the state machinery; people like Jacob Siketho Mukasa (alias Panic), an accomplished engineer in energy and brother of Brian Mukasa, the landlord of the cottage where I stayed in the suburb of Marlborough. Jacob spoke a bit of Zulu and was well-connected to the governing party, the ZANU-PF, and to the intelligence structures of the Central Intelligence Organisation (CIO). He knew every corner of Harare and all the people around, and I felt I was in good hands every time we were together.

Out of the blue, at the end of March, I came across my name on the amnesty list that was faxed from our Johannesburg offices. I immediately began preparations for going home. With the assistance of the International Organisation for Migration (IOM), within a short space of time I had secured a ticket and could ship some of my belongings – mainly books – to South Africa. I agreed to accompany about five other comrades on a flight to South Africa. All of them had been injured during their time in exile or training in Angola and were disabled; some of them in wheelchairs. In early April 1991 we drove off to the Harare airport.

MY REPATRIATION AND HOMECOMING (1991 – 1994)

As we were approaching the airport, I felt overwhelmed by the excitement of leaving Zimbabwe for my own country. At the same time, with all the stories I had heard about people being arrested or kidnapped at Jan Smuts Airport (now OR Tambo International Airport), I was asking myself what I would do if this happened to me. Would I scream for help? Would I fight back and cause a fuss at the airport? I decided to let it be. Once I touched home soil it would be okay.

The one-hour and thirty-minute flight felt like a whole day. I spoke little in the plane, wondering who would be waiting for me at the airport. My family had told me that someone was going to fetch me. Since arriving in Harare, I had from time to time called home to make my family aware that I was in Zimbabwe and that I was preparing to return home, depending on how the amnesty process went. What did Jan Smuts Airport look like? When I left in 1976, I had never been there, or for that matter, to any airport. Was there going to be drama or not? The gap of almost 15 years away from home was narrowing by hours, minutes and then seconds, and then the plane touched down on the tarmac at Jan Smuts.

I was one of the last passengers to leave the plane as I was accompanying comrades who needed assistance to disembark. I remained calm. I was holding the passports belonging to the comrades I was with. SAA personnel came to assist those needing wheelchairs, and we were taken straight to the immigration desk for our documents to be stamped. As we approached the exit gates, I saw throngs of people waiting, and as I got nearer, I identified my mother first, then my sister Nini, and my brother, Fana. There were some relatives, neighbours and children around them. I had to first part with my comrades, whose relatives were also there to meet them with great excitement at their homecoming. I gave their documents to their families and made sure each one had been met. I was greeted with hugs from members of my family. Others in the welcoming party introduced themselves, but my mind didn't register anything except the overwhelming excitement of arriving home and seeing my family at last.

On the drive home along one of the highways, I sat in the front seat of one of the two kombis that ferried us. My mother asked if I still remembered this highway, but there were no highways when I left the country, although I had a hazy memory of the beginning of the construction of the Soweto highway to town via Booysens in around 1975. Throughout my life in exile I had never imagined a highway. Now I was really impressed by the smooth ride from the airport to Soweto. I silently registered that this was the South Africa we were fighting for, and I was now back to finish the last bit before we were fully liberated and in control of our destiny. We entered Soweto and as we went past the Baragwanath Hospital (now Chris Hani Baragwanath Hospital), the biggest hospital in Africa, everything fell into place.

By the time we reached our street in Rockville, I felt as if I was daydreaming. Finally, the kombi stopped at the gate of number 2018 Budaza Street. What a feeling to be back home! People who had come to see this boy, this man who had disappeared in 1976 were waiting for us to arrive. Nieces and nephews I had not yet met were waiting to see this uncle they had heard about but never seen. His name had only been mentioned in special family gatherings or in whispers at night, after endless police raids. Among the people gathered at the house, there were neighbours, parents, brothers and sisters who came to enquire about their sons, daughters and family members who had also disappeared in 1976 and in subsequent years. To my surprise, I heard about the disappearance of some people for the first time. I didn't know that they had also skipped and left the country.

Whenever a name was mentioned, I would think carefully before I gave an answer, as I was cautious not to give false information about anyone.

I occupied centre stage at this special reception and the jubilation was palpable. I was among people who had no picture or knowledge of what life in exile was like. The questions that were thrown at me, created an image of exile as one big country, one house and one home, where people met and knew each other. There was no time to try and explain or rectify false impressions. I simply didn't have answers to many of the questions I was asked. I needed time, days if not months or years, to explain what exile was like, how we lived, what we could and could not do, and how my 15 years away from home were spent and experienced.

My elder sister, Siza, had done what she did best by preparing various scrumptious dishes for my homecoming. It was the best meal I had eaten for many moons. After prayers, which preceded the meal, and singing, which accompanied such special occasions, I consumed the delicious food. I couldn't quite believe what was happening. Throughout my first meal at home, people arrived and left and then others arrived with greetings and cries of happiness. I was asked how it felt to be home and whether I still recognised this face or that one. I was shocked by how many faces had disappeared from my memory, and how this phenomenon impacted on me.

It felt as though I was waking up from an awfully long sleep and dream. Had I adequately prepared for this homecoming? Not at all! By the time evening came, so many people had arrived and left and I had hardly moved out of my family yard. Now and then, I stood up to stretch my legs, wandering around to the back of the house, which had dramatically changed since I had been away. As soon as I was on my feet, someone else would arrive and I was called back to the dining room. At one stage Refilwe Tshabalala turned up and I felt as though I last saw her yesterday. When everyone had left, it was time to engage the little ones; the nephews and nieces. The nieces were the most inquisitive. At one stage Nciki (Ncikazi Merylin Dlamini), Siza's last born, who was then almost three-years old, asked me: 'Uncle, where are you going to sleep?'

Thando (Noluthando Tshabalala), Maggie's last born, then almost five-years of age, giggled uncontrollably.

Pointing at the full, bright moon, I asked: 'Do you see that moon up there?'

'Yes', they responded, looking up, obviously confused about how the moon was connected to the question that was put to me. 'As soon as everyone in the house goes to bed, a stepladder from the moon will fall down and I will climb up the ladder and go and sleep inside the moon.'

'Ooh!' They squeaked simultaneously, full of smiles and visibly baffled. They decided there and then that they were going to wait and see this spectacle. This uncle has brought wonders with him, they must have told themselves. I felt cornered but I was enjoying every minute of it. I felt that the 15 years of an uncertain life in exile was bearing fruit in my interactions with these smart and cheeky little ones. By the time people were gone they had long fallen asleep next to me and had to be carried away to their beds.

There were backrooms in the yard that were built during my absence, and I went to sleep in one of them. Maggie treated me like a king, as this was her sleeping place. I felt proud of her. I slept like a log and was up early to catch the sensation of the early morning breeze at home in Rockville. Oh, it felt great to be home!

By the time the girls woke up I was loitering in the yard, and they came rushing up to me and asked, how my sleep in the moon was. With a stern face, I let them know that I was disappointed that they went to sleep without watching me ascending to the moon. Then I told them that I had just landed from there and they missed it by seconds. They looked puzzled.

I assured them that I was going to make sure the spectacular event was live for them that same evening. I could sense how pleased they were to hear this from me – the novel uncle.

Neighbours who heard about my arrival started coming and things carried on from where we left off the previous day. I didn't want to rush things. I was eager to see the ANC offices in town, but I told myself that I must take it easy. All along I kept asking about family members and neighbours and I would be reminded that so and so was deceased. This one passed away just after my departure and that one was recently buried. It would take more than a day for all this information to sink in. I repeatedly asked about people who I had already been told were no longer alive. I discovered that the brain doesn't record experiences that happened from a distance and outside of one's immediate environment in the same way. Days and months after my return, I found myself enquiring about people who had passed away when I was in exile. I felt embarrassed by this, but everyone seemed to understand that my mind was adapting to an environment I had been disconnected from for 15 years. I was comforted by the fact that nobody thought I was being deliberately forgetful.

A few days after my return, I ventured to town by taxi and visited the ANC offices. The offices were in a building belonging to the Munich Reinsurance Company of Africa on Sauer Street. The ANC occupied two floors of this building. I met a few comrades who had been in exile, and it was a good feeling to be among familiar faces. I came across people from the UDF structures and the mass movement, whose faces I recognised from the media.

This proved I was back in my country, and I immediately felt comfortable about the environment. I enquired about the offices of the Secretary-General, and was directed to his office. He was pleased to see me and informed me that I should start work the following Monday. Sindiso Mfenyana and Papi Moloto were already working in the Secretary-General's office, and I was to join them. The preparations for the national conference of the ANC, taking place in Durban in a few weeks' time, were already underway.

While at the ANC offices I was told about resettlement money that was to be collected from the offices of the South African Council of Churches (SACC), where the National Coordination Committee on Repatriation (NCCR) was operating from. The NCCR was formed in May 1990 as a nonpartisan body, and consisted of members of the ANC, PAC, AZAPO and church representatives from the SACC. I had no idea how much was being offered for resettlement. I didn't have a cent to my name, I had no identity document, no bank account, and no home of my own – there was nothing in my name. What about personal security? Did I need security? This question was left unanswered.

I had been told where to take a taxi back to Rockville. On the way back home, I wondered when the negotiations would take place and how the ANC would handle them. The taxi dropped me at the corner of Vundla Drive and Budaza Street and I was back home. 'Didn't you get lost?' Someone asked and I responded: 'Me, get lost?' I got messages that so and so, from such and such a place, had come to visit me and had waited and left, promising to come back the following day. This happened from time to time when I was away from home. It was fine with me.

There were certain things I couldn't share with anyone regarding my future plans. I wondered, for example, how long I would work for the ANC and whether there were opportunities for working outside the ANC. What about a teaching career at a university? What about suggesting that the ANC establishes a school of its own, like SOMAFCO in Tanzania? What about establishing a political school to bring all the segments of the mass movement together? Clearly, there were different experiences of the struggle as it unfolded over the years, and there were going to be different approaches going forward. Some had remained at home and worked underground, some were imprisoned on Robben Island and other jails, while others were bringing experiences from exile. These questions preoccupied me, but I didn't discuss them.

What about the SACP? How strong was its influence in South Africa? How deeply did the masses of our people understand the difference between the ANC and the SACP? Was the SACP expressing and interpreting the political situation in the country correctly? What about its cadres, especially those who remained and were operating in the country? How well grounded was their Marxist interpretation of ideas? How were these ideas affected by the collapse of socialism all over Eastern Europe? Was the party going to operate above ground and recruit outside the ANC? What about the trade unions? Were they aware of the mammoth task ahead of them? Were they going to continue to be in alliance with the ANC, or would they be independent?

The youth of the country, both black and white, had suffered most from what happened in the country. They fought each other in different and opposite trenches. White boys had been conscripted into the police and defence forces. They saw black people as terrorists and their enemies. They killed them in South Africa and attacked them across the borders, although some whites refused conscription for various reasons. The black youth had been traumatised by the events of the past decades. The school boycotts, the states of emergency, the street fights with the police and the rampant killings throughout the country must have left imprints and trails in the psyches of many.

I mulled over these issues and as I did so, asked myself more questions. My immediate concern was to make a contribution to my organisation, so that we could negotiate for the principles of the

Freedom Charter to be incorporated into a new constitution for the country.

My Comrades and Friends

It was good to be back home but I couldn't help thinking about the friends I left the country with in 1976. We left in groups, never alone. The song, 'Sobashiyaabazali!' was on our lips. It encapsulated our mission in the outside world.

> 'Sobashiy' abazaliekhaya
> Savuma, sangenakwamanyeamazwe.
> Baba noMama,
> Laphosingazi' khona
> Baba noMama
> Silweli' nkululeko!'

> 'We left our parents at home.
> We agreed, and we moved into other territories.
> Dad and Mom
> Where we knew nothin'
> Dad and Mom
> We are fighting for freedom!

Our homecoming, which we had longingly anticipated, was a very different experience from our departure. Apart from those repatriated from Tanzania by the UNHCR, who were mainly students, most exiles came back alone or in small groups like me. In the 1970s, when we left the country, we were full of daring and willing to make every sacrifice to ensure that the struggle for justice was won. We left secretly, without informing the people we loved: our parents, siblings, girlfriends and boyfriends that we were skipping the country and crossing borders into other countries. Our loved ones welcomed us and celebrated our return, and we were overwhelmed to be united once again with the people we had left behind. However, the way in which we had imagined victory would come to our shores was very different to the reality. We had changed in many ways, and between 1976 when we left and 1991 when we returned, the people, the country, the territory had also changed.

While freedom and democracy were in the pipeline, the political climate was very tense. The country had been politically ravaged and conflicts and warfare were widespread, later intensifying into massacres. Sadly, most of this took place within the black communities, although there were running skirmishes with the government's security forces.

We had grown up in several ways too. Many people, both inside and outside the country, had matured politically and were reasoning quite differently about the situation in the country. While some were cautiously optimistic; others saw doom and gloom everywhere. Some exiles returning with their families, had been physically scarred in the rough bushes of Africa, and the psyches of countless returning exiles had also been scarred. Many did not make it back home. The remains of bosom friends and comrades were buried in many countries of Europe, the United States, Canada, and especially in countless African countries, from south to north and east to west. Some were buried in the very lands that had accommodated us as refugees running away from the terror of the racist regime. Among these there were those who found it impossible to survive in political, economic and cultural contexts that were alien to them.

The causes of death were manifold: illness; old age; suicide; internecine fights in camps, and battles against other forces, as had happened in Angola.

In all the organisations and formations, there were those who died at the hands of people who were supposed to protect them. Death did not discriminate; young and old were not spared. We, the survivors, had to tell our families, and the families and friends of people we grew up with, that some exiles would never return.

Until I was back home, I had limited knowledge about who had left the country and who had remained. I was shocked by the number of families that came to see me, enquiring about their sons and daughters. Nearly all young men in my street and neighbourhood had followed our paths. Because of the way we left and the conditions we experienced, there was no way we could meet except by chance, as had happened to me.

Did I prepare for this homecoming? Not at all! There was no way I could have. Nothing could have prepared me for the heart-breaking discovery on my return that Koli (MK Gazelle), the one person I wanted to meet and thank for his farsightedness and the influence he had had on me, was dead.

Amid the happy welcome I received on my arrival, I was delighted to meet Mxolisi, one of my bosom friends and brother to Koli. He was as excited to see me. He enquired about the whereabouts of his elder brother and I was quick to indicate to him that Koli would be coming back in a few days' time. I knew this because of a conversation with Victor Billy Mokgatle (MK Billy Dambuza), who was with Koli in Addis Ababa. Mxolisi was delighted. It meant a lot to him to receive this news from me. I could see the anticipation and excitement in his eyes. Victor had also made me aware that Koli was not well; his health had deteriorated since he returned from Zambia. Even so, he was preparing to come back home.

While talking to Mxolisi and his sister, Rose 'Lolo', I didn't want to bother them by telling them about Koli's arrest and imprisonment in Zambia. I thought it would be better if he himself related the incident to his family. Sadly, Koli died in Addis just a few days before flying back to South Africa. This was a week after my own arrival, and it was the most devastating news that marked my return home. I couldn't imagine how I was going to communicate this tragic news to his family. Delivering the message to Mxolisi and the family was one the most challenging tasks I had had to perform. They wanted to know what had happened to Koli so suddenly. I had no answer. Did he die in hospital, or did he die in a house or in a camp? Who was there with him at the time of his death? I couldn't answer their questions.

Addis was far away and I relied on those who had lived with Koli, those that he served with in the trenches of the frontline states, those that commanded him and those he commanded himself, to say something about Koli. At that moment, I had nothing to add.

I didn't know all the people and comrades that had worked with him. Some had come back and some were still in exile.

Friends and comrades like Brian (MK Scratch), Siphiwe 'Gebuza' Nyanda (Ret. Gen. Nyanda and ambassador), George Sipho Nene (ambassador) and others, came to see, speak to and comfort the family. It was as difficult for them as it was for me, although I was the only one who had known Koli and his family well before we left the country. I tried to explain that Koli had faced an unfortunate situation in Zambia, linked to a shooting incident which resulted in his detention. I had to describe the conditions of the Zambian jail and how Koli's health was affected by this. As I was doing this, I knew that what I was saying was not easing the family's pain about the death of their brother and son.

The most agonising time was completing the paperwork and making preparations for the body to be repatriated to South Africa. When Koli's body was finally brought back to South Africa, arrangements were made for his funeral.

The funeral was a very sad moment for me. I had hoped that Koli and I would be able to share whatever moments we had missed when we were in exile. We bade farewell to Koli, another giant that was going silently. I promised myself to continue in his footsteps so that his sacrifices were not in vain and would be known by future generations. His encouraging words to me, highlighting education as the key to the liberation of our country will stay with me forever. Koli embodied ANC policy in all his interactions. He had been a good ambassador and spokesperson for the cause of the struggle and the ANC. He dared to enter unfamiliar territory and was able to motivate and capture the minds of many during the 1976 uprisings and beyond. He did his training in Novo Catengue in Angola and was later sent to the Lenin party school in Moscow, to continue his political education. When I heard that he had been roped into the department of information and publicity, I knew that this was what he was good at, and it reminded me of the days at home when we used to listen to Radio Freedom. He served in the frontline, in Mozambique, and apparently even distributed literature to various embassies located in Maputo.

The signing of the Nkomati Accord in 1984 between Mozambique and South Africa resulted in Koli's unit – and many of our people operating from Mozambique – being kicked out of the country. He left for Tanzania and was later deployed to Lusaka. After a few years he set up office in Addis Ababa. When Godfrey Josiah Madileng Motsepe, who was the chief representative, left his post for South Africa, Koli doubled up as the ANC's chief representative. It was at this time that he met his death.

Just as I was trying to absorb the shock of Koli's death, the family of Selby (MK Larry Makhaya) approached me to find out if I knew anything about what had happened to him. I was expecting this, as I was close to Selby and the family knew this. I couldn't escape this encounter. As it was, I was preparing myself to meet with them to find out if they had taken note of media reports that Selby was killed by the security police in around 1981. This information came to be known in 1989 after Butana Almond Nofomela, a South African security policeman, who had been sentenced to death for murder, spilled the beans about the existence of a police assassination squad that killed opponents of the regime.

Afraid of the gallows Nofomela divulged these secrets to fellow death row prisoners, among them, Jabu 'Dubu' Masina (from Rockville) and Sibusiso Masuku, nicknamed 'Mantolo', who passed this information on to Lawyers for Human Rights (LHR).[2] While pursuing the matter with 'Dubu' and Sibusiso Masuku, LHR found out about this squad, which led to Dirk Coetzee escaping from South Africa. Coetzee corroborated Nofomela's story and the existence of the squad to Jacques Pauw, a journalist with the *Vrye Weekblad*. Coetzee also revealed more information about the gruesome slaying of civil rights lawyer Griffiths Mxenge in 1981, and disclosed that Sizwe Kondile was shot and burnt and Selby Mavuso was poisoned and then shot, and his body was burnt too.

Coetzee and Generals Jan Viktor and Jac Buchner founded Vlakplaas, the headquarters of the South African Police counter-insurgency unit in the west of Pretoria. Coetzee was the commander of Nofomela, David 'Spyker' Tshikalanga, Joe Mamasela and Brian Nqulunga. Fearing for his life, he was helped by Pauw and Max du Preez, the founder of *Vrye Weekblad*, to find his way to the ANC in exile. This information was in the media and besides the Vrye Weekblad, the *Mail & Guardian* and the *New Nation*, a popular newspaper read mostly by black people, carried these articles and exposes.

I remember very well that I was in Athens, reading the ANC News Briefings with clippings of these reports. At some stage, while reading about what happened to Selby, tears started falling from my eyes. I was at the office but nobody around me knew Selby. I felt lonely as I could not share this terrible information with anyone. It took me days and days to absorb and process the news. It was the first time I had heard what had happened to one of my bosom friends – and that was almost a decade ago.

According to Coetzee, Selby and another MK cadre were abducted from Matola, Mozambique, by the SADF Special Forces that had – under cover of darkness – entered Mozambique and attacked and killed fourteen MK fighters on 30 January 1981. When the Special Forces returned, they handed the two over to members of the Security Branch. At that time Coetzee and his people were in charge. They tried without success to recruit Selby as an askari (anti-apartheid combatant turned spy), but failed. On 11 October 1981, Coetzee, Koos Vermeulen and a few askaris drove Selby from Pretoria into the bush near Komatipoort along the Crocodile River.

It is alleged that they decided to use him as a guinea pig for a poison supplied by a certain general in police forensics. The poison was mixed in a soft drink and given to Selby. He collapsed and spent the night squirming in pain and babbling incoherently, but he didn't die. As this was going on, Cotzee and his men were braaing meat and drinking alcohol. It was said that the next morning, they tried to poison Selby again. Again, this exercise was ineffective, and they decided they would shoot him. Before this happened, Joe Mamasela chose to teach Selby how to pray.[3] He forced Selby to kneel and recite the Lord's Prayer. Selby bowed and was made to recite the prayer many times. When he stopped, Mamasela kicked him in the face while the other policemen laughed raucously. It is said that Selby fell many times while trying to kneel and recite the Lord's Prayer. This went on for hours, until his face was unrecognisable. Koos Vermeulen forced Selby and another person, called Peter Dlamini,[4] a former MK member, to lie on the ground and he shot them both in the back of the head. They then burnt their bodies on the fire they were braaiing on and threw the ashes in the Crocodile River.[5]

Did the Mavuso family know about this? Had they read the articles in the newspapers but not believed it? Were they asking me to confirm if this was true or not? How was I to handle this and where would I start? Selby's family didn't know that I had never met Selby in exile. Among the first letters from my mother, while I was in the GDR, she indicated that Fana and Selby had followed me and left the country.

Although I trusted my friends in West Germany, I decided I would not send my parents letters again to avoid getting them into more trouble if my correspondence was intercepted. With two of us in the family gone, the apartheid security police might have decided to keep my parents under strict surveillance.

Then came the correspondence from Trizzer (MK David More) in which he indicated that he was with Fana and Selby and that they were okay. I was happy to hear that they were with me in the ANC and at the same time worried that this must be putting a lot of strain on my parents. Another letter from my mother followed telling me about the rumours of Selby having been seen at John Vorster Square, and that evidently he was severely injured. His family had rushed to the police station, and been told that he had been released.

I didn't hear anything more about Selby until the newspaper reports implicating Coetzee. I wasn't aware that he was kidnapped from Maputo during the attack in January 1981. As with Koli's family, I had to be cautious about where to start and what to say to Selby's family. I told one of Selby's sisters that I would come and speak to the family. I was buying time so that I could get more information from my comrades who had returned from exile. I also asked my sister, Maggie, what people knew about Selby from the media. What had been generally accepted by our people and what was still in doubt? This was long before the TRC was established. Families relied on friends of their sons and daughters, or friends of brothers and sisters for information that they considered to be reliable and trustworthy. I was caught up in the middle of this.

The Mavuso family, like the Ngqase family and other families whose sons and daughters from my neighbourhood had left for exile, were like family to me. Selby's family came to settle in our street in around the mid-1960s. The authorities had built the Mavuso family home on an empty space between two houses. At the time there were many such empty spaces between houses in Rockville. The Mavuso family came from Orlando East. There were five children: Dobsy and Dolly, the elder sisters, followed by a brother Lesley 'Kid' and then a sister Abigail Vombo. Selby was the last born and of my age, and he was in the same class as I was at school at Ndondo.

Maggie told me that they knew what had been reported in the media about Selby. No one, meaning the authorities, had been to see the Mavuso family to explain what had happened to him. From all the information I was able to gather, I decided that I would confirm that Selby was no longer alive. It was possible that the information reported by the media was correct. I told them that with time the truth would come out. I remarked that Dirk Coetzee, the man who revealed how Selby was killed, was now with the ANC but not yet back in the country. They listened to me, but I was aware that this was not bringing any relief to their anxiety.

Notwithstanding the available information, some members of the family hoped that he might still be alive and was hiding somewhere. I did not go along with this because Coetzee's version was too convincing. The matter remained unresolved and nerve-wracking for some years. The TRC was only established in 1995 and started hearings in 1996, where Dirk Coetzee, Joe Mamasela and others once more gave their version in the killings in which they were involved.[6]

The events surrounding the death of Sakie (MK Oupa Moloi) who was killed by our own comrades in 1981 at a camp in Camalundi, Malanje, Angola was also still pending. In 1991, the ANC had not yet released the findings of the Stuart Commission Report (1984). The reports of the Skweyiya Commission (1992), the Motsuenyane Commission (1993) and the TRC (1995–1997) only came later. Again,

I had no official admission from the ANC that Sakie was killed by ANC cadres in Angola (this came out in the findings of the Stuart Commission Report). Friends and comrades like Thiza and Mandla Mangethe, who might have been able to shed some light on what had happened, were not yet back in the country.

I was not sure how the ANC intended engaging families of those that met their deaths in exile, including those who were alleged to have been killed by our own people. I told myself that senior members of the organisation would take this responsibility upon themselves. I spoke to Secretary-General Nzo, about it. He assured me that the ANC would set up a task team to deal with these matters.

Before the first internal commission was established by the ANC in 1992, there were media reports, such as the report by Paul Trewhela, Inside Quatro of July 1990, about how the ANC tortured and killed some of its own cadres in Angola on suspicion that they were secret agents, spies, agents provocateurs and hired assassins in the employ of the South African Government's security services. A group of these cadres escaped from the ANC in Tanzania and landed in South Africa in April 1990. With the assistance of sympathetic church bodies, they addressed a press conference in Johannesburg to put forward their side of the story. The event, which was attended by South African and international media, made headlines. Afterwards, another group organised itself as an association of Returned Exiles Committee (REC) and became vocal on these matters.

All these groups were making grave allegations about ANC detainees being beaten with iron bars, bicycle chains and barbed wire while they were in captivity, that there were summary executions, and that some detainees had simply disappeared without trace. It was then that President Nelson Mandela undertook on behalf of the ANC to fully investigate all these allegations. The image of the ANC was at stake before political negotiations about the future of the country started. In March 1992, the appointment of an Internal Commission of Enquiry (the Skweyiya Commission) was announced.

I decided to confide in Sakie's uncle, Garage Radebe. I told him that Sakie was killed in an ANC camp in Angola. Other members of the family wanted details from me. I was unable to provide any more detail. Like Selby's family, Sakie's family assumed that we had been together in Angola. I informed the family that I hadn't seen Sakie since we parted in Tanzania, but we did exchange letters. I said the ANC intended to address these matters as soon as it was settled in the country. I empathised with the family because my explanations didn't bring closure. Instead, they were left with a huge gap in their hearts. Another member of the family, Sakie's (Oupa) cousin, Sakie Radebe, the son of Garage Radebe, known as 'Small Sakie', had been severely tortured by the police and had brain injuries. After he and Sipho (MK Themba Mlotshwa), followed us into exile, 'Small Sakie' had decided to return home from Lesotho after a few weeks in that country. He was arrested and interrogated by the police, who decided he was a trained guerrilla and was being stubborn when he told them he knew nothing about the ANC.

The various commissions never got to the bottom of what happened to either of the two boys. When the TRC convened, the ANC submitted a comprehensive statement taking collective responsibility and Sakie's (Oupa) name was mentioned, with reference to the Stuart Commission report. Sakie's (Oupa) family never received an explanation from the ANC about his death in Angola, or any compensation from the state. The same applied to 'Small Sakie' and his family.

During the time of the TRC hearings, I was out of the country serving at the United Nations in New York from May 1995 to May 1996, and in Germany from May 1996 to August 1998.

My Family

Several members of my family had passed away while I was out of the country. My brother, Jotham, died in 1980, my father in 1981, and my grandmother in Mamelodi, Lena, in 1984.

The lives of my brothers, Joseph and Jerry, had remained largely unchanged in the 15 years that I had been away. They were both unemployed, unmarried and without children.

My elder sister, Siza, was still employed at the five-star Carlton Hotel and had retained her position as the best sous-chef on special demand. Her character as an introvert had not changed. She had never spoken much about her work, allowing it to speak for itself. She was short-tempered and when it came to sloppy work and untidy environments, her voice was loud. As a teetotaller, like our mother, she detested anyone speaking to her under the influence of liquor. Unfortunately, her situation changed radically after 1994, when the Central Business District began to deteriorate and crime in the area escalated, which led to corporate businesses migrating north to places like Sandton and Rosebank. When the main Carlton Hotel was closed in December 1997, about 300 personnel were laid off. A few were retained, including my sister. After holding on for a few months hoping to get new investors and a casino license for the hotel, the hotel finally closed in April 1998. My sister's only domain for 26 years, the Carlton Hotel, crumbled.

The real pillar of the family was the last born, my sister, Maggie. In 1976 she was already studying for her Junior Certificate (JC) at Sekano-Ntoane, having started in the same year in Form I with the likes of Paul Msimang (MK Spokes Masaka 'Fapla') from Rockville, Joseph 'Joe' Ndhela (previous surname Moyane) from Chiawelo and the former chief executive of the Premier Soccer League (PSL), and a younger brother to Tom Moyane (the former Correctional Services and SARS

Commissioner who schooled at the same time with me at Sekano), and Naphtali Manana. Naphtali, together with Johnson Lubisi and Petrus Mashigo, was sentenced to death on 27 November 1980 for his role in an attack on Soekmekaar police station, but in 1982, their sentences were commuted to life imprisonment by President Marais Viljoen. I happened to have been in the same class – from Form I to Form V at Sekano – with Naphtali's elder brother, David, an outstanding and hardworking soccer player during our days.

Maggie fell pregnant in 1977 and gave birth to her first child, a boy named Thulani, in March 1978. Thulani's father, Ivanhoe Mpumelelo Mzamela Kambule came from a family living in the same street in Rockville. He paid lobola and they got married after 1983.

When, at the initiative of the Council of Unions of South Africa (CUSA), the National Union of Mineworkers was formed in 1982, Maggie applied for an advertised job and started work as an administrator in January 1983. Looking back to those years, she rightfully considers herself as a founding member of the NUM, which grew extremely fast in the following years. She remained with the union throughout the 1980s as it successfully campaigned for the rights of mineworkers, especially after the great 1987 strike, and to end the job reservation system in South Africa. In later years, the union played an important role in forging unity among the workers' federations and anti-apartheid forces. With her experience of so many years she left NUM to join the Soweto Civic Association (SCA) in 1989, when people in the townships were starting to create an alternative system of community development that was in strict opposition to the apartheid system. The SCA, as part of the South African National Civic Associations (SANCO), provided leadership for communities on taking ownership of their own development long before democracy was achieved in 1994.

After the 1976 uprisings with Fana and me gone, Siza and Maggie were the ones who kept the fires burning at home and kept the family together, as they were the only ones who had permanent jobs. Maggie's contribution sustained the family with financial and other contributions – my parents, my brothers, her two children and Siza's five children.

My brother, Fana

My parents had written to inform me that my younger brother, Fana and Selby had followed in my footsteps, skipping the country soon after I did. Trizzer 'David' wrote to me in 1980 confirming that they were both safe. I heard nothing more about Fana until I met Koli in Tanzania in 1982 and he told me that Fana had been arrested. Subsequently, the letters I received from my mother confirmed his arrest in Pretoria. After this, it all went quiet as Koli, who was in Mozambique, indicated to me that there was no news from home. He pointed out that rumours emerging from operations people were that the police were trying hard to turn Fana against the movement. I tried on my own to follow every piece of news regarding MK operations at home or trials of those arrested, but I never came across Fana's name.

My mother had indicated that after his arrest, the police threatened to arrest my uncle and his wife and the whole family in Pretoria. I knew that if Fana was hiding in my maternal grandparents' place, those suspected of harbouring him would be at risk because this is how the system worked. I tried to make sense of what had happened but I didn't have all the facts. I had read about the arrest of Mandla 'Mendoza' from his relatives' home in Daveyton in the news briefings in 1978 and wondered whether Fana would be tortured to the point that he informed the police about his mission into South Africa. I grappled unsatisfactorily with these questions. As with Mandla 'Mendoza' and Selby, there were far more questions than answers.

Chapter Five

When I saw Fana at the airport, my first reaction was gratitude that he was alive. I was obviously very keen to hear about what had happened since we last saw one another. However, there was a lot of catching up to do with other members of the family and it would be a couple of weeks before Fana and I could have a conversation.

Soon after my return, my mother sat me down one day and explained how my father's life, hers and the lives of everyone in the family, were turned upside down with our departure into exile. In the early days, especially during the night, when my parents heard any movement outside the house, they woke up to check if Fana or I had returned.

My father's health deteriorated. He was already very ill when we left, but from the time of our departure, ill health became part of his daily life, until death took him away. Our absence added to my mother's sorrow. She never stopped praying and hoping we would come back one day. As many families were similarly affected, they formed bonds of solidarity to help deal with the stress, and they passed information among themselves whenever they heard of news about their children. They were careful because they were supposed to report to the Protea police station if they received any news about their children's whereabouts.

In the beginning, families had to report once a week, later it was once a month, and as the years passed, it was whenever there was something they had seen, or suspected or heard from neighbours. When someone got detained and the police knew that that the detainee was your child's friend, they would come fetch you and ask you if you heard anything about your own child. The police would try to turn neighbours against one another and to implicate them by saying they had heard from someone that they had seen their child.

It was only when my parents received my letter from Germany that they felt relief that I was still alive. I had been careful not to disclose that I was in East Germany or to give any information that might have facilitated any follow-up. My mother's response to my letter made it clear to me that while my world had changed radically through my association with the politics of struggle and the ANC, my parents' world remained as it was when I left it behind.

When I asked my mother about Fana, she told me that when he was caught, they were all afraid that he would be hanged or sent to Robben Island. My mother was not aware of the activities that Fana had been involved in and it was evident that she still didn't know. She told me about how the police threatened to arrest her brother, my uncle Hezekiel and his wife, Thelma, if Fana refused to collaborate with them. My grandmother, Lena Mbono Nhlapo, was still alive, and likewise she was threatened with arrest as the legal owner of the house. In addition, the police got to know that my mother had visited Fana in Mamelodi before his arrest and threatened to charge her for breaking the law.

Fana's arrest on 23 April 1982 was a year after my father's death in February 1981. The police took my mother from Soweto in her mourning garments to go and see Fana at a police station in Pretoria where he was being held. She was shocked to find that he had been tortured and was in pain. Communication between the two of them was difficult in the presence of the police, who were saying things like: 'You see, your son is a terrorist. You protected him, but we can save him'. These were black policemen implying that they could save Fana from repercussions from their white colleagues, who were only too keen to show Fana how terrorists were dealt with. My mother was whisked away and taken back to Soweto.

After this, the police tried to use family members in Pretoria to convince Fana to work with them. Fana disappeared for a long time. My mother prayed that he would not disappear for good or be killed by the police. Nobody knew what really happened after this. Fana's arrest gave the police the upper hand, a psychological victory in a sense, because they could play family members against each other and at the same time gain power over Fana's emotions. Fana was actually used in court cases involving some of the members of his unit. He did not have to appear in person, nor was his name mentioned, as the courts were in possession of his testimony.[7]

It would take more than a year before Fana reappeared in Mamelodi at my grandmother's place, always in the company of other people who were not known to my family and were obviously police. The visits were remarkably short, and then he would disappear again. The police were playing mind games with the family. After some years of living like this, Fana asked the family in Mamelodi to organise for my mother to come and see him on a specific day. It was then that Fana asked her to initiate contact with the Ntebe family in Rockville. For what purpose? He wanted to pay lobola for Audrey Nonzwakazi 'Maki' Ntebe, his girlfriend from our neighbourhood, with whom he had started a relationship before he left the country.

My mother asked Fana what had happened since his arrest; where he worked, and what type of work he did. Fana was evasive and said that he would explain later. Lobola was paid and after this, he married Maki, the mother of his daughter, Nomalungelo 'Lungi', who was born just before he left for exile.

I knew Maki, a beautiful girl, light in complexion. Like me, she was a member of the Rockville youth and table tennis club at Elkah Stadium. She was the only girl that played competitive table tennis with us, boys. I never met her after the June 16 uprisings or when I came back from eNgoye. Fana and Maki were both doing their matric at Orlando High in 1975/1976. I never knew of her pregnancy and how this was overseen by my family. I was surprised on arriving back from exile to find out that their daughter, Nomalungelo 'Lungi' was born in October 1976. Now, because of Fana's circumstances, the lobola and marriage were strictly a private affair, without the customary fanfare and involvement of family members. Only my uncle from Pretoria, who had been threatened with arrest, was involved from my family side.

When I saw Fana for the first time on my return, he behaved quite normally, not showing any signs of emotional stress. After the brief from my mother, I had an opportunity to visit him in Soshanguve, where he lived. That is when I discovered that my younger brother was masking, as he had become an alcoholic and a human wreck. On my arrival at his place, he had already downed a few bottles. Since this was my first visit, I made no remark about this. I indicated to him that I was pleased that he had settled, established a family and built a house. I told him that the next time I paid him a visit, I wanted us to talk about what happened to him after his arrest. I also indicated that I wanted him to know about what had happened to me. He agreed that it would take another visit for us to have this discussion.

On the next visit, by the time I arrived, he had already started drinking and this time I joined him. I asked him what had really happened. He started telling me that they were left with no money by the structures that were responsible for their wellbeing in the underground. I said, 'I hear this, but how did you get arrested?' I didn't get a straight answer. I pressed him for an answer but he wouldn't budge. Realising that I was getting nowhere, I told him of my concern about his drinking, reminding him that our older brothers used to drink and started fighting among themselves. I impressed on him that we had a responsibility to help our mother, who was still doing piece jobs and no longer young. Apart from my mother, Maggie was the only member of the family who was employed and there was a need to alleviate the financial burden on her. I also told him that his friends that he grew up with, who I had met since coming back, were saying that he was not easy to find because they wanted to visit him too.

Because of Fana's drinking, every day of the week, Maki was finding it very tough living with him. There were now two additional children besides Lungi: Nontuthuzelo, a girl, and the last born, Andile, a boy. Fana had sided with the police, and I told myself I was not going to ask him about the details of his job again. I came to know that many who had turned against their comrades and joined the police started drinking heavily.

While at school, Fana had received distinctions in many subjects, including mathematics. He was not an ordinary cadre in MK; he belonged to a highly specialised trained group that would be known as an elite force in a regular army or police force. The order to create such a unit came from President Tambo in 1979, when marking the centenary of the Battle of Isandlwana. The unit's main task was to make the presence of MK felt inside South Africa, thus raising the spirits of demoralised black South Africans.

The first such trained cadres were known as the G5, and they were Zacharia Solomon 'Solly' Shoke (Ret. Gen – head of the SANDF and MK Jabu Lukhele); Nicholas 'Nicky' Hlongwane (MK Mteleki Nsizwa); Marcus Thabo 'Abie' Motaung; Simon Thelle Mogoerane, and a fifth member who committed suicide just before their departure from Angola. Led by Hlongwane, the unit fell under the Transvaal Urban Machinery commanded by 'Gebuza' Nyanda, assisted by Johannes Malekolle Rasegatla (MK Leonard 'Len' Mpanza), operating from Liberdad, Maputo, Mozambique.

Members were trained to use combat weapons like firearms and assault rifles, and some specialised in explosives, limpet mines, bombs, missiles, rocket launchers, and so on. A few more cadres were trained to augment the G5 members from time to time, which led to the creation of the G6 and G7. This is where Fana came in. He was joined by, among others, Linda Jabane 'The Lion of Chiawelo' (MK Gordon Dikebu); Bobby Tsotsobe; Suzman 'Kid' Nkopane Mokoena;

Jerry Semano Mosolodi; Theophilus Dlodlo; Sydney Molefe, and Gabriel 'Budis' Molepo.

This was a 'trial and error' mission as there were no textbooks to teach how these missions were to be conducted. They were to hit police stations, railway lines, and other symbols of apartheid and try to return safely to their hideouts, which were actually dugouts in the bushes around Pretoria and Johannesburg. They had undergone survival courses and had no fixed place to stay. They had to use abandoned mine shafts or make dugouts on farms and keep their arms caches with them. In a unit, only one of them was to know where the ammunition was located. They were to spread into the Johannesburg/Soweto area, the East Rand and Pretoria surroundings. What followed were attacks at Moroka, Orlando and Booysens police stations in Johannesburg. The Mabopane and Wonderboom police stations, the Capital Park and the Rosslyn sub-stations followed.

Fana specialised in explosives and limpet mines and his unit, the G7, which operated in Pretoria was under the command of Shoke. Other members were 'Kid' Mokoena; Gabriel 'Budis' Molepo; Theophilus Dlodlo, and 'Bruce'. 'Abie' Motaung was the coordinator and the link between the units. Targeted attacks succeeded in raising the profile of MK, and politically, that of the ANC in the country.

Even in places like Germany, we were able to follow some of the heroic deeds undertaken by these units through the ANC News Briefings, the BBC and VOA radio stations. There were other attacks in some parts of the country during this time, but these units in the Pretoria, Witwatersrand and Vaal (PWV) area, were close to the seat of government and for this reason they were incredibly effective. Considering that the cadres involved in these missions were aged between 23 and 27 years of age, they were seen as the brave lions of our struggle.

This was dangerous work and not without casualties. Some

hideouts were discovered by passers-by; some cadres were arrested, and some of the units' members paid the ultimate price of death by hanging, because in the eyes of the apartheid regime they were terrorists. This was the case with the 'Moroka Three' – Motaung, Mosololi and Mogoerane. There were askaris who helped engineer arrests. Fana's evidence would have been damning as he had planned and executed some of the attacks.

I began to engage with Fana regularly, but it was long after his death in 1995, while writing this memoir that I discovered that another member of Fana's unit, Suzman Mokoena, had moved into my grandmother's house in Mamelodi with Fana at the beginning of 1982, and they had been operating from a backroom for about four months before their arrest.

For the type of mission they were involved in, this was the riskiest thing to do. According to Suzman, at some stage , there were communications breakdowns with the coordinators of the units and the two had indicated that they needed to be moved out, possibly to Swaziland, to allow for the situation to cool off.

There were a number of adults and children staying at my grandmother's place. Besides my grandmother, there was my uncle with, his wife and children. My two aunts, my mother's younger sisters, Emma Masombuka (nee Nhlapo) and Jumaimah Pule (nee Nhlapo), also stayed in Mamelodi, within walking distance of my grandmother's house. Some of my aunts' children – my cousins – were Fana's age, and they would frequent my grandmother's place almost on a daily basis.

Fana got arrested first, and then Suzman, who was in the backroom at the time, was arrested. They were put in separate cars, in a large police convoy. After being subjected to severe torture, Suzman faced a one-man trial in which Ratha Mokgoatlheng (a former and well-regarded soccer player known as 'Jimmy Greaves', who became a judge of the High Court), was the defence lawyer. The judge wanted to impose the death sentence, but gave him twenty years. While Suzman was serving his sentence on Robben Island he was brought back to Johannesburg to stand in another trial,[83] but the authorities failed to show evidence to implicate him. He was sent back to Robben Island, and as a result, he acquired two different prison numbers from the notorious island. He was only released in 1993.

Fana's situation worried me, and I sought help from other quarters. When we came back home from exile, the question of askaris was a big issue in the country, although there was no official party position on the matter. While I was preoccupied with this state of affairs, other matters came to the fore and made headlines in the media: the torture and killing of cadres within the liberation movements (both the ANC and the PAC) in exile. It was clear that this was being orchestrated and that securocrats were behind it.

There was also the report by Paul Trewhela, Inside Quatro, in July 1990. The ANC had not prepared for this, and quickly reacted by setting up the Skweyiya Commission (Report 1992) and the Motsuenyane Commission (Report 1993). Another report came from the Douglas Commission (1993). By this time, the Stuart Commission Report of 1984 had not been released by the ANC. The TRC was still to come.

As Chris Hani was Chief of Staff of MK (before he stepped down in 1992 after being elected as the new Secretary-General of the SACP in December 1991), I sought his advice on how to deal with Fana's matter. He said to me, 'Comrade Khulu, tell your brother to leave whatever he is doing, he must come back home.'

I organised for many of Fana's friends and some comrades who did training with him in Angola, to talk to him. Many did their best to engage with him so he could adapt to the new situation. Among these was Norman Phiri, who had come back after a rough time in the ANC, including being incarcerated at Quatro. My family, relatives and Fana's wife, tried to help, all in vain.

One day in September 1995, he drove all the way from Soshanguve to our home, in Budaza Street, Rockville. Finding my mother alone, he relaxed in one of the bedrooms we used to share as boys. It was known as the 'boys' room'. After some time when my elder sister's kids were back from school, he took his pistol, went to the bathroom inside the house, locked the door, pointed the gun at his head and pulled the trigger. I received a call at work. It was early in the morning in New York, where I was now based as one of the deputy ambassadors to the United Nations. A few days later, on 26 September 1995, he died at Baragwanath Hospital. I flew back from New York for the funeral.

Back to the ANC

According to plan, I started work at Sauer Street on a Monday before the end of April. It was a good feeling to be a worker in the city again after so many years away. What was missing was public transport. Prior to 1976, buses and trains ferried the bulk of workers from Soweto to town and back to the township. Now, minibus taxis were the main mode of transportation.

As I started working, the ANC was moving to new offices, a 22-floor building located at 51 Plein Street, the head office of Shell, known as Shell House. Preparations for the 48th ANC National Conference in Durban (2–6 July 1991) were underway. Among other things that Sindiso and Papi were already dealing with was the Secretary-General's draft conference report.

While we were getting ready for the conference, we were well aware that the whole country was anticipating this conference as it was the first national conference to be convened on South African soil in three decades, and the first since the unbanning of the ANC. Everyone knew how crucial this gathering was going to be to determine a common future for South Africa and its people through negotiations.

The conference came and the results spoke for themselves: the ANC was able to unite all its factions, from the underground structures to the UDF; from those who came from Robben Island to those who had been in exile. The newly elected executive was an expression of this unity, with Nelson Mandela as president, Oliver Tambo as chairperson and Cyril Ramaphosa as Secretary-General. The ANC opened its doors for new members to join and was ready to proceed to the negotiations.

The results also spoke to me directly about my future. Do I resign and start doing something along the lines of my profession, or do I stay? I didn't even have a chance to think about it when a directive about my future was issued to me. The day after the conference closed on 6 July 1991, Ramaphosa arrived at the ANC offices and went straight to the office of the ANC's secretary-general. I was alone in the office as others were still on their way back to Johannesburg from Durban.

I opened the office for Ramaphosa, and we sat down and began to plan how to build the necessary structure to enable the office to function at its maximum and meet the demands that came with the mandate of the office. While we were talking, he said to me, 'You know all the comrades who are from exile, therefore you will coordinate all the meetings of the National Executive Committee (NEC) and the National Working Committee (NWC). That's your responsibility from now on.'

I was not clear what coordinating the meetings of the NEC and NWC would entail. I had worked in the secretary-general's office in Lusaka and had more or less continued this work since my return, but this was totally different to what I used to doing. It proved to be one of the most challenging jobs I had ever done, but I enjoyed every minute of it.

Chapter Five 266

The period from 1991 to 1994, was generally known as the 'negotiations period'. Political prisoners were being released from various prisons in the country, mainly from Robben Island, and exiles were returning home. The country was going through many political changes, and at the same time there were challenges and violence fuelled by the politics of the time.

There were significant milestones during this period: the National Peace Accord (14 September 1991), the Patriotic Front Summit, (25 October 1991), CODESA I (20–21 December 1991) and CODESA 2 (15 May 1992).

There were also incidents of violence and brutality during this time: the Boipatong massacre (17 June 1992), the Bisho massacre (7 Sept 1992), the assassination of Chris Hani (10 April 1993), and the attack on the World Trade Centre in Kempton Park by the right-wing Afrikaner WeerstandBeweging (AWB) on 25 June 1993.

After the Bisho Massacre, on 26 September 1992, Nelson Mandela and FW De Klerk signed a Record of Understanding, establishing an independent body to oversee police operations.

On 23 September 1993, the Tricameral Parliament passed the bill for the establishment of the Transitional Executive Council (TEC) whose main function was to ensure free and fair elections. On 9 March 1994, the intransigent bantustan, Bophuthatswana folded.

The Secretary-General then appointed Sophia de Bruyn (known as Aunt Sophia de Bruyn) to take overall responsibility for all staff at the ANC headquarters. With her vast experience of running the Institute for Namibia in Lusaka as part of the UN management, Aunt Sophia, proved to be a great asset to the ANC. Her task was to start a full HR department from scratch and to develop policies and guidelines, with assistance from HR consultants. Under her leadership, training, ethical conduct and a dress code for ANC personnel, became important. Patrick Msomi (MK Moses Swanepoel), a diligent hard worker, assisted Aunt Sophia in her office.

In 1991 typewriters were still in use; computers were just being introduced. The first list of ANC staff interested in receiving training on how to operate a computer using WordPerfect and MS-DOS was compiled. The training took place at the Liberty Life Centre in Braamfontein. Only two males put themselves forward. I was one of them. At that time, most male comrades considered computers to be an extension of typewriters and their use reserved for women. They laughed at us.

The work of ensuring the implementation of decisions and resolutions made by the NWC and NEC was demanding and crucial. Marion Sparg joined the Secretary-General's office to coordinate this work, as well as carrying out other responsibilities. At the beginning Gill Marcus, as a member of the NWC, assisted as Secretary of the NWC. When the negotiations started, this position became more crucial because of the volumes of documentation that came from the various committees at the World Trade Centre in Kempton Park, where the negotiations were taking place. Reams of information had to be packaged and sent through to the NWC and NEC for decisions. Later, Donné Nicol joined the team.

The Secretary-General was responsible for organising NEC meetings. As soon as the officials determined the dates for a meeting, I was directed to organise it. Everything was left to me, beginning with sending out notices and finding a safe venue. The country was fraught with political tensions at the time and an attack of an NEC or NWC meeting was always a possibility. For this reason, information about the venue of a meeting was withheld until absolutely necessary..

My work involved identifying a venue and dealing with logistics down to the finest detail, including food and accommodation. I demanded to know from the owners of the venues who the caterers were and who would handle the food. The venues had to be secured by our own ANC security personnel. Reddy Mampane was head of security, and he allocated Gary John Kruser (Ret. Gen), among others, to liaise with me. They had to clean and electronically sweep the rooms where the meetings were taking place. It had to be done shortly before and the rooms had to be locked and guarded until the following day before the start of the meeting. Most meetings lasted two to three days. From time to time, one-day meetings were held when the need arose.

I had to liaise with the treasury, and our Treasurer-General Thomas Nkobi, who assigned personnel to assist, among them Vusi Khanyile, who later established the Thebe investments company.

Venue, food and accommodation had to sometimes be paid for in advance or with deposits. Accommodation was always a big challenge, especially if it was not at the same venue as the meeting. I never used the same venue twice and I made sure I always found a venue where ordinary people could see our leadership. For example, I used the Ipelegeng Community Centre in White City Jabavu, Diakonia Ministry in Central Western Jabavu in Soweto, the JISWA centres in Mayfair and Lenasia, the Rand Inn and Holiday Inn hotels close to Shell House. For a quieter environment I would use the Methodist Church in Bonaero Park in Benoni, the Aloe Ridge Hotel and Heia Safari Ranch in Muldersdrift. All these places became the centres where the leadership debated, deliberated and took very vital decisions about our nation.

The provincial, regional and local structures were configured differently in the four provinces in those days. In Natal there was: Northern Natal, Southern Natal and Natal Midlands; in the Cape: Western Cape, Eastern Cape and the Border regions; in the Free State: Northern and Southern Free State, and in the Transvaal: Northern, Western and Eastern Transvaal and the PWV regions.

Organising the logistics for transport and flights was a nightmare at the beginning. There were no cell phones then. Preparations required phoning all provincial and regional offices of the ANC; notifying secretaries of the meetings; sending the agenda, and confirming people attending and the mode of transport that would be used. Information on flight bookings needed to be made by headquarters and times of departure confirmed individually by fax. Those flying in needed to be collected from Jan Smuts Airport and taken back to the airport when the meetings were over. There were drivers with the transport department, under the direction of Andrew Mlangeni, who were assigned this task and who worked with me and contributed immensely to the success of the NEC meetings.

Travel arrangements for the 82 members of the NEC, especially for those coming from a region like the Western Cape – Albie Sachs, Kader Asmal, Abdullah Mohamed Omar, Reginald September, Alan Boesak and Tony Yengeni – had to accommodate individual work schedules, which meant they arrived at different times. For the first NEC meeting this was extremely challenging. Later, a more efficient management system was introduced.

I counted on Prudence Gugulethu Motlanthe (nee Mtshali), who worked with the Secretary-General, Cyril Ramaphosa; Bartinah 'Tinah' Ntombizodwa Netshitenzhe (nee Radebe, ambassador), who worked with the Deputy Secretary-General, Jacob Zuma, and Sibongile Mahlangu and Audrey Mohlamme. They all worked in the Secretary-General's office and had different responsibilities, but were always ready to assist me in the execution of my responsibilities.

Even today the first NEC meeting after Durban remains embedded in my memory. It was like a reunion of the founders of the Youth League (some were NEC members before the banning of the ANC). Founding members of MK; former Robben Island prisoners; the exiled leadership; UDF and civil society leaders, and the Women's and Youth Leagues were all there. These meetings empowered me to interact directly with the national leadership at head office. They also provided an opportunity to work intimately with the provincial, regional and local leadership structures of the ANC.

The ANC had limited financial resources. In around 1992 to 1993, the organisation ran out of funds and was not able to pay salaries one month. The staff was up in arms. Mandela and Ramaphosa, called a meeting with all staff and assured them that the matter would be addressed as quickly as possible. Mandela summoned Advocate George Bizos to his office.

I was assigned to accompany Advocate Bizos to meetings with some of his acquaintances at three different locations in Johannesburg one evening. We met mostly Greek businesspeople who, when Bizos explained the situation in the ANC, opened their coffers and made donations. The following day I took the donations to Nkobi's office. Within a week Bizos had mobilised enough funds to keep the ANC going.

The shortage of funds also affected issues like accommodation during the two- or three-day NEC meetings. Only the top six officials were allocated single rooms. For the rest I had to allocate a room per pair. This was not an easy assignment with NEC members, including the provincial and regional members. I couldn't wait for them to start arriving and then try to pair them in rooms We would have had no time to attend to other matters, like seeing to it that the conference room had been properly equipped with the material we requested, all documentation was ready, and so on.

In one of the meetings at the Aloe Ridge Hotel, I organised for Steve Tshwete and Joe Slovo to share a room. My simple logic was that they were both pipe smokers. In the morning of the following day, Joe Slovo, approached me at breakfast and calling me aside, pleaded to be paired with someone else, because he didn't have a good sleep. Tshwete had allegedly woken up in the middle of the night and started smoking his pipe. I apologised and promised to find someone to swop rooms with him.

Fifteen minutes later, Tshwete came to take his breakfast and he also summoned me to where he was standing. He said, 'Hey, I could not sleep last night because Slovo was wheezing the whole night'. He pleaded with me to find another room. Again, I apologised. I knew I had to act quickly. This was not the end of it; two other roommates complained that morning. Thankfully, by the end of the day all the concerns had been successfully resolved.

It was remarkable that there were no leaks from NEC or NWC meetings. Secret documents issued to individuals the previous day or during the meetings, had to be returned to me when the meeting ended. I kept a register for this.

One day, I was in the car en route to one of the NEC meetings in Muldersdrift. Someone else was driving and I was in the passenger seat. Mac Maharaj, who had asked for a lift, was sitting on the back seat. I told the driver to take the off-ramp at 'Doctor William Nicole'. Mac laughed so loud, that I got irritated. He asked me to repeat what I just said. I did so. He said, 'You fool, you are still in exile. It's not Doctor William Nicol, but William Nicol Drive (written William Nicol Dr). I was stunned because this is what I had been saying to people since my arrival in South Africa and no one had ever corrected me.

One of the more tense NEC meetings I ever experienced was when, for the first time, a member of the ANC and NEC was elected to a position in the top six outside of a national conference. This is how former President Thabo Mbeki came to occupy the position of the national chairperson. This was occasioned by the death of OR Tambo in 1993. Mandela lobbied for either Kader Asmal or Mac Maharaj to replace Tambo but he was not successful. The NEC had to take a political decision by vote because the meeting did not agree with

Mandela's suggestion. This was the first time the NEC had taken a decision by vote. Up until then, all political decisions taken by the NEC were taken by consensus. Maharaj withdrew after the debate on this matter, but Asmal went ahead to contest in a secret ballot. Before the election took place, I indicated to Asmal privately that from what I had picked up in informal discussions taking place outside the meeting, especially after engaging with Winnie Mandela and Peter Mokaba, the majority in the house was not going to vote in his favour. He said, 'Mandela wants me to stand!' He was humbled by the results of the elections conducted by myself and Zola Skweyiya, who was then head of constitutional development department.

'Bra Phiri'

The story of 'Bra Phiri' is painful and hilarious at the same time. His full name is Ndabakayipheli Wilson Macozoma (MK Phiri 'Ball of Fire' Nkosi) but he was popularly known as Phiri or 'Bra Phiri' among the *Qiniselanis*. His father, Mntakwende, died when Bra Phiri was very young, so when he applied for his passbook he used his stepfather's surname, Macozoma. No one in the ANC would say they didn't know Bra Phiri as his presence was felt between Lusaka and Livingstone in Zambia, and between Dar, Kongwa, Morogoro and Dakawa in Tanzania. I first met him in Dar in 1976 when he transported people from Kinondoni with his unmistakably big French truck, the Berliet GLR type, named by Bra Phiri and Bra Ted Baholo, as the 'Ball of Fire' because of the loud noise it emitted when changing gears. The two painted that name, 'Ball of Fire', on the back of the truck. I also travelled in this truck on my way to Magadu. Several comrades were always passengers to and from Dar and Morogoro.

Bra Phiri was slender and just a bit taller than the average person. He was a jolly person, never angry and always helpful. He delivered food and other essentials to several places where the ANC people were based, and also to areas across the borders. From the docks in Dar, he collected items that came from the Soviet Union, GDR and Nordic countries: food, clothing, etc., and took them to our storerooms, and from there he distributed goods in Zambia and Tanzania. In this way, Bra Phiri was all over the place. Sometimes he took students from Morogoro to Dar so that they could go swimming at the beach, and after a day or two he transported them back.

As I was in charge in Magadu, I came know Bra Phiri very well. He was the most trusted driver in the ANC and in the early days, the organisation would sometimes second him to drive the leader of Frelimo and the first president of Mozambique, Samora Machel, when they were still in Kongwa in Tanzania. I left him in Dar when I went to study in the GDR, and I was overjoyed in 1980 when he joined me in the GDR for a year or two. He did some vocational training and thereafter he left. He was also with our delegation when we attended the youth conference in Hungary that year.

The next time I met Bra Phiri was in Harare in 1990 when I was preparing to return home. It was at Thoy Nthongoa's (MK Thoy Tshabalala) place. Thoy was simply known as 'Bra Thoy'. Patricia, his partner, and their beautiful daughter, Mamusa Khanyeza were also there.

Once the ANC was unbanned and Mandela visited countries like Zambia, the prospect of returning home was accompanied by mixed feelings: we were excited but also fearful. Some of us had been away from home soil since the 1960s, some since 1976, and some since the mid-1980s.

I felt that the June 16 generation – the *Qiniselanis* – were in touch with the political and social environment prevailing at home. This was not the case with many of the older generation of the 1960s, the 'Mgwenyas', as some came from areas that no longer existed because

Chapter Five

of forced removals, and had no one to connect with to prepare them for their return to South Africa.

In a conversation with Bra Phiri, I expressed joy for cadres like him, who left home so long ago, imagining that he would be happy about the prospect of returning home. Certainly, he was happy, but the look on his face didn't show any sign of it. He indicated that his information was that the people who had lived in the place that he came from had been relocated and he didn't know where to.

In exile, there was a strict norm in the ANC not to ask comrades exactly where they came from at home and what their real names were. Breaching this norm could get one into serious trouble. But the atmosphere suddenly changed after the unbanning of the organisation. There was more freedom to ask personal questions. I asked Bra Phiri where he came from. He said he came from the Old Brakpan location. I was amazed. 'Old Brakpan location is my place too', I exclaimed. I told him that some members of my extended family, on my father's side, were from there.

He shouted back excitedly, 'What, you know this place, Old Brakpan location?' I told him that the people from that area were forcefully moved, the same as us in 'Western', and they were relocated to a place called Tsakane, which I knew very well. He smiled, evidently immensely relieved. I said to him, 'Let's make a deal; when we go back home, I will help you find your people'. We shook hands and laughed over the Zimbabwean beer we were drinking.

Every time I visited Bra Thoy's place the topic of me helping Bra Phiri find his family came up. I left Bra Phiri in Harare when I came home. In April 1992, he called from Harare telling me that he was coming to South Africa by taxis and asked whether I would be able to collect him from Park Station. 'Yes, of course!' I said. On the morning of 28 April, I met him at the station and brought him to Shell House as Park Station was within walking distance of the ANC offices.

After work, when Bra Phiri had met with the security department, I dropped him at a house in Yeoville that was used to accommodate those who had nowhere to go and were still searching for their next of kin. I regarded this 'house of exile' as the second exile for the unlucky ones. I visited Bra Phiri from time to time, assuring him that I had not forgotten my promise to him.

In the meantime, he had work to do organising with the security and transport departments to bring ANC trucks back from Lusaka and Dar, and he was expected to return to Harare. Sometimes, he walked to the offices in Plein Street. For somebody who had been on the road for years in trucks, cars and motorbikes, this was rather strange. He would pop into my office to remind me of what I had promised him when we were both out of the country and I didn't want to disappoint him.

I spoke to Tinah Radebe about my mission to help Bra Phiri. Tinah was a down to earth person, a youth activist par excellence and an extremely popular community member in the township of Tsakane, Brakpan. She remains the only person I know who was honoured by her community by giving her a brand-new house and naming a street after her in Tsakane before 1994. This was because in her early teens she had taken up a dispute between her community and the authorities. The confrontation was over the provision of houses and rent increases and Tinah stood her ground and led from the front. When people from the old location were brought to Tsakane, there were also those who were tenants in the yards of those who owned houses in the old location. With this relocation, the authorities had built houses for the residents but not for the tenants, who were put in shacks, known as Kwavezinyawo, in Tsakane.

> *'Kwavezinyawo is the name of a section in Tsakane location. When the town council moved the people from Brakpan location to Tsakane they promised to provide the people with*

> *decent housing and proper social facilities. When the people arrived in Kwavezinyawo they discovered that the council did not fulfil its promises. Kwavezinyawo is a small, untidy and overcrowded place. The name itself refers to the size of the houses which are so small that the people are fond of saying: when you sit in these houses your feet stick out of the doors. The people, however, decided to come together to form a home-seekers' association. They united to fight the council and succeeded in improving their living conditions.'* [9]

Tinah became one of the leaders of this community at a time – from 1983 to 1985 – when the confrontation between the communities and the Development Board and councillors, over rent increases and the resultant boycotts, were at their peak.

At the same time, independent trade union activity was increasing, student politics and school boycotts were intensifying and UDF structures were being established in the townships. Tinah became a community and youth leader at the same time. She was detained many times under the state of emergency and at one time she was imprisoned with the likes of Albertina Sisulu, Jessie Duarte (current deputy secretary-general of the ANC), and many others.

Although I still have relatives in Tsakane, I relied on Tinah, 'the mayor'. She assured me that she would assist me in finding Bra Phiri's family. One Saturday in May we embarked on this mission. We used a car belonging to Welile Nhlapo, who I had persuaded to join the Secretary-General's office because of the increase in the amount of work in the office. He was with DIA under Thabo Mbeki at the time, and he moved over to share my office.

The three of us went past Yeoville to fetch Bra Phiri and set off for Tsakane on the East Rand. We stopped in the middle of Ndabezitha Street, at a place that was close to Tinah's house, and questioned a few people in the streets about the whereabouts of people with the surname Bra Phiri gave us. Many people had no idea who we were talking about.

After a while, someone advised us to go to the older section of Tsakane, known as the 'Xhosa' section, where we might find people who knew the name. We slowly drove to this part of the location. We decided to lock the car and walk the streets, and even enter some houses to make enquiries. This was risky, because at this time tensions were high in the townships because of the ANC – IFP conflict, but there wasn't another way. People were on high alert and looked at us with suspicion.

We tried two or three houses before coming across an old lady, who scrutinised us from the gate of her house. She was about to turn away when I called to her and told her we were not from this part of town and were looking for a certain Macozoma, who used to reside in the old location in Brakpan. She thought about this for a minute, clearly trying to retrieve information from her memory, then said, 'I know that man, he must have died many years ago. He used to work for the old rails (the South African Railways).' The three of us looked at 'Bra Phiri' and he nodded with a smile and affirmed that his old man used to work for the railways. We collectively let out a sigh of relief.

Here was a person who knew Bra Phiri's father, who was evidently no longer alive. She asked us if we knew a certain street not far from where we were, then when we explained once more that we didn't know the place, gave us directions to a house where a woman lived who might know about the old man's relatives. She was certain that this person would be able to give us information. We were not in a hurry. We drove slowly to the street the old woman had indicated, and without any effort, found the woman we had been told about. This woman was able to point out the specific house we were looking for.

It was now early afternoon and our mission was on track. There were cars parked outside the house and several people seated in front of the house, some on chairs and some on the grass. From the look of things, a big party was going on. We realised that it wouldn't be a good idea to approach the group and start asking questions, especially if it was the wrong place. It could lead to trouble for us.

We decided to go to the back of the house, although this would mean walking past the people and could be interpreted as disrespectful. There didn't seem to be an option. At the back we found a young boy and I asked him to call his mother. He disappeared and then returned and beckoned us to enter through the kitchen door.

An elderly woman in her sixties came into the kitchen from the inside of the house, and politely greeted us, sitting opposite us on a seat that was more elevated than ours – like a bar chair. After politely exchanging greetings, I explained that we were not from Tsakane but were looking for a certain family, and were not sure if we were in the right place, but someone had directed us to her house.

I introduced myself but deliberately refrained from introducing my companions. I questioned her directly: 'Did someone in this family, sometime in the early 1960s, disappear?' She moved on her seat, shifting her position, her eyes moving from her right to left, clearly sizing us up.

I didn't know what was going on in her mind. I expanded my question: 'Did one of the sons in this family disappear in the sixties?' I was certain she understood me now and she was grappling with how to respond to me. The whole conversation was in Zulu. I had to be down to earth and sensible in the best way I could because this event happened almost 30 years ago. To meet strangers in your house who had no appointment with you and were there to question you about something that had happened so many years ago, was not an everyday event.

She took a deep breath and said, 'Mfa'nami, ngangin' abafana abathathu.' ('My child, I had three sons…') One day my eldest took his brothers to Park Station in Johannesburg. Two sons came home, and this one was never seen again. They told me their brother said that they were meeting some people, who never came. The two decided to come home and I don't know what happened to him.'

The temperature started rising inside me, and I knew then that we were at the right place. I was in charge, but I was not one hundred per cent sure because up to this point, Bra Phiri didn't reveal any emotion. I was looking at him from the corner of my eye. Tinah and Welile remained cool too, no emotions. I realised this was not enough. The lady was again sizing us up and I allowed her to do that, thinking that perhaps she might recognise Bra Phiri. Nothing happened! With a sideways glance, I noticed Bra Phiri's face and eyes were changing, like a hunter about to pounce on his prey, but his body was motionless.

I followed up with another question, asking the lady what happened since then. She responded by saying she had literally given up on her son, Ndabakayipheli. This was the first time I had heard the name, and from where I was seated, at the far end of the room, I was able to watch her but also follow 'Bra Phiri's reaction.

On hearing the name, a suppressed smile broke through on Bra Phiri's face. I knew that I must press the final button, and I asked the lady directly, 'Is there someone among us here who looks like your son?' She looked at me again, looked at Welile, and then at Bra Phiri and their eyes met. I could feel that they were intensely examining each other. Within seconds the woman screamed so loud, the people from outside came rushing in thinking there was some trouble in the house.

The old lady was shouting, 'My son, my son, Ndabakayipheli, ooh my son…!' They were hugging and by the time she took a pause, she called out to her other two sons, 'Here is your brother! Here is your brother! Can you recognize your brother?' The two brothers were among the group of people that had rushed in when the mother screamed, and they looked at each other, deep in shock. They did not even recognise Bra Phiri when we passed them entering the yard.

Chapter Five

After this breakthrough, I was able to introduce Tinah and Welile, who were smiling joyfully at what had just happened. We were informed that one of the brother's was celebrating his birthday and that is why the whole family, including the grandchildren were around. They showed us where the main table in the house was. People made space for us to join the party.

Food was prepared for us, and more bottles of beer were put on the table to celebrate the return of the long-lost and forgotten son, Bra Phiri. The whole atmosphere was joyful and breath-taking. Bra Phiri's mother remained in tears throughout our stay.

After an hour or so with the family, we had to excuse ourselves, so that we could return to Johannesburg while it was still light outside. Bra Phiri was confused about what to do and he grabbed his cap and started bidding farewell to his family. The three of us instantaneously called out, 'No, Bra Phiri, you remain here, this is now your home!'

Arrangements were made for Bra Phiri's brothers – Zwelakhe and Petros Marago – to fetch his items from the Yeoville 'house of exile'. My promise was fulfilled, thanks to Tinah and Welile! You can imagine how I felt on this day – happy and relieved. The experience was unforgettable!

We drove back and dropped Tinah at her house in Tsakane, where she was spending the weekend. Welile and I continued to Shell House where I had left my car. We parted in good spirits and I drove towards Birch Acres in Kempton Park where I now lived.

I related the extraordinary events of that day to Nomvume Magaqa, with whom I was living, and to her two lovely daughters, Lunga and Nonhlanhla (Lunga Nene and Nonhlanhla Nene). This experience was probably the most fulfilling moment of my return home.

NOTES

Preface

1. South African Democracy Education Trust. (2004). *The Road to Democracy in South Africa*: 1970–1980 (Vol. 2). Unisa Press. Page 147–148
2. Makobe, D. (2012). The Bulhoek Massacre: Origins, Casualties, Reactions and Historical Distortions. *Scientia Militaria – South African Journal of Military Studies*, 26(1). https://doi.org/10.5787/26-1-237

Chapter One

1. 'Mbata' is the old way of writing Mbatha. The Zulu alphabet and phonics underwent a change in the 1950s with certain words changing how they were written, e.g., 'ta' and 'pa' became 'tha' and 'pha'.
2. See reference (1) above, Nhlapo became Nhlapho.
3. "Mamelodi is a township located in Gauteng Province and is part of the City of Tshwane Metropolitan Municipality. It is bordered by Magaliesberg Mountain on the northern and eastern sides and the Pretoria-Witbank highway on the south. Mamelodi is built on a farm in Vlakfontein. The name changed in the late 1950's to Mamelodi, the name given to president Paul Kruger by the Blacks because of his ability to whistle and imitate birds. Mamelodi also means 'Father of Melodies'." https://www.south-africa-info.co.za/country/town/632/mamelodi.
4. The two acts combined reinforced each other - The Township Amendment Act, Law 34 (Transvaal): The residence in town were restricted to domestic servants. (1908) and The Gold Law, Act 35 (Transvaal): There was an absolute prohibition of Indian traders to reside or carry-on trade in proclaimed areas (1908).
5. South African History Online (SAHO), Johannesburg the Segregated City.
6. Owen Crankshaw, Class, Race and Residence in Black Johannesburg, 1923–1970 in: Journal of Historical Sociology, Vol. 18 No. 4, December 2005 ISSN 0952-1909), page 354 -355.
7. Ellen Hurst, Tsotsitaal Chapter, University of Cape Town, Publications, November 2018 DOI: 10.1057/978-1-137-01593-8_18.

8. Parnell, Susan and Gordon Pirie (1991) Johannesburg. In Anthony Lemon (eds) Homes apart: South Africa's segregated cities. Bloomington: Indiana University Press pages 129-145. See also: Indian Community in Lenasia, SAHO.

9. Estelle Bester, The Dube Story in Heritage Portal, Thursday, April 19, 2018 – http://www.theheritageportal.co.za/article/dube-story).

10. Miriam Duduzile Zondo, born on September 18, 1954 lived with her grandmother eZitandini at number 1993 Nuse Street, Rockville, when she was at Ndondo Primary School. Otherwise her mother and family were in Zulu section, Rockville.

11. Before Cyril Ramaphosa left Sekano-Ntoane he was an active member and chairman of the SCM and when he arrived at Mphaphuli High in Venda, he was elected to the same position.

12. Mxolisi Dlamuka, Harry Gwala, Political Militancy and State Trials, 1960-1977.

13. Kendal Harrison, Tribute to Arnold Napier Boyce, in http://wiredspace.wits.ac.za/handle/10539/20638.

14. During the writing of my memoirs, I discovered that Pat Chabane was Collins Chabane's elder brother. I did not know this until both were deceased.

15. Nelson Mandela, 'Black man in a white court: Nelson Mandela's First Court Statement, 28 October 1962.

16. Nelson Mandela's statement from the dock at the opening of the defence case in the Rivonia Trial, Pretoria Supreme Court, 20 April 1964.

17. The Road to Democracy in South Africa, Volume 2 [1970 – 1980], 2007, page 326 – 327. See also: Majeke, The 1976 Soweto Uprisings.

18. Prof Keith Breckenridge, 'Cross of Gold: The gold, liquor and pass laws and the problem of identification, 1895 – 1899', 2008/27, University of KwaZulu-Natal.

19. Sean O'Toole, Apartheid was the spoke in South African cycling, Mail & Guardian, 7 March 2013.

20. Volkskas Beperk (Peoples' Bank) a cooperative loan bank founded in 1934, became a commercial bank in1941. In 1991, as South Africa's largest

Afrikaner bank, it merged with the United Building Society, the Allied Building Society and Trust Bank to form the Amalgamated Banks of South Africa (ABSA).

21. In 1998 I was appointed as Deputy Director-General and as Acting Director-General in the Department of Home Affairs under Minister Mangosuthu Buthelezi.

22. I never heard anything about Gilbert Mazibuko until I left the country, and when we were in exile, we heard he had passed away and his family confirmed this.

23. John Vilakazi: I knew John (John Magwegwe Vilakazi, MK Thabo Mkula) who was my senior at Sekano-Ntoane and his siblings (brother Nina, sisters Linda and Zamo (married to George Nkosi) well as we lived in the same street in Rockville. John and Nina, together with Koli (Kolisile Koli Ngqase, MK nom de guerre Ephraim Gazelle) were peers of my brother Jerry, and Koli was the elder brother to Dennis Mxolisi, who was my peer and one of my bosom friends.

I only happened to know John's extended family relatives when I was already in exile. Through John's correspondences with me, I learned that there was a relationship between the Vilakazis and Msimangs families. To start with Meinrad 'Mendi' Themba Msimang, who I first met in Dar, Tanzania in 1976 (born in Marshalltown on December 8, 1928, and the second child of seven siblings) was the son of Vangile Martha Vilakazi and Mjele Msimang. The brother to Martha was therefore an uncle to Mendi and his siblings, and father to John's father, meaning John's grandfather. Mendi Msimang's siblings are: 1. Sister (late); 2. Mendi (late, father to Khosi, Mabutho, Zimpande and Mandla); 3. Sebastian Nhlanhla (late brother, father to Paul (MK Spokes Masaka 'Fapla'), Velaphi and Ntsika); 4. Sinda Msimang (brother, father to Mzimuhle, Hlula, Mazwi and Sabelo); 5. Bheki Msimang (late); 6. Sister (in Lesotho) and 7. Bongani (brother, in Lesotho).

Paul (('Fapla') was with my sister, Maggie, in the same class at Sekano-Ntoane. I only came to know Hlula after coming back from exile and he later worked with me at the South African Mission to the United Nations in New York. The Vilakazis and Msimangs families are also related to the Twalas of Rockville (George Twala's family).

Chapter Two

1. Ambrose Makiwane, Tennyson Makiwane, Temba Mqota, Pascal Ngakane, Joe Matlou, OK Setlapelo, Tami Bonga and George Mbele. The group was mainly against the ANC's 1969 Morogoro Conference decision to open its membership to whites, coloureds and Indians.

2. Trial of 22 of 1969: These men and women were arrested in May 1969 and were held in solitary confinement for seven months until they appeared in court in December 1969. They were charged under the Suppression of Communism Act, 1950 (Act 44 of 1950) – renamed the Internal Security Act in 1976 – in a case known as 'State vs Samson Ndou and 21 others'.

   >Mr Lawrence Ndzanga;
   >Ms Rita Ndzanga;
   >Ms Winnie Madikizela Mandela;
   >Mr Samson Ndou;
   >Mr David Motau;
   >Mr Jackson Mahlaule;
   >Mr Elliot Shabangu;
   >Ms Joyce Sikakane;
   >Mr Joseph Snuki Zikalala;
   >Mr David Dalton Tsotetsi;
   >Mr George Mokwebo;
   >Mr Joseph Chamberlain Nobanda;
   >Mr Samuel Solomon Pholoto;
   >Mr Simon Mosikare;
   >Mr Douglas Mtshetshe Mvemve;
   >Ms Venus Thokozile Mngoma;
   >Ms Martha Dlamini;
   >Mr Owen Vanqa;
   >Mr Peter Sexforth Magubane;
   >Mr Paulos Matshaba;
   >Ms Shantie Naidoo;
   >Ms Nomwe Mamkhala.

3. From the Political Report by Oliver Tambo of the National Executive Committee to the National Consultative Conference of the African National Congress, on 17 June 1985, Kabwe, Zambia.

4.
- a. Wolff Geisler, Jürgen Ostrowsky: South Africa: Racism, Imperialism, Liberation Struggle. An introduction. Pahl-Rugenstein, Cologne 1978, ISBN 3-7609-0364-9.
- b. Military cooperation between the Federal Republic of South Africa and South Africa in the nuclear and conventional sectors. In: Booklets for German and international politics. Vol. 23 (1978), H. 2, pp. 4-12.
- c. Wolff Geisler (Ed.): Arms export (=FRG + Third World. Vol. 2). Magazin-Verlag, Kiel 1982.
- d. Wolff Geisler, Gottfried Wellmer: DM investments in South Africa. Southern Africa Information Center, Bonn 1983, ISBN 3-921614-40-6.
- e. AIDS: Origin, Spread and Cure. Bipawo, Cologne 1994, ISBN 3-9803883-1-X .
- f. The mass diseases of mad cow disease are caused by the artificial dissemination of retroviral parts which have been grown in Campylobacter microbes. Self-published, Cologne 1996, ISBN 3-9803883-4-4.
- g. Jubilee murders: authors and methods of mass murders. Self-published, Cologne 2014, ISBN 978-3-9803883-6-8.
- h. Bankers over the swastika: Target of Adolf Hitler's financiers. Self-published, Cologne 2014, ISBN 978-3-9803883-5-1.
- i. Klaus Pokatzky: Wolff Geisler: With lust against the mighty. A doctor who became an expert on South Africa in his second job. In: The time .No. 28/1986.

5. Statement by the Central Committee of the SACP on the activities of the 'Gang of 8', The African Communist, Second Quarter, 1976.

Notes 286

Chapter Three

1. ANC Summer School, Sechaba, November 1980.
2. Letter from Sakie, 20 December 1978.
3. Letter from my parents, 02 November 1978.
4. Letter from my parents, 11 April 1979.
5. Letter from David Trizzer, 09 June 1980.
6. Letter from David Trizzer, 30 June 1980.
7. We Fight, We Produce, We Learn, in Sechaba, November 1982.
8. South Africa and Netherlands had signed a cultural exchange agreement in 1951 followed by a Cultural Accord in 1953. The Nederlands Zuid-Afrikaanse Vereniging (NZAV) in Amsterdam was the institution responsible for executing this agreement. The AABN rallied against this agreement as it was seen a collaboration with the apartheid system.
9. Conference "Cultural Voice of Resistance" held in Amsterdam and organized by the Dutch Anti-Apartheid Movement in December 1982.
10. Letter from my parents, 02 November 1978.
11. Letter from Sakie (Oupa Moloi), 20 December 1978.
12. Letter from my parents, 11 April 1979.
13. Letter from Sipho Pewa (Themba Mlotshwa), no date (early 1979).
14. Letter from Sakie, no date (mid 1979).
15. Letter from Sipho Pewa, no date (late 1979).
16. Letter from John Vilakazi (Thabo Mkula), 05 September 1982.
17. Letter from John Vilakazi, 17 January 1983.
18. Letter from John Vilakazi, 20 Januariy 1983.
19. Letter from Koli Ngqase (Ephraim Gazelle), 29 April 1983.
20. Letter from John Vilakazi, 27 November 1983.
21. Letter from my mother, mid 1983.
22. Letter from my mother, end 1983.

Chapter Four

1. Report to the Pan Africanist Congress Consultative Conference in Arusha, June 27th-2nd July 1978

2. Dr Teboho J Lebakeng, They Blunted Us, June 16, Exile and Homecoming, pages 45 – 49.

3. Ibid. Page 49.

4. Ibid. Page 49.

5. Ibid. Page 56.

6. For her secondary level after standard VI, Miriam Duduzile 'Dudu' Zondo, my home girl and classmate at Ndondo Primary School in Rockville, had left for Inanda Seminary School, near Durban, one of the oldest schools for girls in Natal. When she passed her JC, with a first class for that matter, the authorities had indicated that she might not be accepted for her matric level because of her 'bad behaviour' – a euphemism for involving herself in students' politics and raising relevant questions.

    Her school used to be visited by students from around Durban, from the Durban-Westville and the Natal's Medical School universities, what Vanessa Noble calls the "epicentre of political radicalisation and mobilisation against apartheid epitomised in the story of Steve Biko and the Black Consciousness Movement" (*Dan Ncayiyana, A School of Struggle: Durban's Medical School and the Education of Black Doctors by Vanessa Noble. Scottsville: University of KwaZulu-Natal Press, 2013. Review*).

    She decided to take her matric at Orlando High and that is where she got more involved in the students' politics of the day, and she became a member of the SRC that prepared for the marches on June 16th, 1976. She was one of those the police were keen to arrest when she escaped into Swaziland in April 1977. If she had not fled, there was a high possibility that she would have been one of those charged in the trial of the 'Soweto 11', charged with sedition, that followed. This was so because Tsietsi Mashinini and Khotso Seathlolo – respectively the first and second leaders of the Soweto Students' Representative Council, SSRC – were already outside the country and were listed as co-conspirators in this trial of the 'Soweto 11' (Caryle Murphy, South African Judge Convicts 'Soweto 11' Students of Sedition, Washington Post, May 1, 1979).

In Swaziland she fell ill and was seen by a doctor who prescribed her some medicine, assuming that she was suffering from stress of running away from the police in South Africa. Like us before, the UNHCR flew her and a large group to Tanzania in May. She faced the dilemma of arriving in Dar and having to make choices between the ANC and PAC or be declared a refugee. Seeing more friends in the PAC, and having lived with PAC persons in Swaziland, it was easy for her to decide to be with the PAC. Having done that and after settling in Tanzania, she fell ill again and had to be hospitalised.

The doctor at the hospital asked her if she knew why she was in hospital. She only knew that she was not feeling well, and the doctor told her she was pregnant. With Dudu confused, the doctor in attendance called for a nurse to explain to her that she was carrying a baby. A baby boy, named Sizwe, was delivered later and became the first child born in Dar from the 'June 16' generation in the PAC. He was nicknamed the youngest 'soldier'. Anyway, Dudu was adamant that she wanted the baby taken back to South Africa. UNICEF in Tanzania organised a ticket for her to fly to Botswana. Around October 1978, she arrived unannounced in Gaborone with the baby.

Her sister in South Africa was supposed to collect the baby from Gaborone. The plan did not work. As there was no other alternative at the time and connecting with the structures of the PAC in Botswana, she got to know that Justice and Tshepiso were bound for South Africa and ventured back home with them and her baby.

7. Lebakeng, page 66.
8. The five APLA members Joe Bhembe (Titus Soni) a former bodyguard of Potlako Leballo, Reuben Linda Zwane (Daniel Monogotle), Gilbert Nhlapo, Abham Tatu and Shindo Mahlangu were tried in a Tanzanian court and sentenced to 15 years in prison for the killing of David Sibeko. The sentence was reduced to 10 years on appeal.
9. Interview with Richard Mtwetwe Nyide.
10. Truth and Reconciliation Commission, Armed Forces Hearing, PAC / APLA, Date: 7 October 1997, held at: Cape Town, DAY: 1.
11. The People's Armed Forces of Liberation of Angola (Portuguese: Forças Armadas Populares de Libertação de Angola) or FAPLA was originally the armed wing of the People's Movement for the Liberation of Angola

(MPLA) but later (1975–1991) became Angola's official armed forces when the MPLA took control of the government.

12. Luthando Dyasop, Out of Quatro – From exile to exoneration, A Memoir, Kwela Books 2021, page 118.
13. Stanley Manong, If We Must Die, 2015, page 207.
14. Stuart Commission Report: http://www.anc.org.za/show.php?id=87 * Mwezi Twala, Inside MK: Mwezi Twala – A Soldier's Story, page 62-63. Luthando Dyasop, Out of Quatro – From exile to exoneration, A Memoir, Kwela Books 2021, page 122–123.
15. Stuart Commission Report.
16. Paul Trewhela, The Dilemma Of Albie Sachs: ANC Constitutionalism and The Death of Thamizulu, A Death in Exile, page 36. See also: Bandile Ketelo et al, 'A Miscarriage of Democracy. The ANC Security Department in the 1984 Mutiny in Umkhonto we Sizwe', Searchlight South Africa No 5, Jury 1990. pp40-41.
17. Stuart Commission Report.
18. Joseph S. Jackson, Roots of Revolution: The African National Congress and Gay Liberation in South Africa University of Florida Levin College of Law, jjackson@law.ufl.edu 2019.
19. Letter from Reginald September 198
20. Report of the Symposium on Culture against Apartheid held at the Ergenidion Foundation, Athens, from 2 to 4 September 1988
21. 1st Conference during the Hellenic Presidency to EU Ministry of Foreign Affairs of Greece "Frontline States. How to counter SOUTH AFRICAN DESTABILISATION" October 20-21, Athens, 1988.
22. Lakis Chalkias, Ode to Nelson Mandela - https://m.youtube.com/watch?v=Qx2RgXOmyhl
23. World Peace Council, 8 to 11 February 1990, Athens, Greece.
24. Truth and Reconciliation Commission, Human Rights Violations, Submissions - Questions And Answers, Date: 15.08.1996 Name: Godfrey Josiah Madileng Motsepe, Case: Jb00606 – Pretoria, Day 4.
25. Letters to The Editor, by CA Georghiou, Charge d' Affaires a.i. South African Embassy, Athens, in: Athens News, March 11-12, 1990.

Chapter Five

1. The Green Book contains the political philosophy authored by Libyan leader Muammar Gaddafi, published in 1975. It was inspired by The Little Red Book of Chairman Mao Tse-tung. It consisted of three parts: The Solution of the Problem of Democracy: The Authority of the People; The Solution of the Economic Problem: Socialism, and The Social Basis of the Third International Theory. The theory rejected capitalism and communism, including representative democracy. Instead, it proposed Direct Democracy overseen by the General People's Committee and allowed direct political participation for all adult citizens.

2. My Interview with Jabu 'Dubu' Masina on 2nd January 2022. He asserts that he passed the information on to Shucks Sefanyetso, not SibusisoMasuku. For my book I decided to use both Dubu's and Sibusiso's versions.

3. Peter Harris, In A Different Time, the inside story of the Delmas Four, Umuzi 2008, pages…255 – 256.

4. "According to Ms Gertrude Dlamini [KZN/NM/100/NQ], her son, Peter Nkosinathi Dlamini from Nqutu, went into exile in 1978. Before he left he had been regularly harassed by Security Branch members as a result of his involvement in political activities at the University of Zululand. After he left, the Security Branch visited his mother's home and asked for him. She was later informed that her son had been kidnapped and brought back to South Africa, where he was forced to become an askari, and was later killed.

    Dirk Coetzee stated that Brigadier Willem Schoon, fearing that Dlamini would return to the ANC, decided he should be killed. In 1981, Dlamini and ANC operative VuyaniMavuso were taken by Dirk Coetzee and Major KoosVermeulen to a spot near Komatipoort. Mavuso had been captured in the Matola raid, and after unsuccessful attempts to 'turn' him, it was decided that he too should be killed. The two were given 'knock-out' drops obtained from General Lothar Neethling. These and subsequent drops did not have the desired effect. Eventually the two were shot by KoosVermeulen and their bodies burnt, while the operatives had a braai." TRC Final Report, VOLUME 2 CHAPTER 3, The State inside South Africa between 1960 and 1990, https://sabctrc.saha.org.za/originals/finalreport/volume2/split/BMvolume2_s1ch3_pg94.pdf.

Notes 291

5. a) Peter Harris, In A Different Time, the inside story of the Delmas four, Umuzi 2008, pages...255 – 256.
   See also: b) The commander of Vlakplaas was granted amnesty for the killing, while a Vlakplaasaskari was granted amnesty for his role in the attempt to recruit Mr Mavuso (AC/2000/163 and AC/2001/279). http://sabctrc.saha.org.za/victims/mavuso_selby_aka_bab.htm, and c) Former security police captain Dirk Coetzee was granted amnesty for the murders of several anti-apartheid activists, including Selby Vuyani Mavuso. http://www.iol.co.za/news/politics/amnesty-for-dirk-coetzee-1.69191?ot=inmsa.ArticlePrintPageLayout.ot.

6. During the hearings of the TRC I was out of the country and on tour of duty serving at the United Nations in New York, USA from May 1995 to May 1996, and in Germany from May 1996 to August 1998.

7. The Road to Democracy in South Africa, Volume 2 [1970 – 1980], page 496.

8. Interview with SuzmanMokoena.

9. Staffrider, Vol. 8 Nos 3 & 4, 1989. Special Issue, page 150.

ABOUT THE AUTHOR

Dr Khulu Mbatha was until the end of 2021 the special adviser on international relations to President Cyril Ramaphosa (2018 – 2021). He also served as an adviser to President Kgalema Motlanthe (2008 – 2014). Under President Mandela he was in the Ministry of Foreign Affairs, as the right-hand man of Minister Alfred Nzo, the Foreign Minister. He then joined the Permanent Mission of South Africa to the United Nations in New York before President Mandela appointed him as the Consul-General to Munich.

During the Presidency of Thabo Mbeki, he was the Deputy Director-General of the Department of Home Affairs under Minister Mangosuthu Gatsha Buthelezi and was appointed as the first CEO of the Road Traffic Management Corporation (RTMC) in the Department of Transport by Minister Dullah Omar.

In April 2020 Dr Mbatha, in collaboration with the Nelson Mandela Foundation, launched his 'Negotiating Democracy' exhibition, which traces the negotiation process from the release of Nelson Mandela to the signing of South Africa's Interim Constitution. The exhibition was located at the Nelson Mandela Centre of Memory. until the end of March 2022.

Dr Mbatha is an accomplished professional, academic, diplomat, columnist, exhibitor, and author, who speaks fluent German and is conversant with the Greek language. He has over 45 years' experience in the field of international relations and earned his Master's degree and PhD in Philosophy from the Friedrich-Schiller University in Jena, Germany.